Depletion

Advance Praise for *Depletion*

"This is a highly original, important, and engaged conceptual and practical reflection on depletion—a multifaceted concept central to understanding challenges to sustainable and equitable elements of social reproduction and provisioning of livelihoods. Strongly recommended reading for those interested in the dynamics of social reproduction in conditions of global capitalism."

—Isabella Bakker, York University

"*Depletion* is an important, innovative contribution to the political economy of care. It argues that the work of care entails depletion of physical and mental health, which diminishes the well-being of carers. Public policy can support replenishment of their capacities, but to prevent depletion requires transformation of social and economic relations to redistribute both care and resources. This book is essential reading for all courses on international political economy."

—Diane Elson, University of Essex

"This book develops an original discourse on the concept of depletion, which describes the current burden of unpaid and paid women's work, and proposes a formidable journey through the different political economy landscapes. This book is a must for anyone who is interested in understanding the living conditions of women in the world today and possible ways for women to overcome their depletion."

—Leopoldina Fortunati, University of Udine

"What an impressive combination of materials and methods, all brought together incisively in a brilliant conceptualization of depletion. A true tour de force!"

—Nancy Fraser, New School for Social Research

"This book provides critically important insights into the crisis of care, using the profound yet relatively unrecognized concept of depletion: the multiple and varied human costs of social reproduction. We ignore these costs at our peril; as Rai shows, they affect individual lives and livelihoods, but also society, economy, and even the planet. Anyone who is envisioning a more equitable, just, and viable future for humanity needs to read this book."
— Jayati Ghosh, University of Massachusetts, Amherst

"A stunningly original, immensely timely, and profoundly important dissection of the human cost of social reproductive labor. Eloquent and at times deeply harrowing, this is an essential reference point for all subsequent debate on this vital topic."
— Colin Hay, Sciences Po, Paris

"Shirin Rai's *Depletion* offers a conceptual breakthrough in feminist political economy. Beautifully written, brilliantly argued, methodologically clear, this is the book with the highest of stakes. It contains a planetary warning, offered from a feminist perspective, and suggests strategies to reverse the current course of human and nonhuman depletion of resources. It should be read and built upon by activists, scholars, policymakers—by all who wish this world could be otherwise and are willing to work for it."
— Aida A. Hozic, University of Florida

"This important book provides innovative tools for theorizing capitalism and for political organizing that puts people's well-being ahead of the drive for private profit. Rai advances the 'depletion' as a complement to feminist political economy's concept of social reproduction. Weaving together time-use studies, participant observation, and in-depth interviews, Rai offers superb ethnographies of depletion in the lives of women and children, revealing the ways in which gender, race, class, disability, and age inequalities play out in daily life."
— Meg Luxton, York University

"*Depletion* is a tour de force. In it Shirin Rai brilliantly develops the concept 'depletion through social reproduction' originally co-created with Hoskyns and Thomas. Drawing on diverse methods, the book sharply illuminates gendered, classed, and racialized facets of reproductive labor by women in New Delhi, child carers in Coventry, and the Xolobeni community in Western Cape. While laying clear the resulting harms, the book importantly reflects on ways of challenging and transforming the circuits of power underlying the unequal division of care."

—Rianne Mahon, Carleton University

"From individual homes to the global household, everyday lives and structural inequalities are all affected by what 'counts' as work and whose work gets counted. This fundamental insight informs Rai's always groundbreaking critical research and astute analyses. Focusing here on the everyday enables Rai to rearrange and enrich how we understand multilayered and interactive, visible and invisible, emotional, biophysical, economic, and geo/political harms of depletion, while demonstrating the urgency of reversing depletion and productively exploring strategies for doing so."

—V. Spike Peterson, University of Arizona

"Shirin Rai has done it again! *Depletion* is a highly welcome contribution that pushes us to see beyond settled perspectives. Firmly anchored in the situated lives of carers around the world, the book surfaces the true costs of reproductive labor under capitalism, bringing into focus unusual sites, such as migration, the care labor of children, and environmental activism. Deeply grounded theoretically, full of rich empirics, and with its eyes firmly trained to the future the book is an eye-opener with profound policy implications."

—Elisabeth Prügl, Geneva Graduate Institute

Depletion

The Human Costs of Caring

SHIRIN M. RAI

OXFORD
UNIVERSITY PRESS

Oxford University Press is a department of the University of Oxford. It furthers
the University's objective of excellence in research, scholarship, and education
by publishing worldwide. Oxford is a registered trade mark of Oxford University
Press in the UK and certain other countries.

Published in the United States of America by Oxford University Press
198 Madison Avenue, New York, NY 10016, United States of America.

CIP data is on file at the Library of Congress

ISBN 978–0–19–777772–5 (pbk.)
ISBN 978–0–19–753554–7 (hbk.)

DOI: 10.1093/oso/9780197535547.001.0001

The manufacturer's authorised representative in the EU for product safety is
Oxford University Press España S.A. of El Parque Empresarial San Fernando de Henares,
Avenida de Castilla, 2 – 28830 Madrid (www.oup.es/en or product.safety@oup.com).
OUP España S.A. also acts as importer into Spain of products made by the manufacturer.

For all those who experience depletion and struggle to reverse it
Also, for Jeremy

Contents

Acknowledgments

No work of this length can be the product of the labors of one person; I have many debts to acknowledge in the writing of this book.

First, I would like to thank Catherine Hoskyns and Dania Thomas, my co-authors of the paper "Depletion: The Cost of Social Reproduction" (Rai, Hoskyns, and Thomas 2014) which outlined the concept of depletion. I thank them for our collective labors in writing that paper but also for their generosity of spirit in encouraging me to extend that work by writing this book. It was Diane Elson's (2000) insight about depletion that sparked our interest in the issue and led Catherine Hoskyns and I to try to develop this concept further. I am thankful for Diane's support of this work.

I have sought and received the help of institutions, many friends, colleagues, and my family. The University of Warwick allowed me to take a sabbatical and funded a small methodological project that helped clarify ideas about measurement for Chapter 2. I worked on this project with Florian Reich, Piotr Bodganski (Warwick), and Chris Payne (Office of National Accounts)—I sincerely thank them for their patience in explaining the mysteries of numbers, modeling, and regression analyses, as well as showing curiosity about the concepts of care, caring, and social reproduction. Also at Warwaick, my colleagues in the IPE Cluster in the Department of Politics and International Studies (PAIS) critically engaged with the book through organizing a workshop which helped me enormously in sharpening my arguments— thanks to Mouzaiyan Khalil, Chris Clarke, Juanita Elias, Dominic Kelly, Nicola Pratt, Lena Rethel, Ben Richardson, Sharifah Sekelala (Law), and Mat Watson; I am deeply grateful.

In 2016, I was Ford Professorial Fellow at the Jawaharlal Nehru University Institute for Advanced Studies (JNIAS); I was also supported by a UKERI project grant at the University of Warwick on *A Working Day: Depletion, Entitlement and Survival*. Most of the research and fieldwork for Chapters 3 and 4 were undertaken during this period. JNIAS provided me with space and time to do this research but also much more. I was acutely aware throughout my stay in JNIAS that my friends and colleagues at JNU were under tremendous pressures as the student movement in opposition to the government policies in Kashmir escalated into a full-fledged attack upon the university and its students, several of whom were charged with sedition. It was a fraught time, despite which they engaged with my work, for which I am grateful: Mangai Arasu, Pratiksha Baxi, Upendra Baxi, Uma Chakravarti, Bishnupriya Dutt, Niraja Gopal Jayal. For supporting me in my everyday life with their friendship and concern, I thank Bindu Dewan, Prema Baxi, Geeta Sudan, and Vidhu Verma.

I would also like to thank M. S. Merian at R. Tagore International Centre for Advanced Studies (ICAS:MP), New Delhi for the Visiting Fellowship in 2019 that allowed me to write two chapters of the book and, more important, engage with a whole new set of colleagues and gain their insights about my work through seminars delivered and conversations had over delicious food at weekly lunches and endless cups of tea and coffee: thanks to Martin Fusch and Shail Mayaram, codirectors of the Centre and Laila Abu-Er-Rub, who made me welcome. Thanks also to Geeta Sudan, who made it possible for me to have a home base in New Delhi.

I moved to SOAS, University of London, in 2022 to take up a Distinguished Research Professorship, which allowed me the time away from teaching to work on the book and to engage with new colleagues and get their feedback; I am grateful for this. In particular, I would like to thank Alessandra Mezzadri, Hannah Bargawi and Sara Stevano for welcoming me into the feminist political economy group at SOAS and for engaging with the arguments presented in this book.

I would not have been able to write Chapters 3, 4, and 5 without the intensive fieldwork I undertook in New Delhi and Coventry, with women and children who opened up to me and to the researchers working with them—they were honest, frank, and reflective and did not shy away from discussing difficult everyday issues of care. Although I cannot name them here, I am deeply indebted to them for their time and their understanding of why their participation in this research was important. My immense gratitude to Pujya Ghosh and Annie Piironen for their work in interviewing and shadowing research participants during these two projects. Both were completely engaged with the themes of the projects, sensitive in the way that they approached the research participants, and respectful of their lives and their stories. This book would be poorer without their excellent work.

In Chapter 6 I have used photographs by Thom Pierce. Based in Cape Town, South Africa, Thom is a recipient of the 2016 Piclet prize for contemporary African photography and the 2016 PDN storytellers award. His wonderful, political work can be seen at https://thompie rce.com/. I am enormously grateful to Thom for letting me use his beautiful and deeply political work without monetizing it.

I would also like to thank Ricardo Morales for letting me use the image of his beautiful screen print *8 Hours* in Chapter 1.

Chapters 1 and 2 draw on, reprise, and extend the original paper that I co-authored with Catherine Hoskyns and Dania Thomas, "Depletion: The Costs of Social Reproduction" (2014), *International Feminist Journal of Politics* 16 (1): 86–105. Thanks to Taylor and Francis for the necessary permissions to do so.

I presented the different chapters in seminars in many locations and received excellent and robust feedback, for which I am grateful—as visiting professor in the Department of Gender Studies (2012–2015 and 2021–), LSE, from Sumi Madhok, Ann Phillips, Ania Plomien, and Wendy Sigle, and from the Governance Group at Carleton University, Dorothy Buss, Shireen Hassim, and Rianne Mahon, among others. I am grateful to colleagues who participated in the Workshop on Depletion, Law and Harm that I organized with funding from the Global Research Priorities program, University of Warwick—Beth Goldblatt, Jean Grugel, Rosie Harding, Briony Jones, Rianne Mahon, Fionnuala Ní Aoláin, Ania Plomien, and Ann Stewart; this resulted in a Special Section coedited by me and Beth Goldblatt for the *European Journal of Gender and Politics* in 2020. Generous funding from the Warwick Monash Alliance Research Fund in 2018 provided resources to fund two remarkable postdoctoral fellows—Jayanthi Lingham and Melissa Johnson—who helped me and Jacqui True, Monash University, to extend and refine my initial research methodology developed in New Delhi for Chapters 3 and 4 as the Feminist Everyday Observatory Tool (see Chapter 2); this work also produced an excellent report (2020) and article (2024) authored by Jayanthi and Melissa on how conflict affects social reproduction and depletion.

Thanks also to friends and colleagues who have critically read and discussed with me all or parts of this book: Donatella Alessandrini, Molly Andrews, Kate Bedford, Paul Bywaters, Juanita Elias, Diane Elson, Samanthi Gunwardana, Aida Hozic, Niraja Gopal Jayal, Toni Haastrup, Jayanthi Lingham, Wendy Luttrell, Sumi Madhok, Alessandra Mezzadri, N. Neetha, Ruth Pearson, V. Spike Peterson, Parvati Raghuram, Jeremy Roche, Kanchana Ruwanpura, Birgit Sauer, Sara Stevano, Jacqui True, Stefanie Woehl, and Sussane Zwingel. The comments of the anonymous reviewers were immensely helpful in revising the manuscript; I thank all three of them sincerely.

Thanks also to Angela Chnapko, commissioning editor, OUP, New York, for her encouragement and her patience. Several conversations at the International Studies Association conferences over the years helped shape the book, and her enthusiasm for the project was always encouraging. Thanks to Alexcee Bechthold for all her help with putting the manuscript together through production. Special thanks to Mouli Banerjee for her incredible editorial help in chasing down endless references at the end; I could not have managed without her support. Hinduja Dhanasegaran, Project Manager for OUP, was critical in managing the final revisions and copy editing of the book, which she undertook with a calmness and efficiency that I really appreciated; thank you.

Finally, I would like to thank my family: my sons, Arjun and Sean, who have always provided the emotional scaffolding I have needed for completing this long and protracted project, and my husband, Jeremy Roche, without whose unstinting support and care this book could not have been written. He read the whole manuscript with close attention and discussed its gaps with me with care. If we are thinking of transformation as a strategy of reversing depletion, then successful shifts in gender roles are needed; I have experienced this because of Jeremy's political commitment, his love, and his labors.

The gaps and omissions in this book are, of course, my own.

Shirin M Rai
Leamington Spa
2023

Introduction

Care, Social Reproduction, and Depletion

In New Delhi eight women lead different lives, going about their everyday life/work. One craves for friendships she has let go because she does not have enough time to invest in them; another augments her caring resources through depending on her mother and mother-in-law for household help; and still another feels the relentlessness of her social reproductive labor in the rhythms of her baby's needs.

Meera walks to work; she climbs over a fence to save 20 minutes because the gated community that she works in has shut all gates but one, which makes her journey longer. She does this because she needs to finish her work quickly in order to be able to collect her children from school and go home to do all the household chores before helping her children with their homework and then making dinner.

In Coventry children look after parents and grandparents who are differently abled or are sick. They find some time for themselves supported by an NGO, where three social workers work with them through play. The social workers are overburdened and underpaid. The parents of the children worry about the effect of the care responsibilities on their children—on their friendships, school time, bullying, and homework.

A community in Eastern Cape, South Africa, worries about the mining company that could destroy their land and way of life. How, they ask, will the traditions bound up in the soil and the histories etched in the trees and the everyday economies of fishing be affected if they are thrown off the land? The worry takes political form as well as cultural resistance. Violence lurks around the corner—people have been killed resisting. And the constant worry dissipates energies and affects everyday well-being.

Depletion. Shirin M. Rai, Oxford University Press. © Shirin M. Rai 2024.
DOI: 10.1093/oso/9780197535547.003.0001

These are some of the stories of depletion—of individuals, households,[1] and communities—discussed in this book. Why do these stories matter? Why does depletion matter?

Depletion Matters

Reproduction of life doesn't just happen—it is labored over, in different contexts and with differential resources, unequally. In all countries, in all classes, races, religions, and cultures, women perform these labors more than men. But these women are classed, raced, and located in deeply unequal ways and therefore experience depletion differently and intersectionally. Bhowmick (2022, xi–xi) writes, "[Middle class] Indian women are burdened with so much housework and caregiving that they are leaving their hard-won financial independence, dropping out of schools, and dropping off the labour force. . . . These women soldier on, unhappy, stressed and overworked; knowing they deserve better . . . but not knowing how, or whom, to ask."

Women, many who cope with this work in contexts of poverty and of violence, are constantly told that their everyday labor—both paid and unpaid—to maintain the rhythms of life-ecology do not count in/ as production. And yet we rely on this work every day and know that without this work we will not survive—as a global population, culture, and community. However, as a global society we fail to recognize this labor in our everyday lives and we continue to deny its appropriate inclusion in discourses about work, in our national budgets, and in policy frameworks. The exploitation of this work of life-giving and maintenance depletes lives and generates crises of care that threatens not just livelihoods but lives. The denial of this work is institutionalized through our methodologies of accounting for work, through our ideological positioning of domestic work, through cultural and social gendered norms. Fundamentally, we continue to take this work for granted, as given, always available, "infinitely elastic" (Elson 2000), costless.

The human cost of social reproductive labor—depletion—is extensive and multifaceted. As the stories in this book illustrate, it affects individuals, households, and communities; it endangers society, the economy, and indeed the planet, even as it is drawn upon as a "free good" available to plug deficits in our collective everyday regimes. Environmental unsustainability and depletion endanger future generations. So does depletion through social reproductive labor—labor that is mobilized to care within the home, labor that maintains life by combining paid and unpaid work, acknowledged and unacknowledged work. The failure to acknowledge this varied labor is a social deficit that needs to be addressed urgently: "Every day in 2017, approximately 810 women died from preventable causes related to pregnancy and childbirth. . . . About 295,000 women died during and following pregnancy and childbirth in 2017. The vast majority of these deaths (94%) occurred in low-resource settings, and most could have been prevented" (WHO 2019). Oxfam India's (2019) report on inequality showed that "performance of unpaid care work was a trigger for violence on women" and its Household Care Survey 2019 found that "in households where men and women express greater acceptability of beating women, women there spend 42 minutes longer on paid and unpaid care work and 48 minutes less on leisure activities" (see also Bhowmick 2022).

And yet the women I met on my journey through the research for this book also gave me hope. They were not just feeling stressed and overworked, although they were; they did not just feel their labors were unrecognized, although they did. They were also active agents in managing their lives, their families' well-being and coping with the structural disadvantages that they encounter with the resources available to them—friendships, family support, bought in domestic labor. They strategized to cope and they managed to survive and even thrive, even as depletion continued to mark their lives. Through narrating these stories, I argue that our lives, and the lives of future generations, are dependent on the work we call social reproduction, the reproduction of life itself, which can be and is being eroded through depletion.

So what does the depletion lens (together with the social reproduction lens) allow us to recognize, assess, measure, and address? The book makes four arguments: first, that the unequal system of social reproduction that leads to depletion harms those who care. This harm through depletion is multifaceted and affects everyone engaged in social reproduction, but unequally, and affects life that needs to be sustained and reproduced. Second, the strategies of reversing harm cannot be successful if society as a whole—states, markets, individuals, nonstate and collective actors—does not acknowledge in measurable ways this harm. Further, mitigatory strategies alone for reversing depletion can only be limited and unequal and indeed can intensify harm for some. State intervention in addressing the unequal distribution of social reproductive work is essential, if not sufficient, for replenishment as a strategy of reversal of harm. Third, a vision of a "good life" for all, rather than for only some, must include human as well as planetary care. Depletion of our environment is entangled with capitalism's pursuit of cheap nature (Moore 2015) and harms us and future generations (IPCC 2023). Fourth, the recognition of depletion as harm must recognize the location and histories of inequalities that cast long shadows on the current care regime—race, gender, and class are vectors of this inequality.

While previous scholarship has discussed the role of social reproduction in sustaining capitalism, the costs of social reproduction have been only partially understood and analyzed. In this book, I argue that through focusing on depletion, we can begin to reveal the full costs of social reproduction, to understand the circuits of power that circulate through different regimes of care and how these might be challenged and reversed. In essence, *depletion fundamentally affects the material conditions of reproduction and maintenance of social life, and the struggles for reversing depletion can help us think through the transformation of social reproduction.* As Mau (2021, 11) argues, "the struggle for wrenching the conditions of life free from the grip of capital takes place on all levels and across the entire social totality"; reversing depletion is critical to this struggle.

The book frames depletion as harm—historic, present, and anticipatory—to argue that social reproduction is not cost-free, that it differently depletes people in ways that have both affective and material consequences for individuals, households, and communities and for their environments. Depletion results when the outflow of social reproductive labor exceeds the inflow of resources, tipping those affected over the threshold of sustainability. Consent does not mitigate depletion, just as love does not make social reproduction less depleting. Depletion through social reproduction is a concept that also bridges the worlds of paid and unpaid work—paid work is affected by unpaid work in the home and vice versa. There is now accumulated evidence that women face a disadvantage in the labor market because of their mothering roles (Grimshaw and Rubery 2015), which translates into persistent gender and race pay gaps (racially minoritized women experience these two together; Ishizuka 2021). In turn, growing income inequalities, continuing gendered and racialized violence, declining state and social infrastructure investment, precarity and migration, and sedimented gendered social norms, all affect how social reproductive work is carried out and who carries its burdens and costs. Depletion as a concept also helps us connect ecological harm and harm to individuals, households, and communities through unrecognized and unvalued resources that are extracted, accumulated, and mobilized in the service of national capitalist development.

The book also draws attention to planetary depletion and the harm this does through nonrecognition and neglect in different contexts—gendered, intergenerational, intersectional, and locational. The acceleration of the environmental crisis because of continued pursuit of immediate profit and consequent disregard for worsening conditions of living and livelihood—droughts, floods, rising sea levels, fires—has resulted in increasing depletion at different rates and magnitudes across the world. This increases the pain for people over time as capitalist accumulation, labor extraction, and ecological trauma deplete people as well as the everyday ecologies that are so important to sustaining and perpetuating life (see Puig de la Bellacasa 2017). Both the communities in the Global North that think themselves protected from the depredations of climate change (Bittle 2023) and the communities that are already being displaced because of it in the Global South are being depleted, albeit at different rates.

If depletion is complex, so of course is its reversal—it evolves over time through what Nancy Fraser (2016) has called "boundary struggles" over the economy, polity, and households. Feminist agendas for change have been particularly difficult to implement—there is a long gendered history of waiting uncomplainingly for change to come about (Wolf 1985; Sangari and Vaid 1989). There seems to be always more important things ahead in the queue—protecting male breadwinner jobs, prioritizing growth, investing in infrastructure building—all of which means less money for investing in social infrastructure that supports care work. Waiting can add to depletion—physically but also mentally; impatience is regarded as being unreasonable, especially in times of crisis. Reversing depletion is not easy also because it is anchored in structural inequalities of gender, race, and class, which are essential to the reproduction of capitalist social relations. State policy to address issues of social provisioning and welfare builds on "the state's unique legal and sanctioning power regarding the production and 'management' of [gendered and] racialised categories" (Peterson 2020, 180) and of gendered and minoritized groups. This, in turn, is generative of un/intended differentiated discriminatory practices, policies, and outcomes (180). Further, as Beverley Mullings (2021,153) has argued in the context of the history of slavery in the Caribbean, while "it is important to disentangle 'race' from gender in these hidden histories, recognizing full well that this may be impossible for Black women whose location at the intersection of these oppressive systems points to a multiplicity of ways that they were dispossessed."

The struggles to reverse depletion thus take different forms in different temporalities—from mitigation to replenishment to transformation (see Chapter 1)—as capitalism itself evolves. They occur not only within circuits of capital accumulation but also through "the efforts of working people to thrive and flourish" (Naidu 2023, 94). Thriving and flourishing, however, are not innocent concepts in capitalist societies. They can denote a focus on growth, on consumption for nonessential goods and services, and one could argue, also, for some, mitigation built on the labor of others. On the other hand, alternative approaches to a "good life" are reflected in collective processes of struggle protecting ecological landscapes from extractivism and challenging modernity's entrapments while pointing to the enchantments of new imaginaries and solidarities (Federici 2019). We will see examples of these struggles in different chapters, through the attempts to develop networks of friendship (or laments at not being able to do so), depending upon extended family networks, through strategies of self-care, wherever possible, and through challenging and holding the state accountable. *Depletion: The Human Costs of Caring* outlines these struggles through individual negotiations and community mobilizations.

Strategies to reverse depletion need to change unequal social relations fundamentally. However, if we want to avoid generating new forms of waiting—waiting for revolution—then we also need to strategize in the everyday. As I have argued elsewhere, "if we see successful transformation not as a single revolutionary event but as a bundle of changes that may add up to transformation in the long term, then we may see some elements of that bundle emerging through . . . struggles for gender equality and the valuation of social reproduction" (Rai 2018, 11).

Next, I outline the conceptual differences between care and social reproduction and the relevance of this debate for the understanding of depletion in different contexts. I argue that social reproduction itself needs to be locationally decentered, taking into account the long histories of colonialism and racism, to better understand the entanglements between past, present, and anticipatory harms of depletion.

Care, Social Reproduction, and the Value of Care

Concepts matter to analysis.

"[C]are is a species activity that includes everything that we do to maintain, continue, and repair our 'world' so that we can live in it as well as possible," write Fisher and Tronto (1990, 19). The term "care" is often used interchangeably with "social reproduction"; I did this earlier. Debates on care and social reproduction have been wide-ranging, with different approaches to the relationship between production and reproduction, on the regulation and governance of reproductive labor and the racialized nature of this labor (Mezzadri 2021).

Care is a capacious concept. Care is an immediately understood term from our everyday interactions and empathies, in part because care work emphasizes the care of persons, which takes place in households and communities in all societies; it is, as Laugier (2020) argues, entangled in the ordinary (see also Gilligan 1982; Nodding 1992; Tronto 2013). Care is cognitive, affective, and embodied (Gilligan 1982; Hamington 2004). Care has been defined as "a life-affirming action and an important part of human relationships which does not necessarily represent an unwanted burden" (Dowling 2021, 20). But the etymology of the word points to exactly such a burden—the Latin root of "care" is in the word *caru*, meaning sorrow, grief, and anxiety; as Dowling points out, "one only need think of the image evoked by the term 'carefree,' being without a worry in the world" (20). The link between depletion and care here is obvious, but also overlooked.

Studies on care focus on how to better attend to the needs of others and how care can be better supported in an unequal welfare society (Conradi 2020; Raghuram 2016). The complexity of care is seen as embedded in family/household, state, market, and nonprofit institutions, in a "care diamond," as Razavi (2007) called it. And, of course, care scholarship reveals its gendered and cross-generationally unequal practices—women care longer hours than men in all countries of the world, although both boys and girls support families, but in different ways, and those who need care also participate in caring, for example older people and children (Chapter 5). The practices of care and caring are also understood as racialized, with people of color mobilized in low-paid, insecure, and poor conditions of work (Hamed et al. 2020; Lingham, Rai, and Akhter forthcoming). Increasingly, scholarship on care is concerned with the care not only of human beings but of the nonhuman, and indeed planetary care and how the depletion of the two are connected and must be reversed (Bauhardt and Harcourt 2018; Buckingham 2020). Finally, care is, as Tronto (2013, 10) has argued, a "problem for democracy" because of its unequal nature—the dependence of those needing care, the valorization but not valuing of those who care.

"Social reproduction," on the other hand, is an awkward term—inelegant and jargonistic and unrecognized in popular parlance. The reason I prefer to use it is that although the two concepts overlap, I find that "care" is largely used as a normative and relational concept, which captures the emotional aspect of labor well. "Social reproduction" is also relational, but it is a more structural approach to understanding how life is reproduced and maintained within the capitalist system. Theorizations on social reproduction are embedded in historical debates on labor within Marxism: its reproduction and value; how reproduction and production, exploitation, oppression, and accumulation are intertwined; and how women are treated as a reserve army of labor within capitalism, which itself is embedded in long histories of gendered and racist expropriation (Bhattacharya 2017; Bhattacharyya 2018; Farris 2019).

Marx and Engels in *The German Ideology* saw "production of life" as both a "natural" and a "social" relation. Radical and Marxist feminists developed this insight into a theorization of social reproduction. The Wages for Household campaign in the 1970s made a radical move by asserting not only the importance of housework to social reproduction but also that this labor is value producing (Dalla Costa and James, 1972). Producing and maintaining life contributes to capitalist production and indeed subsidizes it through the unremunerated labor of life-making. Further, the commodification of care makes caregiving a goal-oriented task rather than a relational one, adversely affecting the care receiver too. New forms of wealth extraction through financialization, debt, and "affective remuneration"[2] also throw light on the changing nature of social reproduction (Roberts 2015, 3, 4). Technologizing of caring—robots, panic buttons, CCTV—can make abject the relationality of care; think, for example, of the conditions of work under surveillance-led exploitation, depleting the lives of the caregivers and the lack of human touch affecting the well-being of those in receipt of care (see Wright 2018). Finally, extractive approaches to labor and the planet are increasing the burdens of maintaining life for the poorest, increasing the burdens of social reproduction, and in so doing intensifying depletion (Federici 2019).

Social reproduction therefore conceptually helps me to understand capitalism and its reproduction "and restores to the economic process its messy, sensuous, gendered, raced and unruly component: living human beings" (Bhattacharya 2017, 19). It gestures toward intimate relations in the home, includes paid and unpaid work to reproduce and maintain life (care scholarship tends not to focus on reproduction but on maintaining life), not just through "caring" but also through reproduction of ideologies that legitimize existing social relations. Further, and importantly, social reproduction through its focus on capitalist social relations reveals how "relations within commodity production become dehumanised. . . . Social relations take the form of money relations" (Foreman 1977, 71),[3] which pushes relations of care and caring into that marginal space where care might be valorized but is not valued (Dowling 2016). This results in both family life and work life being experienced as depleting. Through its emphasis on issues of value, exploitation, and property regimes under capitalism, social reproduction also connects the precarity of systems of reproduction of life with those of environmental and planetary sustenance essential for the maintenance of life by revealing "linkages between exploitation and extraction not only in relation to women's labour, time, and bodily integrity, but also in relation to nature and its plunder" (Mezzadri et al. forthcoming; see also Mies 1986; Mies and Shiva 1996; Chapters 1 and 6). Further, social reproduction, as a concept, "makes visible the systems of life that support the labour process, both daily and intergenerationally, in sites of production along global supply chains" (Fernandes et al. 2023, 1), from the world factories producing cheap goods to mining and agriculture and services of care and caring. However, as Winders and Smith (2019, 873) argue, "in this moment of deepening precarité, when certain human beings are rendered into raw labor power, bare life, or 'remaindered' as entirely disposable bodies . . . social reproduction itself is under siege";[4] depletion through social reproduction and depletion of social reproduction thus go hand in hand.

As I see it, social reproduction needs generate demands for labor that are met in part through commodifying, feminizing, and racializing care by marketizing aspects of it, while the nonmarketized elements, entwined though they are in market regimes, remain unpaid and not counted as work. As we will see in Chapters 3 and 4, buying in domestic labor is a way of mitigating depletion for those who can afford to do so; those selling their labor experience an increased depletion (Stack 2019). Social reproduction is also entangled in the social histories and geographies of care—what is marketized varies across place and over time.[5] These marketized and nonmarketized elements of caring also continue to be framed in histories of gendered exploitation and racism, which affect the social relations of production and social reproduction, abjection of labor, depletion of lives, and, as we shall see in this book, struggles to reverse this. However, care remains an aspect of social reproduction as an everyday practice and remains embedded in systems of governance—who can care, where can care take place best, how are care and caring organized, exchanged, funded, and regulated? Negotiations and struggles take place over these questions in both private and public spheres, at individual and social levels, at local and global scales. The scholarly and activist work on care and social reproduction, however, suggests that the labor of both remains unrecognized, unmeasured, and unaddressed, and that this needs to be reversed.

In this book I argue that if we do not value the work of social reproduction, we risk intensifying depletion.

Decentering Social Reproduction

Location matters.

Social reproduction is a spatial as well as a temporal concept (Winders and Smith 2019; Bryson 2007; Chapters 2, 3, and 4). Standing in one place rather than another, whether it is along the boundary of class or race, caste or sexuality, of formal and informal work, of waged and unwaged labor, provides vistas and possibilities of social reproduction and depletion that converge as well as diverge (Mezzadri et al. forthcoming; Madhok 2020; Mohanty 1995; Said 1978). As Ferguson (2008, 42) notes, "it's not just what we do to reproduce society, but where we do it that counts in an imperial capitalist world" (see also Cusicanqui 2012). The critiques of Global South and Black feminists have led to the opening up of the debate on class- and race-based experiences as being vectors of exclusion, within the theorizing of social reproduction, and of the marginalization of political demands resulting from these (Bannerji 1995; Cantillon, Mackett, and Stevano 2023).

Some recent interventions, such as social reproduction theory, have treated social reproduction as an integrated system of oppression of women (Bhattacharyya 2018), although composed of circuits of power lying outside processes of value generation (Mezzadri 2020, 2). This largely Global North perspective overlooks the importance of informal work in the labor landscape of the Global South (Naidu 2023; Hassim and Razavi 2006; Mies 2014),[6] which means that depletion in the doing of this work also remains unrecognized. Challenging binaries of formal/informal, paid/unpaid, valued/valorized can help us understand the fuzziness of time and regulatory systems in the doing of paid and unpaid work, much of it done within the home. Therefore, bringing into focus both social reproduction and depletion in the Global South requires a pluralizing of these concepts and approaches (Mezzadri et al. forthcoming).

Black and racially minoritized feminist scholars argue that both race and gender are foundational concepts of colonialism, colonization, and coloniality; that this allows for the continuing subordination of women and indigenous and marginalized communities in the Global South (Lugones 2008; see also Connell 2014; Oyěwùmí 1997). The long histories of exploitation of those engaged in global care chains and subject to violence and depletion haunt the debates on social reproduction (Davis 1983; Sacks 1989). The argument is that if location is taken seriously, the family form as well as the understanding of production and social reproduction and the place of labor/work in capitalism would have to be rethought. Intersectional analyses of social reproduction have tried to show how locations and identities shape and are shaped by capitalist social relations and in turn shape the form of capitalist production and of social reproduction (Crenshaw 1989; Brenner 2000).

This has serious implications for the analysis of depletion. If the binary that is generated in the Global North between productive and reproductive realms is not always sustainable in the Global South, then different forms of depletion become relevant to our discussion, based on the premise that social reproduction is endogenous to capitalist production (Naidu 2023, 100). For example, despite rapidly increasing urbanization in the Global South, different labor regimes are in play in the rural areas that are dependent on internal circular migration (Mander et al. 2019; Breman 2009). This is also the case in precarious, informal labor markets, where most women work. Global Southern cities and deeply unequal agriculture depend on this precarious, informal, migrant labor (Sassen 2005). Postcolonial, national development strategies in the Global South in the 1960s and 1970s also led to the mobilizing of female labor in global factories where women worked across home/work boundaries and where gender frames shaped their everyday identities as well as capitalist production (Elson and Pearson 1981; see also Ruwanpura 2022). At the global level, multi-earner households of the Global North often mitigate their depletion by buying in migrant labor, generating global care chains and global households (Safri and Graham 2010; Lutz, 2018). This reproduces North/South inequalities that are reflected in the possibilities and curtailments of maintenance of life itself down the care chain.[7] Blurring the boundaries between production and social reproduction leads to changes in the organization of both.[8]

Further, as the social infrastructure erodes under regimes of austerity in the Global North, we see the social reproduction debate increasingly focusing on welfare regimes (Fraser 2016). These, however, also differ enormously across North/South boundaries; in some locations the welfare state is almost absent, and in others it is strongly present as a regulator even though its investment in social infrastructure is minimal. This influences the nature of social reproduction—its organization, recognition, valuing (or not), and sustainability (Kunz 2010). As we shall see in the chapters that follow, the state is almost entirely absent from the narratives of women organizing everyday life in India (Chapters 3 and 4); the family and the community matter more. In the UK, the state provides an inadequate support infrastructure for children who care, with NGOs supplementing this support (Chapter 5). In South Africa, on the other hand, the state confronts the Xolobeni women violently. Often, critical approaches to North/South relations fail to acknowledge gendered labor as an important arena of contestation (Lugones 2008; Bakker and Gill 2019).[9]

Without decentering the analysis of social reproduction and, through it, of depletion a North-centric approach can also "undermine efforts to build solidarities across labouring classes and political movements, as the identification of 'hierarchies' of contributions to capitalism may weaken the redistributive claims of some classes and communities" (Mezzadri 2020, 2; also see Banks 2020; Federici 2019).

The concept of social reproduction therefore needs further stretching when faced with different regimes of public and private life, of blurred distinctions between family labor and work and marketized labor and racial and gendered distortions (Davis 1983; Mies 2014). These differences are important, even as globalization of regimes of care are folding in varied forms of reproduction (Banerjee and Kotiswaran 2021) to better serve the state's and capital's needs to constantly decrease the costs of "living labour" (Farris 2019, 112). However, as Tuck and Yang (2012) remind us, decentering (or decolonizing) is "not a metaphor." Recognizing difference cannot be a fantasy of "easier paths to reconciliation" (4) relying on the understanding and even forgiveness of the exploited, just as consent does not legitimize the inequalities of social reproductive work.[10] This can mean, as Fellows and Razack (1998, 335) have argued, that white women can be engaged in a "race to innocence"—"the process through which a woman comes to believe her own claim of subordination is the most urgent, and that she is unimplicated in the subordination of other women"—poor and racialized, nannies, cooks and cleaners, and surrogate life-givers, for example.

Entangled as depletion is with social reproduction, it too needs a decentered lens. I build on these debates also in attempting to decenter my own understanding of social reproduction and its depletion effects by taking location—of class, race, and North/South relations—seriously. I think through these issues across different cities, forms of social reproductive work, and struggles to reverse depletion (see Chapters 1, 3, 4, and 6). Building on this varied and rigorous scholarship and debates on social reproduction, in my work I use the term as including the following:

1. Biological reproduction, which includes birthing/reproducing labor and the provision of the sexual, emotional, and affective services that are required to maintain households and intimate relationships. Here it is worth referring to how social reproduction attaches itself to gendered subjects, who are then subjected to unmitigated social, economic, and political depletion.

2. Production in the home, of both goods and services, incorporating some types of home-based agriculture, different forms of care, as well as social provisioning and voluntary work directed at meeting needs in and of the community. Here depletion can be seen in outflows attached to both paid and unpaid, formal and informal labor.

3. Reproduction of culture and ideology, which stabilizes (and sometimes challenges) dominant social relations (Lazlett and Brenner 1989, 382–383; Hoskyns and Rai 2007, 300).

This is important as issues of consent, "cultural" and normative dominant discourses about the gendered nature of work, and the legitimizing of social hierarchies of labor are reproduced as well as suffered through social reproduction regimes. Clearly, as noted above, these definitions cross the divide between paid and unpaid work and illustrate the complexity of the relationship between the two, as does the measurement of value and of depletion. Measuring social reproduction and depletion is, I argue, a form of recognition and therefore critically important to our understanding of (1) their marginalization, (2) their effects on individuals, households, and communities, and (3) data mobilization in the struggles to reverse depletion.

Depletion, as a concept, also decenters—focusing on the costs of social reproduction allows for light to be cast on relationships that invoke love as well as pain, joy as well as exhaustion, solidarity as well as exploitation. Depletion decenters middle-class notions of care that obfuscates the complexity of the labor of care by revealing the circuits of power in which social reproduction is enmeshed, which depletes individuals, households, and communities with different intensity, leaving significantly diverse routes out of it depending on their socio-economic locations.

Mapping the Book

It is always difficult to introduce a project in a way that piques interest but also provides an accurate roadmap. As I attempt to do so here, I also want to reflect upon not just the shape of the book but also the substance of individual chapters—why these particular issues, actors, spaces, and temporalities? Depletion is the thread that binds all the chapters together. In different forms, intensity, scope, and manifestations, it helps me develop the argument that is at the heart of this book: that depletion harms and needs to be reversed.

Straightforwardly, the book is divided into six chapters. Chapter 1, "Depletion, Harms and Struggles to Reverse Them," builds on and revises an article I wrote with Catherine Hoskyns and Dania Thomas outlining and explaining the concept of depletion (Rai, Hoskyns, and Thomas 2014). As I look back on the substance but also the process of writing that paper, I think of coffees, cakes, lunches, and laughs as we worked to conceptually outline and explain depletion through social reproduction (DSR). DSR is a tipping point when the outflow of labor exceeds the inflow of resources of sustainability for individuals, households, and communities and is a powerful tool for understanding the consequences of nonrecognition of the value of domestic work to national economies, as well as the harm that might accrue in the doing of this work at both a systemic and individual level. Issues to do with gendered harm as well as questions about how depletion might be reversed through strategies that are individual as well as social movements and community mobilization are discussed. I also address some gaps in the original paper—specifically on issues of ecological and human depletion and of race and social hierarchies more generally, and the importance of their recognition in the understanding of depletion. Further, while we proposed a model for measuring depletion, I don't think we tested it. This meant that we were not able to fully reflect on the challenges of measuring something as complex as the human cost of doing social reproductive labor.

I address these issues of measurement in Chapter 2, "Measuring Depletion in Multiple Registers." However accurate, should we, can we measure human relations? What do we gain and lose by emphasizing measurability? Why do we need this model at all? Can this support the overall feminist argument about valuing unpaid domestic labor? Analyzing the different ways to measure social reproduction, I suggest that the model presented in Rai, Hoskyns, and Thomas (2014) to calculate depletion has limitations of measurement as well as the power to make the argument for depletion and how this affects gender justice. I discuss other feminist methodologies such as time-use surveys to research, reveal, and (potentially) reverse the depleting effects of social reproduction (Budlender 2010; Rao et al. 2021). However, noting the limitations of these, I outline a novel approach to researching depletion, which uses both shadowing and time-use surveys but also qualitative narrative interviews. Jacqui True and I have called this method FEOT—the Feminist Everyday Observation Tool.

I use this methodology in its prefigurative form in Chapter 3, "A Day in the Life of . . . : Mapping Individual Depletion across Class Boundaries," by asking the question "What did you do yesterday?"

Analyzing the time used in social reproductive and paid labor by eight women across class boundaries in one day of their lives in New Delhi, I find that depletion, like social reproduction, takes many forms and is inflected deeply with class relations as well as gender inequalities. Tiredness, loneliness, and an erosion of self are related to the relentlessness of social reproductive work, which families and communities do not always recognize as important. Thinking through these eight lives was salutary—the micro practices of care reveal themselves as deeply embedded in structures of capitalist work regimes as well as in everyday demands framed by cultural and social norms. Depletion runs through these lives, even though each one has a different set of resources to draw upon and mobilize to mitigate it. This matters because it allows us to analyze human stories of labor and depletion, of rewards and alienation, of what works and what doesn't and cannot work in terms of personal strategies of survival as well as of thriving, in the absence of state support, for those engaged in social reproductive work in the city.

Bringing paid and unpaid work together is the arc of everyday travel for social reproduction: commuting. In Chapter 4, "Depletion on the Move: Commuting and Social Reproduction," I think through how, together with unpaid social reproductive work, traveling to work is also unpaid labor that subsidizes the urban economy in neoliberal cities. Travel, done over space, requires not only time (thus stretching the margins of work-time) but also affects the body (increased tiredness), the sense of security (safe or unsafe travel can decrease or increase the sense of insecurity), reputations, family status, and wages (the money spent on travel could be seen as a subsidy given to the employers). The state investment at varying levels in physical but not so much in social infrastructure also affects this equation. I explore these issues through a close discussion of two stories—of an Indian domestic worker, Meera, and Sangeeta, a journalist. Class divides them, but for both, their travel to and from work increases their depletion.

Depletion moves across generations. Care of children preoccupies much of the work on caring, rather than care *by* children. However, children also care, and their labor is also not recognized; indeed, it is often seen to be exploitative and therefore something to be discouraged—through national and international policy and legal framing. Chapter 5, "Depleting Futures: Children Who Care," builds on a pilot project conducted in Coventry with children between the ages of 8 and 16. I found that caring by children often takes place through mundane, everyday activities. Austerity years have eroded the support systems necessary to poorer families' social reproduction, with the gaps being met by the family—women, men, and children. Depletion associated with this work affects children—in terms of their education, levels of anxiety, friendships, and exclusions—and their households in different ways; class and race, gender and economic policies shape the regimes of care as well as the costs of care.

Caring of the community also needs planetary care. Building on an examination of a protest movement against mining in the Xolobeni community in South Africa's Eastern Cape, I focus on the gender effects of proposed corporate extractivist mining in Chapter 6, "Postcards to the Future: Anticipatory Harm and Struggles against Extractivism." This chapter also builds on the concept of social reproductive work as cultural and ideological reproduction. I argue that the deep connection between gender relations, environmental contexts, and temporalities of depletion can occur through anticipating the harm to communities and their life-worlds. Through reading Thom Pierce's photographic portraits of the members of the Xolobeni community, I explore not the harm that has been done but harm that is yet to happen. This visual lens is a powerful way to think through the costs of resistance as well as of social reproduction.

In the conclusion, "Building Solidarities to Reverse Depletion," I briefly bring together the arguments of the book and reflect upon how the concept of depletion through social reproduction travels through the different political economy landscapes. In particular, I reflect upon the various strategies for measuring and reversing depletion that I have explored in the book and look forward to seeing if and under what conditions these might be useful in changing policy frameworks that address women's work.

Depletion argues that strategies for recognizing, measuring, pluralizing, and reversing the harms of depletion are urgently needed in the context of the growing costs of care and caring for our social and ecological worlds.

1

Depletion, Harms and Struggles to Reverse Them

The daily rhythms of social reproduction reflect the costs of care and caring as Annie Ernaux (2018, 49–50) writes about her life after marriage, "Space shrank, time took on a regular rhythm, carved up by work schedules, the day nursery, bath time . . . Saturday shopping. . . . Our melancholy at seeing a personal project fade into the distance—painting, writing, or making music—was compensated by the satisfactions of contributing to the family project. . . . [We] denied the value of things [we] nonetheless felt obliged to do without knowing why."

In this chapter I argue that while social reproductive work provides an underpinning of everyday life, it is also depleting. I suggest that the work of social reproduction—the acts of caring that fulfill but also drain and exhaust—make for the Janus-faced nature of social reproduction in capitalist societies that is valorized but not valued and that willful and sanctioned unknowing and care/lessness about valuing social reproduction are the foundation of depletion.

Building on the discussion about care and social reproduction in the introduction, I outline below the conceptual framework of *depletion through social reproduction (DSR)*. The work on depletion I present in the first part of this chapter was outlined in the paper I published together with Catherine Hoskyns and Dania Thomas (Rai, Hoskyns, and Thomas 2014). We built on Diane Elson's (2000, 28) insight that without support, unpaid domestic work can be depleting. Depletion is a concept and a reality that people intuitively recognize but cannot pin down. In our paper we expanded on and conceptualized what we mean by depletion, identifying three sites of depletion, outlining its harmful effects and how it can be measured and reversed. Here, while I retain most of the conceptual framing of depletion set out in that paper, I also

Depletion. Shirin M. Rai, Oxford University Press. © Shirin M. Rai 2024.
DOI: 10.1093/oso/9780197535547.003.0002

extend the discussion by examining some of its gaps: issues of race, the environment and the place that the state could and should occupy in supporting strategies that are and can be mobilized to reverse depletion. Finally, I review and comment on how this concept has been used in different contexts and disciplines since we wrote the paper and evaluate how this work helps expand the concept of depletion through cross-disciplinary approaches in different geopolitical contexts.

Depletion: The Everyday Cost of Social Reproduction

Does the non/malrecognition of the value of social reproduction undermine the possibilities for achieving gender justice? This is the question that has animated my work on depletion. As noted in the introduction, feminist political economists have long worked on the issue of nonrecognition of social reproduction in national economies and the consequences of this in the context of crises of capitalism (Edholm, Harris, and Young 1978; Mackintosh 1981; Waring 1988; Picchio 1992; Elson 1998; Bakker 2007). Methodologies such as time-use surveys and modeling have been developed to estimate the value of unpaid work (Esquivel et al. 2008; Budlender, 2010). While this rigorous and powerful work has resulted in some change—see, for example, the call for recognizing the value of care work in the 2015 Sustainable Development Goals (5.4)—there is little change in the way GDP is calculated, policy framed, and priority given to either social reproduction or depletion that accrues through this labor.

In the context of the 2008 financial crisis, Catherine Hoskyns, Dania Thomas, and I felt that this nonrecognition of social reproductive work was particularly important in the context of the long history of austerity policies—from structural adjustment policies of the 1980s to the austerity policies after the 2008 financial crisis—when state support for welfare regimes that support social reproduction, where present, eroded sharply and were rolled back where they were minimally available. We wanted to render visible the phenomenon of depletion that accrues, when social reproductive work is unsupported, by conceptualizing it and showing how it can be defined and measured as well as reversed (Rai, Hoskyns, and Thomas 2014). We hoped that if we could show that the denial of the value of social reproduction causes actual harm to those who work to reproduce and maintain life, the argument for valuing social reproduction and reversing depletion would be strengthened. Of course, this book is being written in the shadow of another crisis, the COVID-19 pandemic,[1] which has again revealed the deep inequalities of gender, class, and race, has intensified depletion, and has posed new and old questions about the place of social reproduction, care and caring and their costs in our lives. As a carer during COVID-19 told us, "[T]here was never any help and I remember, you know, I'd go to my mum's, take her shopping, my whole day would just go doing that and I was flat out when I got back and then I had the kids and obviously there was no going to the gym for me then either because it was all lockdown. I couldn't run away from my house. I'd go on little walks, even that was difficult to fit in sometimes" (UCL-008, in Lingham, Rai, and Akhter forthcoming). The exhaustion and desperation is evident here.

Here, I build on that earlier paper and outline the concept of depletion and show also how it can be expanded to better understand the harms of racial discrimination and environmental depletion.

Depletion occurs in different contexts and sites: individuals, households, and communities, each embedded in and interconnected with the other (Rai, Hoskyns, and Thomas 2014, 90–91):[2] Everyone has a set of resources (stock), dependent upon their socio-economic position. These resources are used up in doing unpaid social reproductive work as well as paid work. Some of this outflow[3] of resources is replenished through everyday processes such as eating, sleeping and resting. Resource outflows are also affected by "natural wear and tear" such as aging. The difference between the resource outflows used up in the provision of social reproductive work and resource inflows that go into maintaining the current stock of resources available to those engaged in this work is the measure of DSR. DSR can then be visualized as a tipping point—DSR occurs when resources fall below a threshold of sustainability. (89)

These resources are differential and unequal—at an individual as well as household and community levels—and this inequality on grounds of gender, class, and race affects the intensity of depletion experienced. The DSR of the *individual* can be physical as well as mental and might be measured through the Body Mass Index, tiredness, sleeplessness, reduced self-worth, insufficient time for oneself, the loss of friendships, and participation in community life (see Chapters 3, 4, and 5). If they fall below the threshold of normal wear and tear, these factors can deteriorate the well-being outcomes and reduce the capability of the individual to carry out social reproduction in the long run. DSR of *households* may include the decrease in collective household resources—leisure time spent together by members of the household as a result of extensions to and precarity of the working day, long commutes to work because of segregated living (see Chapter 4), failure to manage the consequences of an increase in the number of household members engaged in wage labor and reduced support structures, disposable income to carry out essential repairs to the fabric of the house, and more. The household can benefit to different degrees from the resources of the individuals who constitute it, but it can also exacerbate individual depletion if the recognition and resource allocation within the household is unequal. As Baxter and Brickell (2014 in Bertonali and Boccagni 2021, 57) have argued, this can lead to an increased "gap between normative models and actual domestic experience as an ongoing, relationally and materially based matter of home making and *un*making." The DSR of *communities* that we identified included the shrinking of the commons—of community resources, spaces, time commitments from those mobilized into paid work leading to the erosion of community networks (see Chapter 6). The depletion of communities or a reduction in the collective resources required for social exchange can exacerbate the extent and effects of individual and household depletion. The inequalities that mark communities—of gender, caste, class, sexuality, and race—also affect the ways in which the DSR of both individuals and households is experienced. However, the vitality of communities that are able to address these divisions can also mitigate DSR (Rai, Hoskyns, and Thomas 2014, 90–91). So the sources as well as consequences of DSR are not linear; DSR in one site can and does, we suggested, affect the resources in other sites (89).

The identification of DSR is therefore a complex task that involves paying attention to intersectionalities of class, gender, race, and culture in the doing of social reproduction (Rai, Hoskyns, and Thomas 2014, 91). For example, what is "normal" in terms of wear and tear in different socioeconomic contexts? How does this change over time with access to different resources (see Geronimus, Hicken et al. 2006)? For example, for an individual the threshold could be specified at the point at which their stock of physical and mental health falls below the commonly accepted measure of a minimum standard such as blood pressure or other stress indicator. Similarly, the illness or death of an income earner could be a tipping point for a household if the loss drastically curtails the leisure time of other members (Rai, Hoskyns, and Thomas 2014, 89). Further, the consequences of DSR are harmful and cumulative in that, "depending on their geopolitical, class and gendered positionings, individuals, households and communities with high levels of DSR will be more harmed than others" (97–98; Geronimus, Hicken et al. 2006; Bassel and Emejulu 2017; Kundani 2023).

Depletion and Harm

Depletion *is* harm.

The debates about harm are many and complex, but as a concept harm remains slippery. It is both a normative and a legal concept. It is deployed both at an individual and group level and at the level of physical as well as social injury and as denial of rights. Of course, harm is experienced by individuals, but its affects can and are experienced by communities and societies, intergenerationally and intersectionally. Implicit understandings of the good life are important to understanding harm, which can be seen as "the abrogation of [basic] rights [which] . . . limits the individual's chance to full himself [*sic*] in many spheres of life" (Schwendinger and Schwendinger 1975, 137 in Pemberton 2015, 16). Harm as denial of rights can be enacted through "a range of structural harms, such as racism, imperialism, sexism and poverty," which "contextualises harm within the existing mode of production in which they are embedded" (Lasslett in Pemberton 2015, 20). Social harm is also deployed as a concept to understand the denial of democratic rights; Wilkins (1982) suggests that a consensus on what constitutes a meaningful list of rights concerns—personal liberty, human dignity, and fear of victimization, for example—can help us "prioritize harms that are more injurious than others" (Pemberton

2015, 23). Harms are therefore relational in two ways: through enforced exclusions and through mis- or malrecognition (Pemberton 2015, 30). In this way, harms are structurally embedded but also can be foreseen, predicted, and prevented—or not—depending upon their recognition (Yar 2012). The state and the law thus have an important role to play in the prevention of harm, and as in tort law, ensuring compensation for harm done. Robin West (1987, 81) urges feminist scholars to communicate the magnitude of gender-specific pain through its description and argues that "the absence of a jurisprudential analysis of the concept of harm, and particularly the economists' collapse of the concept of harm with the concept of cost, far from being totally inconsequential . . . has had adverse consequences, and particularly for women" (West 1987, 96; see also Ní Aoláin 2009; Goldblatt and Rai 2018).

This expanded understanding of harms is useful to frame our understanding of depletion as harm. However, misrecognition in legal scholarship is focused on individual and group identities being misrepresented; the depletion framework, however, focuses on the mis- or malrecognition of a category of labor/work. In terms of depletion, harm is structural, is always social, and is embedded in unequal gendered social relations.

Depletion as harm occurs when there is a "measurable deterioration in the health and well-being of individuals and in the sustainability of households and communities" (Rai, Hoskyns, and Thomas 2014, 91). Depletion can be generative of four different kinds of harm. First, *discursive harm* results from mainstream public discourses that negate labor as work in the domestic sector[4] and through this negation affirms gendered social hierarchies and distinctions of class and race. Second, *emotional harm* occurs when those engaged in social reproduction experience negative emotive burdens, for example, guilt about being a "working mother," which condemns millions to believing they are harming their children's present and future (Harris 2010; Walker Gore 2020; Bhowmick 2022). Third, DSR can lead to *bodily harm* as the (non)recognition of the working body within the home. Here we think of accidents in the home because of tiredness, of extended working days leading to burnout, which can also lead to losing a job, and of being unable to maintain friendships and community networks of support. Maternal mortality is another bodily harm associated with the "naturalization" of birthing, underinvestment in maternal health, and privatization of healthcare that both excludes the racialized poor for maternal support and overmedicates those who can access it, increasing rates of C-sections, for example. Finally, we saw depletion as harm resulting from lack of access to formal modes of justice: *harm to citizenship entitlements*. Harm occurs when groups are constituted as "noncontributors" to the economy and therefore as recipients of its welfare rather than citizens with entitlements (Rai, Hoskyns, and Thomas 2014, 91–92; Morris 2010; Broom et al. 2023). These four types of harms are of course entangled with each other and work at all three levels, separately and together. They are also entangled with productivist regimes of capitalism, in its diverse forms.

Take, for example, stigma. State welfare regimes, where present, can be sources of support for some and of shame for others, depending upon their social position. As Kittay (1999, 127) notes in the case of the U.S. welfare regime, it "suffers from at least a double stigma: it is for the poor and it is for women," and because "poverty here, as elsewhere, is frequently associated with matters of race, welfare bears a triple stigma—it disproportionately affects women of color and their children." Similarly, Broom et al. (2023, 56) argue, "The perpetuation of harm-by-design is made morally palatable by devaluing certain subjects and social categories" (see also Shilliam 2018)—single mothers, indigenous people, racialized minorities, the unemployed, for instance. Discursive harm is then reflected in both state and nonstate discourses about those who need welfare as undeserving. This stigma attached to welfare underlines the presumption that only those who are able to "work" in the paid sector of the economy contribute to society and are therefore the model citizens needed in a modern society. All this harms those in a relationship with the state—the welfare/workfare regime is a reflection of this, where the stigma of "not working" does not allow claims against the state in the same way as for those who are deemed to be taxpayers and deserving "working families" (on the deserving poor, see Shilliam 2020, 9–32). Harm to citizenship entitlement is then built on the foundations of discursive harm, and together these have material effects on the health and well-being of individuals (bodily harm), households, and communities through intergenerational "weathering," as Geronimus, Hicken et al. (2006) call it. Becoming a full citizen then comes to mean that women must be mobilized into the paid labor market; globally the discrepancy in labor force participation is around 50% for women and 80% for men (World Bank 2022). This is indeed the preoccupation of many Global South states like India where women's presence in the paid labor market is weak (Deshpande and Singh 2021; Chattopadhyay and Chowdhury 2022; Srija and Vijay 2020). States continue to punish those who care; women often take on paid work to support their families without the provision of adequate childcare (Topping and Butler 2023). This mobilization of women's labor is being promoted in both national and international policy arenas and debates today in the context of increasing national debt, inflation, and emerging banking instability.[5] As before, cuts to state expenditures in many countries are increasing, which has a direct impact on the well-being of people, and particularly on the lives of women: "In 2023, 94 developing countries are projected to cut public spending versus 49 high-income countries. Moreover, the average overall contraction is much bigger than in earlier shocks—3.5% of GDP in 2021. . . . In terms of the human impact, austerity affected 6.3 billion persons in 2021 or more than 80% of the global population, which is expected to rise to 6.7 billion people or 85% of humanity in 2023" (Ortiz and Cummins 2022, n.p.). In the context of these cuts, women's labor continues to be the shock absorber of crises. The non- and malrecognition of care work means that depletion and the harms that accrue from it are also not addressed; indeed under conditions of crises these are intensified in the absence of mitigation of depletion. If social reproduction is a subsidy to capital, so is depletion.

Conceptualizing depletion was therefore also an attempt at developing a counternarrative that helps develop an alternative, transformative politics of care. By examining the rhythms of everyday lives of individuals and households (Chapters 2, 3, and 4), by understanding how to measure the everyday depletion and its costs (Chapter 2), by analyzing the labor of community resistance to systemic attacks upon its collective life (Chapter 6), we can respond to West's urging to record and, through this, recognize the consequences of the ripples of harm felt by individuals, households, and communities and the landscapes in which they are embedded. Pain, like joy, is felt differently; social positionality marks the experiences and articulations of depletion as harm and also affects the resources available to resist harm and to repair. This underscores the importance of intersectional inequalities and exclusions within which depletion is embedded and is reproduced, and refuses the timid and supposedly "gender-neutral" policy initiatives put forward to address harms that do not address exclusions of race and which adhere instead to the ideology of individualism and narrow assimilationism (Kennedy 2018, 132). Further, the experience of the COVID-19 pandemic shows that harm is intensified in times of crises, and as crises are endemic to capitalism, this harm is ongoing (Fortier 2020). Under conditions of austerity, women act as shock absorbers, especially as care responsibilities increase and poverty intensifies, harming women directly and indirectly (79). To meet their care responsibilities, women move quicker and in greater numbers into part-time work or stop working altogether, increasing their dependency. The collapse of household income under conditions of crises and, as we have seen, increasing debt, increases the burdens of social reproduction, intensifying depletion. Not surprisingly, all this adversely affects women's financial position, self-esteem, and mental well-being. (On previous crises effects, see Seguino 2006; Floro and Pichetpongsa 2010; Giuntoli et al. 2015; Hiswåls et al. 2017.) Depletion and crises thus go hand in hand, but depletion also fundamentally marks everyday regimes of care and caring. Strategies to reverse DSR are therefore urgent and necessary.

Reversing Depletion

Rai, Hoskyns, and Thomas (2014, 98–100) outlined three broad strategies for reversing DSR: mitigation, replenishment, and transformation. These three strategies are not fixed, and the boundaries between them are fluid. We separated them out only as a heuristic device. Mitigation is widely practiced by those who can afford it; replenishment is available in some contexts and much less so in others; and transformative strategies are still being struggled for and over. In some ways mitigation and replenishment, while hugely important in themselves, may be seen to take the edge off the crisis of DSR; transformation remains far from realizable at the moment.

Specifically, mitigation is an individualized strategy of buying in labor to support social reproductive work and to lessen the consequences of DSR (Rai, Hoskyns, and Thomas 2014, 98–99; Stack 2019). Here, it is important to note how the long chains of care—across space and time—often reflect increased exploitation of raced bodies of what Lutz (2011) has called "the new maids of the transnational economy." The role of many Global South states in facilitating developmental policy frameworks to mobilize the labor of poor women, particularly in the field of care, and benefit from remittances has been analyzed by feminist scholars (Truong 1996; Elias 2009; Mahon 2020). Other mitigating strategies can include sharing tasks across generations—children (see Chapter 5) and older members of the household helping the primary carer—or by communal and collective arrangements among networks of friends and neighbors. Class and race also mark these strategies—the double burden of doing both care and waged work increases the DSR for those at the "dying end" of social hierarchies, while those able to pay for care are more easily able to mitigate their own DSR. Buying in labor also allows middle-class women to join the labor market, on the one hand, and to use their income to buy in care labor; the circularity of this mitigatory practice is available to relatively few, however. In all these cases, there is a production-reproduction nexus underwritten by state policies that support the gendered division of labor in the sphere of care, which underpins the capitalist system as well as generating higher levels of DSR for those who are poor and marginalized. While mitigation also includes communal and collective arrangements, such as networks of friends and neighbors, the working poor may not be able to afford the time to contribute to collective strategies (see González de la Rocha 2001). This exposes differences in the effects of DSR between North and South and between different classes, races, and regions within particular national contexts (Rai, Hoskyns, and Thomas, 99).

Replenishment includes interventions by both state and voluntary associations and other nonstate actors which assist households to cope with DSR but without addressing its structural causes (Rai, Hoskyns, and Thomas 2014, 99). Young (1990, 55) suggests a comprehensive form of replenishment, for example, by proposing a "social wage," a guaranteed socially provided income outside the wage system.

Universal Basic Income can also be a replenishment strategy, although "its transformative capacity to empower women and to strengthen their role in society should not be overestimated" (Lombardozzi 2020, 317; see also Chhachhi 2022). While obviously helpful in lessening DSR, replenishment strategies are also variable and always in danger from cutbacks in times of economic crises and changing value systems. The austerity policies introduced in many countries after the financial crisis in 2008 led to deep cuts in state spending on social protection (see Dewan et al. 2023; Dasgupta and Mitra 2020); the COVID-19 crisis, for example, led to increased spending on healthcare and the economy but also led to increased governmental debt, which in the absence of a shift in discourse about the importance of social infrastructure is again leading to rollbacks to state expenditure in the name of balancing budgets. Struggles for consolidating and expanding social protection and community networks are important aspects of political action that must accompany this strategy to reverse DSR. Mitigation and replenishment act to "fill in," some of the systemic causes and consequences of DSR, but do not necessarily envisage deeper structural change. Rather, in some ways these approaches, while hugely important, may absorb some of the pressures imposed by crises and distract from addressing DSR through providing much-needed support for ongoing regimes of social reproduction.

Transformation involves structural changes in two dimensions (Rai, Hoskyns, and Thomas 2014, 99–100). The first is the restructuring of gendered social relations. This would mean, for example, both men and women being fully involved in the sharing of social reproduction. This would transform not only the lives of millions of women who largely bear the burden of this work today but would also mean the restructuring of wider social relations, as gender-based inequalities outside the home are challenged to equalize social reproductive work. The second is the issue of the recognition and valuation of social reproduction and therefore of DSR. As Catherine Hoskyns and I have argued elsewhere, "Valuation becomes a communication tool by translating unpaid work into a language that governments understand: money" (Hoskyns and Rai 2007, 302). The question here is whether capital can bear the costs of this valuation; the debates on social reproduction covered in the introduction would suggest not. If they are to be successful, both these transformative arenas need strategies that cut across private/public, North/South divides. Struggles for transforming both these arenas have been ongoing and have seen some successes—formal and informal, legal, constitutional, and discursive—but as yet these successes have not led to systemic transformations. On the contrary, backsliding on gender issues is increasing in different parts of the world. However, if we see successful transformation not as a single revolutionary event but as a bundle of changes that may add up to transformation in the long term, then we may see some elements of that bundle emerging through these struggles for gender equality and the valuation of social reproduction.

As we can see, there is a distinction between mitigatory (individual), replenishing (state/nonstate), and transformative strategies to address DSR, which suggests that while the structural barriers to including social reproductive work within the production boundary continue to exist, we need to be vigilant that addressing DSR does not lead to the privatizing of risk, with mitigatory strategies at one end leading to the increase in DSR down the care chain (Rai, Hoskyns, and Thomas 2014, 100). So the maintenance and extension of social protection that the state provides (replenishment strategy, in our schema) is important to struggle for and over; the defense of social protection then becomes an urgent task in times of crisis. Delivering justice remains tied to both—the transformation of gendered social relations and to addressing maldistribution of resources in capitalist regimes of accumulation, production, and exchange. Recognition, measurement, and compensation of social reproduction and DSR then remain critical political issues for gender equality, as does campaigning for the following:

1. More work on identifying and measuring social reproductive work as well as DSR that accrues through it.
2. Inclusion of the value of social reproduction in the GDP.
3. Gender equality in care work.
4. Policy shifts that recognize the value of social reproduction and the costs of DSR for society as a whole and that support the replenishment of individuals, households, and communities, especially in times of economic crises. I outline the depletion framework visually in Figure 1.1.

Sites of Depletion ↓	DEPLETION AS HARM Embodied, emotional, discursive, citizenship, ecological		
Individual			
Household			
Community	Mitigation	Replenishment	Transformation
REVERSAL STRATEGIES →			

Figure 1.1 Mapping depletion and reversing it.

Recognition of social reproduction and of unpaid labor is then the first step in the struggle for transformation of social relations. By conceptually shining a light on depletion as harm, Hoskyns, Thomas, and I hoped to challenge the gender regime—discursive, political, and socioeconomic—that underpins the non- or malrecognition of social reproductive work, of those who perform it and those who can be harmed by it. We were not seeking a direct correlation here between this recognition and gender justice; rather we hoped that making depletion visible would provide strong evidence for the necessity of recognizing the subsidy that social reproduction pays to global capital and to addressing the human costs of this subsidy. This would, we hoped, also lead to a struggle to accurately reflect the former and to develop strategies to minimize the latter. These struggles are, as Nancy Fraser argues in her conversation with Rahel Jacggi, "[p]erfectly intelligible responses to structural harms, they are neither expressions of 'secondary contradictions' nor embodiments of 'false consciousness'" (Fraser and Jaeggi 2018, 166). They are therefore an expanded understanding of class struggle as social struggle (166).

Conceptual Travels: Studying the Crises of Our Times

Once published, concepts acquire a life of their own, as they should, and travel with those who work with them. These travels can lead to new directions or to cul de sacs; they can generate new debates or contribute to old ones; they can uncover new connections, hitherto not made by the original author(s), in interdisciplinary vocabularies. Like all travel, concepts journey with some baggage that might help or hinder communications across intersectional boundaries; travelers then might have to choose to shed this baggage or to creatively deploy it for finding and making new pathways as they travel with a bundle of conceptual definitions and grids. As I examine the ways in which depletion through social reproduction as a concept has been and can be worked with, I am delighted and awed by the innovative and unexpected connections that scholars are making across disciplines while engaging with depletion, some of which I discuss below.

While we covered a lot of ground in a short (7,000 words) paper, inevitably there were some gaps that became more visible over time. For example, until now I have been building on the original conceptual framework of depletion *through* social reproduction; however, some scholars have used the term rather differently—as depletion *of* and depletion *in* social reproduction (Fernandez 2017; Johnson and Lingham, 2024; Stevano forthcoming). I could argue that through/of/in are within the same parameters and therefore might be used interchangeability. However, depletion *of* social reproduction alerts us to the erosion of social infrastructure supporting care work, adding to the concept's heft. The point that my colleagues and I wanted to make in our paper was about the costs of *doing* social reproduction on individuals, households, and communities. However, we were also concerned that state support for social infrastructure or its withdrawal from this sphere can either replenish or intensify the depletion of those engaged in this labor. So the erosion of social infrastructure— depletion *of* social reproduction—does directly affect depletion through social reproduction.

The concept of depletion has been worked on/with in different contexts and from various disciplinary approaches: the concept has been used to understand the future agendas of feminist international relations (Prügl and Tickner 2018); environment and climate change (Zbyszewska 2018; see also Chapter 6 this volume); debt and microfinance (Guermond et al. 2023); conflict and postconflict politics and violence against women (Basham and Catignani 2018; Hearn et al. 2022); sexual and reproductive health (Tanyag 2018;) race, racism, and global positionality (Gunawardana 2016; Fernandez 2017; the law and the political economy of care (Goldblatt and Rai 2018, 2020; Goldblatt 2022); and, of course, socioeconomic crises, health crises (COVID-19 in particular), and the crises of social reproduction (Lux and Wohl 2015; Brickell et al. 2020; Fortier 2020; Stevano et al. 2021). These interventions have also pointed to some gaps in the article; this is understandable, as we were trying to conceptualize depletion in most familiar spaces, units, and social relations and to understand how we can identify and measure depletion. This was a new approach to an old problem of the nonrecognition of costs of caring that had gone unaddressed. We were concerned with showing that the cost of social reproduction, depletion, has material human effects—it is harmful, and people are harmed by it. Below I assess some of the issues raised by the cross-disciplinary work on/with depletion to reflect upon the ways in which the concept we outlined has been stretched to connect different spheres of life and work; I have learned from this, as I hope is visible in the work that follows.

Ecological, Military, and Economic Crises and Intensification of Depletion

In our work on depletion, we built on the work of environmental accountants (UNSNA 2009; see also Chapter 2); we did not, however, focus on the relationship between our social and natural worlds—the impact of depletion of the environment on human beings and their social lives and, in particular, on the intensification of depletion through social reproduction. The climate crisis and other crises—of health, of war and conflict—make it imperative that we understand the linkages between the everyday and the geopolitical, between depletion of humans and their environs in the broadest sense and between humans who have been separated through the logics of capitalist exploitation on grounds of class, race, and, of course, gender. We need to recognize, as Fraser (2014b) has pointed out in her reading of Polanyi, that the thrust of capitalist crises lies in "the efforts to create 'self-regulating markets' in land, labour and money, the effect of which was to turn those three fundamental bases of social life into 'fictitious commodities.'" Fraser, following Marx, concludes, "The inevitable result . . . was to despoil nature, rupture communities and destroy livelihoods, thus connecting the 'three dimensions of the present crisis: the ecological, the social and the financial'" (541; also see Biesecker and Hofmeister 2010). This underlines a need for a shared political grammar that can help us in making these connections.

Ecological crises are eroding life and livelihoods in different ways, and the poorest, most marginalized, and most vulnerable people are experiencing the depletion of their individual and collective lives in impacts from the climate crisis. However, mainstream economics continues to treat the negative effects on nature—if at all—as "externalities" and does not recognize the fundamental role nature plays for all economic production processes (O'Hara 1997; Jochimsen and Knobloch 1997; Dengler and Strunk 2017; Dasgupta 2021). Others have taken up this aspect of depletion; building on the work of ecofeminists such as Vandana Shiva and Maria Mies, de Chiro (2008, 278, 280) emphasizes that "environmental issues are reproductive issues," and to treat them as such allows us to "jump scales" to understand the impacts of the "current mode of production—corporate globalisation—on the survivability of individual bodies, particular communities, national cultures, and the earth itself." As we saw in the introduction, and as Sturgeon (2009, 104) has argued, "The politics of gender are often both the politics of reproduction and the politics of production—the intertwined ways that people produce more people, manage bringing up children, figure out how to do the work at home at the same time as the work that brings in a paycheck, decide how and where to buy food, clothing, shelter, and transportation, take care of elders, and create and maintain all of the social institutions that surround this work. And all of this is central to whether or not our ways of living cause environmental degradation."

Feminist work is therefore now underway to address this dimension of social reproduction—that the care of the environment and the care of the human and other species need to go hand in hand, and depletion of one leads to the depletion of the other (Goldblatt and Rai 2018; Guermond et al. 2023). Ecofeminism "sees a parallel between the exploitation of women's work and the exploitation of natural resources: both are necessary prerequisites for capitalism but remain widely costless because they are considered as natural and thus free of charge," and therefore "the ecological crisis is linked to the gender order and thus exacerbates the crisis of social reproduction" (Bauhardt 2014, 61). As we will see in Chapter 2, the valuing of nature and the environment through putting an economic cost to its depletion is one of the building blocks of the concept of depletion; the idea here is not monetizing nature or care but seeing value as a form of recognition that has a material basis. It is to acknowledge that the exploitation of both caregiving and nature is not costless, even though they are treated as such in the economy and in societies that privilege profit maximization.

A UN report notes, "Women represent a high percentage of poor communities that are highly dependent on local natural resources for their livelihood, particularly in rural areas where they shoulder the major responsibility for household water supply and energy for cooking and heating, as well as for food security" (Osman-Elasha 2009, n.p.). Access to water, for example, is clearly affected by environmental and climate change rhythms, and also affects the everyday rhythms of social reproduction: "A study of 24 sub-Saharan countries revealed that when the collection time is more than 30 minutes, an estimated 3.36 million children and 13.54 million adult females were responsible for water collection. [And] one roundtrip to collect water is 33 minutes on average in rural areas and 25 minutes in urban areas" (UNICEF 2016, n.p.). The lack of water then lengthens the working day of women and depletes their energies and adversely affects their physical health, causing back pain, dehydration, and also anxiety about sexual violence on the long walks to collect water. Further, the lack of access to land and recognition as farmers means that women, who carry the burden of social reproductive work, are often unable to participate in decision-making about what and how to work and produce from the land (Agarwal 1994). It also negatively affects food security of the gendered households and communities. As Camey Castañeda et al. (2020, xiii) note, "Threats and pressures on the environment and its resources amplify gender inequality and power imbalances in communities and households coping with resource scarcity and societal stress." Bringing together an analysis of climate crisis and financialization of debt through microfinance, Guermond

et al. (2023, 4, 5) note that results from privatization of social reproduction as well as climate adaptation can lead to "necessary coping
strategies and tactics that are physically and emotionally depleting";
microfinance thus is not a "harm-free tool of climate adaptation." As
we will see in Chapter 6, extractive economies and struggles against
these are gaining ground, and women are at the forefront of many of
these but are also being depleted as they cope with burdens of social
reproduction as well as struggles to reverse it.

The shifts in the environment are also affecting spaces and places
through "natural disasters," which are crises of another kind;
capitalism's extraction of resources and making wasteland of regions are neither "natural" nor "developmental" and have significant
human costs, which deplete. The World Bank reported that the climate
crisis, could force 216 million people across six world regions to move
within their countries by 2050 (Clement et al. 2021, 80). The gendered
inequalities in this migratory process have been well documented:

1. as they usually carry family and household responsibilities including taking care of their dependent children and elderly relatives,
it is more difficult for them to choose to leave and organise their
departure; 2. but also because they face major gender-based pressure during displacement. They have less access to relief resources
(shelter, water and food), have specific sanitation and sexual and
reproductive health needs that often go unmet, and are more likely
to endure gender-based violence such as forced-marriage, domestic
and sexual violence, exposure to trafficking, etc. Their physical,
emotional and mental health may deteriorate, in part because of
exposure to violence, the loss of social support networks and heavy
caregiving burdens, which can increase anxiety, post-traumatic
stress and other illnesses. (HABITABLE 2021, n.p.; see also Tanyag
2018; Baek 2022)

All these aspects of climate crisis–related disasters intensify gendered depletion. Further, when migration takes place across national
borders, securitization and bordering make journeys and everyday
social reproductive work more dangerous. This is important to study
further, given that around half of the world's female migration is

"care led"—women moving to look after others' needs (Peng 2019). Depletion of millions is therefore tied to the marketization of care and to mitigation of depletion of some through the labor of many.

Displacement through war and conflict and through the systems that support them, also intensifies depletion. Whether it is war between countries or everyday violence of settler colonialism, depletion through social reproduction increases, although taking different forms (see Tuck and Yang 2012; Chilmeran and Pratt 2019). The gender, peace, and security literature unpacked the importance of the discursive constructions of militarized, masculinized, and/or securitized identities (Enloe 1990; Zalewski and Parpart 2019; Kearns 2017; choi et al. 2022), but until relatively recently it was less focused on the everyday regimes of labor and recognition of the impact of these on/as violence against women. Securing resources for managing everyday economies of the household, the psychosocial effects of violence, the trauma of loss and absence of relatives while often carrying the double burden of productive and social reproductive labor in the context of economic and political insecurity—all this means that women experience greater difficulty in carrying out social reproduction with higher levels of depletion in the sites most affected by conflict (Johnson and Lingham 2020, 2024). As Johnson and Lingham argue, "women experience pressure to present themselves as 'strong' rather than exhausted; as 'enduring' the challenges of unpaid social reproductive labour rather than suffering them" (62). Noting and measuring depletion is one way of ensuring that such gendered "resilience" is unpacked and made visible to understand the costs of domestic labor. Chilmeran and Pratt (2019, 586) develop their reading of depletion in the context of geopolitics of the Middle East to analyze "how states intervene in social reproduction, with differential implications for depletion," to instrumentalize it in Iraq and erase life in Israel/Palestine. And Basham and Catignani (2018, 161) point out that not just wars, but war machines—the military—are a continual site of women's depletion as their labor is a core part of the "materialization of and preparation for" war. If precarity experienced through the uprooting of households and communities is depleting, the outflows of energy expended that goes into rebuilding lives affected by violence also cause depletion as inflows of support dry up.

Economic crises also intensify depletion—in coping with crumbling social infrastructure as well as increasing levels of household debt (Dannreuther 2019). The Global South debt crisis, structural adjustment policies that followed, and, among others, the financial crisis of 2008 all affected not only economies but societies and the everyday regimes of social reproduction, inequality, and depletion. Economic crises have long affected the social infrastructures of societies and therefore can erode support networks and systems that can provide help for social reproduction intensifying depletion (Elson 2000; Rai 2002; Dowling 2016; Hozic and True 2016). Crises affect marginalized groups in particular as they try to engage in productive and reproductive practices under conditions of austerity and economic restructuring (Elias and Roberts 2016). This also allows us to understand the intimate connections between these two sites—Gunawardana (2016, 861) argues that both workplaces and domestic spaces are sites of depletion, "fuelling a cycle of gendered harm through the reproduction of disposability."[6] These harms are experienced differently along the arc of intersectional inequalities; depletion must pay attention therefore to issues of inequality and violence of race and racism, class and class exploitation, and gender inequalities (Chatzidakis et al. 2020).

Intersectionalities of Depletion

While feminist political economy literature has outlined the gendered inequality between women and men and shown carefully and robustly how this affects social relations of exploitation, much more work needs to be done on how race and racism as violence and oppression are an integral part of capitalist extraction and human and climatic depletion, globally (see Bhambra 2021; Hobson 2020). This capitalist extraction builds on a history of colonialism and racism that led not to homogenizing labor but to differentiating it and is generative of relations of inequality among people (Robinson 2023 [1983], 26); "for capitalism to survive, it must exploit and prey upon the unequal differentiation of human value" (Melamed 2015, 76). It becomes clear, then, why gender and racial divisions are, both and together, integral to capitalist development (Bhattacharya 2017, 5). These gendered, classed, and racialized exclusions are visible in different ways: through the erasure of women's labor as "reproductive" rather than "productive" labor, through segmentation of labor markets that are deeply racialized,[7] and through accumulations through dispossessions in regions that are continuously folded into the ambit of capitalism (Harvey 1990; see also Fernandez 2017). The effects of this separation and exploitation are deeply depleting.

Take, for example, the argument made by Geronimus (1992, 207) about "weathering" and race: "[T]he health of African-American women may begin to deteriorate in early adulthood as a physical consequence of cumulative socioeconomic disadvantage." While Geronimus, Hicken, et al. (2006, 826) focused on individual women, I would argue that the experience of long-term weathering also affects households and communities within a racialized society as well as the rate of wear and tear intensifying depletion for all: "The weathering effects of living in a race-conscious society may be greatest among those Blacks most likely to engage in high-effort coping." And as we shall see in the following chapters, coping and social reproduction go hand in hand. Coping with gendered regimes of labor, of structural violence, and of denial of social reproduction as work "extracts a physical price [from those] who engage in and cope with the stressful life conditions presented to them" (832). Weathering and depletion of individuals, households, and communities in their gendered and racialized sense allows us to understand the long term consequences of racism as of gendered inequalities of global capitalism. Both increase in the contexts of crises—political and environmental.

True (2012) opened up an important line of debate showing how violence against women both underpins and is perpetuated by the process of global economic transformation. Building on this, Elias and Rai (2015, 426) outline three strands of "the violence of everyday life in the global political economy: "(1) the pervasiveness of violence within feminized global zones of work, such as export processing zones or the expanding market for migrant domestic work; (2) women's experience of violence in public spaces, particularly that relating to mobility and public transport; and (3) the relationship between women's subordination in the household and forms of violence."

So the violence of the state, the violence of the home, and the historical violence of colonialism come together as "the location par excellence where the controls and guarantees of judicial order can be suspended—the zone where the violence of the state of exception is deemed to operate in the service of 'civilization'" (Mbembé 2003, 24). They come together in gendered and racialized regimes of oppression and negatively affect, directly and indirectly, the work and workers of social reproduction. This intersectional analysis not only opens up spaces for discussions of violence as a gendered "everyday" phenomenon, but also points to its depleting effects by highlighting systemic and structural violence (see Chapters 3 and 4). As Maya Angelou (2013) writes in her poem "Woman Work":

> I've got the children to tend
> The clothes to mend
> The floor to mop
> The food to shop
> Then the chicken to fry
> Then baby to dry
> I got company to feed
> The garden to weed
> I've got the shirts to press
> The tots to dress
> The cane to be cut
> I gotta clean up this hut
> Then see about the sick and the cotton to pick . . .
> Fall gently, snowflakes
> Cover me with white
> Cold icy kisses and
> Let me rest tonight

Rest, however, is not easy to access as long workdays mark the doing of social reproduction in the context of racialized and classed oppression; the everyday becomes a site of depletion; this is where negotiating space, time, and (structural) violence affects how social reproduction is carried out and who bears the costs of doing this work.

Everyday Rhythms of Space, Time, and Violence: The Doing of Social Reproduction

In this book, I also underpin more explicitly than was done in the original article (Rai, Hoskyns, and Thomas 2014) the idea of how the everyday lens of life and labor helps us understand depletion better. Through the analysis of the everyday presented in the following chapters, I argue that crises intensify depletion and harm differentially across gender, race, and class boundaries and therefore need to be considered together if we are to make sense of and develop a robust framework to not only understand but to reverse depletion. As Rita Felski (2000, 77) notes, the everyday as a concept is everywhere and nowhere; it just is. Building on Lefebvre's work on the everyday, Juanita Elias and I have argued that "social reproductive work can be a drudgery and if not socially recognised and redistributed in an equitable way it produces alienation for those engaged in it—often valorised as 'mother' or 'parent' on the one hand, and framed through specific policy and governmental techniques which incarcerate, make dependent and marginalise, on the other" (Elias and Rai 2019, 7; see also Dowling 2021). Lefebvre (1984) draws attention to the routines and rhythms of everyday life as well as to how the everyday operates as a manifestation of the sphere of consumption that maintains capitalism. It points to the importance of holding our understanding of space and time together, in a productive tension which allows us to study the rhythms of everyday life (Elias and Rai 2019). As Elden (2004, vii) notes, "In the analysis of rhythms—biological, psychological and social—Lefebvre shows the interrelation of understandings of space and time in the comprehension of everyday life . . . [and] shows how these issues need to be thought together rather than separately." For Lefevre (2004, 25), a "rhythmanalyst" is "capable of listening to a house, a street, a town as one listens to a symphony, an opera"; the materiality of the everyday is built into its rhythms. Repeated circadian rhythms of the everyday challenge the linear impulse of modernity; the body anchors these rhythms as it engages in everyday repetitive tasks.

Feminist analyses have pointed to the everyday as a manifestation of maintenance and reproduction of gendered orders (Felski 2000; Smith

1987). They have built on as well as critiqued Lefebvre's theorization of everyday life because it does not focus on the gendered materiality of production, reproduction, and consumption and because gender features in his depiction of everyday life largely as an account of how "boredom" through domestic incarceration is daily experienced by women (Elias and Rai 2019, 6). As Felski (2000, 19) notes, this is not surprising for two reasons: first, the bodily rhythms of menstruation and birthing are seen as their subordination to natural time; second, because women remain primarily responsible for social reproduction and its repetitive tasks—cleaning, cooking, washing, and intergenerational care. In a sophisticated critique of Lefebvre, Felski argues that to equate repetition with domination and innovation with agency is flawed; change is often imposed in neoliberal contexts, while everyday rituals can help us resist the threatened qualities of everyday life (21). However, I would argue that we need to hold these two approaches to repetition together in tension with each other: while repetition can be used as resistance, it is also the case that social reproductive work includes the reproduction of modes of living and stabilizing of gendered hierarchies. Reciting religious texts and songs, celebrating festivals, and endorsing and performing everyday gendered rituals can be seen as sedimenting gendered orders. The two aspects are intertwined and often generate tensions within households and individuals as shifting subjectivities are disciplined.

In our engagement with the concept of the everyday and with Lefebvre's work from a feminist standpoint, Elias and I have discussed the image of the eight-hour day in private and public spaces by the artist Ricardo Morales, depicted in Figure 1.2 (Elias and Rai 2019, 212), which first emerged in the writings of the early 19th-century British social reformer Robert Owen. The day is divided into three spatial/temporal zones—"for work," "for rest," and "for what we will." This notion of an eight-hour day became an important rallying point for trade unions in the early 20th century as they sought to limit the long working day but can now be seen as a frame through which we can query the separation of the three time zones through a demand for a shorter working day (Weeks 2011). We also noted that if social reproduction is not counted as work (as in this image), then it also remains detached from the need for rest or "what we will." (The fact that paid

Figure 1.2 8 Hours.
Source: Ricardo Levins Morales.

work does not mitigate social reproductive work for poorer women is underlined in Chapters 3 and 4 (see also Mezzadri 2020). What this image leaves out, then, is the imbrication of production and reproduction in value generation and extraction. But it does suggest a gendered division of labor that is visually presented as "normal"—the woman in the mill doing paid work, the (male) laborer resting after a long day at work, and the leisure activity (I suppose at the weekend) where the man rows the woman. It is interesting to see, however, the woman reading the newspaper, which does suggest a more radical approach to gender relations that Morales was putting forward.

As I have been arguing, social reproduction takes time, time that is disregarded as work time. One of the questions that we could ask in terms of social reproduction and time is the following: Does valuing time help us value social reproduction (Elson 2012)? As we shall see in Chapter 2, it is not easy to capture time in rigorous and accurate registers; clock time, free time, and rest time often ignore the time-consuming and complex nature of care work within gendered regimes of the household (Bubeck 1995). One important feature of social reproductive work is multitasking: keeping an eye on children, remembering to give the sick their medicine while at the same time making sure they are warm, ferrying children to work, and shopping on the way back, all these everyday tasks often happen not sequentially but cutting across lines of attention; worry about this remains constant. Measures to assess multitasking time are being developed, as we shall see in Chapter 2 (also see Irani and Vemireddy 2020; TGNP 2009). Elias and Rai (2019, 214) focus on social reproductive time, "which includes not only care work, but also leisure time to repair ourselves, to stem the depletion through social reproduction." A key point that we emphasize is the intersection between public/private time which is also framed by private/public resources. A strategic focus on time as commodity in the context of the everyday allows us to see how depletion through social reproductive labor is built into the everyday social economy of the individual, households, and communities and how gendered norms of care secure the discrepancies in different kinds of work.

Social reproduction is not only a temporal but "a profoundly spatial phenomenon . . . [with] its historical emergence as a spatially distinct ensemble of social activities as an artifact of the birth of capitalism itself" (Winders and Smith 2019, 2). Paying attention to space is essential as we reflect on how negotiating spaces in the doing of social reproductive work mitigates or increases depletion as bodies traverse landscapes of public violence and experience tiredness and anxiety (Elias and Rai 2019; also see Chapter 4). As the experience of care and caring during COVID-19 has shown, spaces shift in the context of crises. A research project on racially minoritized families during COVID-19 showed that households experienced both being "locked in" and being "locked out of" familiar and familial spaces of the home, making the tasks of caring more complicated to organize, tiring to do, and emotionally and physically exhausting (Lingham, Rai, and Akhter forthcoming).

Governance of Social Reproduction and Depletion

The issue of valuing social reproduction also introduces an element of governance in different registers. First, as I argue in Chapter 2, rule-making bodies such as the UN System of National Accounts play an important role in recognition of work and the making of economic and social policy. Take, for example, UN Sustainable Development Goals (Rai, Brown, and Ruwanpura 2019, 368); despite many critiques of narrow economic measures of growth, the focus here remains on GDP and per capita growth. This is problematic because the GDP productive boundary excludes much of social reproductive work. This puts SDG 8 in tension with SDG 5, which calls for the recognition of the value of unpaid care and domestic work. As we argued (Rai, Brown and Ruwanpura 2019, 368), "productive employment and decent work for all men and women by 2030 [SDG 8] needs to take into account the value and costs of social reproduction." Not counting social reproductive labor has material consequences for the economy—the national accounts do not reflect and therefore do not adequately remunerate socially reproductive labor, which is of economic value and provides the foundations of the economy (Montgomerie and Tepe-Belfrage 2016). National governments are of course important in this regard; some governments have funded satellite household accounts to calculate the value of unpaid domestic work. While these are not formally part of the GDP calculations, they do give us a clear indication of the contribution this work makes to the economy. As I argue in this book, value is a form of recognition, and we need to recognize the value of labor in order to invest in mitigating depletion accrued through it (Mezzadri 2020).

The second register of governance is that of the law, which regulates social reproductive work in different ways   family law in cases of divorce and tort law in compensation cases (Kotiswaran 2021b; Goldblatt and Rai 2018, 2020), criminal law in sentencing and overlooking the (im)mobilities of families of the incarcerated (Pereyra-Iraola and Guawardana 2019), and penal regulation—all with consequences for mitigation of depletion. Therefore, some have argued that one way of recognizing social reproductive work is through the law. Take, for example, the issue of conditions of work. Building on the depletion framework, Goldblatt (2022, 15–16) has suggested that "housework and care should be fairly allocated and supported in such a way that it can be performed without exhausting, debilitating and depleting those who perform it." While Goldblatt's focus here is international institutions and covenants, for many legal feminists it is the nation-state that is the focus of demands about social infrastructure and welfare regimes (standard social and political policy demands), which opens up possibilities in the law for preventing harm caused by social reproduction that depletes those doing this work. Compensation is a particularly important and interesting area to examine in this regard (Goldblatt and Rai 2018, 173). Feminists have engaged with tort law with different levels of skepticism; Kotiswaran (2021b, 50) argues that it can have significant distributive effects such as recognizing and valuing unpaid work by reference to the market replacement costs or opportunity cost. However, they have also looked to constitutional and international human rights law to gain recognition of the value of social reproductive work (see also Kannabiran 2009).

However, feminists legal scholars and activists have also been skeptical about the power of the law; Kingdom among others (1991) argued for example that any engagement between the law and women is problematic because of the dangers of cooptation of those seeking change into the politics systems of already existing governance. Ní Aoláin and Hamilton (2009) worry about the western legal traditions crystalizing dominant understandings of western jurisprudence at moments of transitions in Global South countries and ask, "While transformation may occur, the pivotal question we raise is for whom?" (381). Gendered cultural assumptions of legal and state bodies can be sedimented through legal judgements and state policies, even as both the law and the state are powerful mechanisms to provide replenishment. This "in and against" approach to the law is needed to understand the potential and limits of seeing the law and the state as routes out of depletion through social reproduction.

The third register of governance is a discursive register, which valorizes motherhood but does not pay attention to its costs. As noted in the introduction, in a careless society not paying attention to care as well as to the costs of caring predominates and goes against the grain of what Simone Weil called "Attention"—the rarest and purest form of generosity. This generosity is rewarding for both those cared for and those who care. But such generosity is not costless; time, effort, emotion, and material resources go into extending this generosity every day, unsupported and unrecognized. The spectacle of motherhood in capitalist societies produces alienating discourses that separate out attention as reification from the labor of care that is mundane and burdensome. I will be arguing in this book that paying attention to these burdens becomes part of the ethics of care and caring, which then presents the possibility of reversing depletion.

In more immediate terms, not paying attention to social reproductive work is leading to (Seabrooke and Tsingou 2016, 71) declining fertility, which is "strongly linked to attitudes and perceptions of behaviour in the household, including the role of unpaid work and depletion in social reproductive capacity (Hoskyns and Rai 2007, Rai et al. 2014), as well as problems with inadequate childcare provision and the lack of support for child-rearing by employers." There are many reasons for declining birth rates in countries like Japan; one of them surely is the social reproduction burden and the lack of good-quality, reasonably priced child care (*Guardian* 2023).

Further, the neoliberal discourse "conceals the depletion of social reproduction in . . . economic development" (Boeri 2018, 174). As governments engage in successive rounds of labor market deregulation, leading to "flexible," precarious, and poorly paid waged work, which in turn increases gender inequalities, we see dangerously high rates of depleted workers unable to adequately reproduce their livelihoods (Shields 2019, 4). And this has harmful consequences for individuals, households, and communities (see also Prügl and Tickner 2018). One manifestation of this discourse is self-provisioning—householders and in particular women are urged, as Dowling (2021, 167) has pointed out, to not only look after the children and the elderly, to volunteer in schools and hospitals, but also to take responsibility for their self-care: "First of all: take care of you, because you are your own most valuable asset. . . . Second . . . because nobody else will." Long and critical histories of other concepts such as empowerment (Parpart, Rai, and Staudt 2012; McLaughlin 2016; Aslanbeigui, Oakes, and Uddin 2010) and resilience show how discourses of the "self" can be harnessed to neoliberal imaginaries to justify state policies of austerity, of withdrawal of state support from social infrastructure, and to valorize liberal feminist subject formations. Depletion through social reproduction as a conceptual framework can, as Mary Daly (2021, 116) points out, "spearhead very interesting and multi-level analyses of the resource conditions under which care (provision and need) is rendered sustainable or unsustainable." Similarly, Fernandez (2017, 142) argues that "the concept of depletion . . . [can be used] as a diagnostic tool to assess the gendered consequences" of capitalist labor regimes and dispossession. So the conceptual journeys of depletion have added much to our initial outline of the concept and have shown the importance of depletion to understanding gendered inequalities and the struggles to reverse these in our crisis-ridden world today.

Summary

I am struck by the length of time since the work on care/social reproductive work revealed the deep inequalities of our societies, and by how little has changed to radically address this issue. In the introduction to this book, I suggested that overlooking these inequalities, indeed by factoring these in as subsidies to capital, intensifies depletion. Reading through the rigorous, interdisciplinary work on depletion again reminds me that evidence produced by scholars is important but also that it is overlooked, or sometimes even harnessed to the dominant discourses of social relations. This is in contrast to the focus of some studies of ignorance that underline the importance of "knowledge that could have been but wasn't, or should be but isn't" (Proctor and Schiebinger 2008, n.p.); my concern is with the active overlooking, unhearing nonrecognition of social relations of care. Through demonstrating the effects of this nonrecognition, I want to demonstrate the costs of ignorance as depletion. Of course, ignorance is not passive but active—sometimes we want to keep the state and capital ignorant of our everyday practices and preferences, whether it is voting choices or sexual inclination or our everyday consumption patterns. However, there are other times when we want to reveal, to make public our concerns—this making visible is important for challenging ignorance; it also bridges the two spheres of life (and indeed the in-between spaces), the public and the private, that feminists have theorized and politicized. The *making* visible has taken many forms, and scholarship is one of these. The evidence that has been produced by feminist political economists to uncover the importance of social reproduction is by now unassailable, and yet we continue to witness the *active* nonrecognition or ignorance by the state and capital, or recognition in the margins, which does not fundamentally shift the boundaries of production/reproduction. Is this book going to make any difference to this active and accumulated ignorance that continues to rule our ways of thinking, our discourses of valorization and valuing, our policy frameworks? Perhaps not. However, perhaps insisting on repeatedly making visible the costs of this active ignorance can help militate against what Giroux (1986, 247) calls "the sheer weight of apocalypse." In the hands of activists against ignorance, which includes women's groups, feminist organizations, and movements for change, scholarly interventions can be important means of political campaigning to reveal what is being systematically kept out of view: the human costs of caring. An intersectional analysis of these costs by taking on issues of gender, class, race, indigeneity, and sexuality is also needed to generate fundamental disturbances in the regimes of exclusion and inclusion, mitigation and replenishment that are operative today. It is therefore not enough simply to recognize the harm done through social reproduction; the terms upon which social reproduction is done must also change.

2
Measuring Depletion in Multiple Registers

Introduction

"While women represent *half* the global population and *one-third* of the labor force, they receive only *one-tenth* of the world income and own *less than one percent* of world property. They are also responsible for *two-thirds* of all working hours," wrote Robin Morgan (1984, cited in Cohen 2013, n.p.) . This was a powerful representation of women's economic marginalization and was immediately taken up and repeated by international organizations (United Nations Development Fund for Women [UNIFEM], United Nations Development Program [UNDP]), NGOs, and women's movements to challenge gendered inequalities. But were the figures correct? And does it matter that they probably were not entirely so (see Cohen 2013)? The power of visualizing marginalization through what appeared to be "concrete facts" was potent. This mobilization of numbers occurred before the current power of Big Data, which has a large footprint and often dictates who gets heard in the public sphere: "[W]hen your big data is corrupted by big silences, the truths you get are half-truths at best" (Criado Perez 2019, xii). So numbers are important both to mobilize opposition to gendered inequalities and to vocalize gaps. Numbers are also partial, contested, and embedded in existing knowledge inequalities.

In our paper Catherine Hoskyns, Dania Thomas, and I developed a model to calculate the costs of social reproduction as depletion (Rai, Hoskyns, and Thomas 2014). In this chapter I reprise the model critically to show both its potential and its limits, which led me to develop the Feminist Everyday Observation Tool (FEOT)[1] to research and analyze the complexities of social reproductive work and its costs. Before doing that, however, I review the feminist debates about measuring

Depletion. Shirin M. Rai, Oxford University Press. © Shirin M. Rai 2024.
DOI: 10.1093/oso/9780197535547.003.0003

gender equality and suggest that a quantitative approach to depletion *can* alert us to the ways in which ontologies, epistemologies, and methodologies play out in our everyday lives and help us make sense of these, so long as we take a critical view of this data. To reach this conclusion, I will also discuss some important measures that have influenced my work, such as the UN System of National Accounts (UNSNA), environmental accounting, U.K. household satellite accounts, and time-use surveys.

Number Critics

Numbers matter.

As noted above, through numbers we can make people and issues visible or invisible, depending on what we measure and don't measure. Marilyn Waring (2012, n.p.) argued that "if you are invisible as a producer in the GDP, you are invisible in the distribution of benefits in the economic framework of the national budget." If recognition is value, as I have been arguing, then how do we represent it? Caroline Criado Perez (2019, xv) in her book *Invisible Women: The Gender Data Gap* explains that the gender data gap is "both a cause and consequence of the type of unthinking that conceives of humanity as almost exclusively male."

Influenced by international development institutions that insist that closing "the gender data gap" would allow for more gender-sensitive policy frames (Fuentes and Cookson 2019), feminist economists have demanded "better measurement," and improving the rigor of data produced to push forward gender equity measures (Deshpande and Kabeer 2019, 2). The argument goes that the bridging of this data gap would then lead to bridging of the gender gap, as policy will be driven by new and robust data on women; the active ignorance that I reflected on in Chapter 1 and the structural framing of policy then become appropriate data questions. In response to this challenge of producing better data, much work has been done to develop different measures to gauge the impact of economic development on women, their empowerment, and equality between women and men: the Gender-Related Development Index, the Gender Empowerment Measure, the Gender Equity Index, and the Genuine Progress Indicator, for example. However, despite attempts, there is yet to be an index that "measure[s] gender differences in responsibility for the financial and temporal care of dependents" (Folbre 2006a, 183) and definitely not one that measures the costs of providing this care. As Liebowitz and Zwingel (2014, 363) argue, "frequently used measures of global gender (in)equality [actually] diverge in important and substantial ways from the notion of gender equality and women's rights as articulated in feminist discourses and internationally agreed human rights norms and as such, fail to adequately measure that which they claim to capture."

The quantification of human experience through research and modeling has its critics, who point to the claims to truth based on quantitative data despite their obvious social desirability biases—when "research subjects . . . choose responses they believe are more socially desirable or acceptable rather than choosing responses that are reflective of their true thoughts or feelings" (Grimm 2010, n.p.)—in the processes of collection and analysis and storage of data. These then "fix" everyday experience and shape our worlds through policymaking or shifts based on these data. The critics also reject what Rose (1991, 675–676) calls "undemocratic numbers": numbers which stand in for knowledge and information and are mobilized "not merely [to] inscribe a pre-existing reality" but to constitute it (see also Hacking 1990). Further, these critics point out that numericalized norms produce deviance, which can lead to, for example, a Eurocentric and/or gender bias in the creation of global indices and their variables (see Jerven 2013; Fukuda-Parr, Yamin, and Greenstein 2014). The point here is that the many different realities across the world are hard to capture in one variable or model. "Not everything that can be counted counts and not everything that counts can be counted," Albert Einstein is reported to have said. Further, this can lead to the growth of an "audit society" (Power 1997) with a "measurement obsession" (Leibowitz and Zwingel 2014), where league tables and rankings of everything guide and nurture this obsession. "Categories of people and behaviour are created to enable counting, comparison, and ranking to take place, affecting how problems are defined and emerge as worthy of attention," writes Buss (2015, 381). This leads to investment in quantitative modes of expertise (Broome 2022). This critique has contributed to the skepticism about statistical models and dependence on quantitative research. The failure of complex predictive economic models to forecast the economic crisis in 2008, for example, also showed up the limitations of economic modeling.

My position on numbers is somewhat more ambivalent: I am sympathetic to the critique, but I also see the value of quantitative analysis. I agree with Muegge (2022, 1) that, "[i]ndispensable for public policy, quantification is neither good nor bad per se; the question is what its specific ramifications are. . . . [T]he real-world impact of statistics always depends on how they are understood, used, and subverted" (also Rai 2016). Building on the feminist debates on representation (Pitkin 1967), I have argued elsewhere that we need to understand numbers and data in three different registers: descriptive, substantive, and symbolic (Rai 2016). Description can serve as "a hypothesis generating procedure"; substantiation can help ask questions about how description becomes policy and who reads the numbers and interprets them with what effect; and symbolic readings can see numbers, measurement, and classification as provocations rather than as claims to truth (Rai 2016; Abt 1987; Federici, James, and Dalla Costa 1975). On this reading, data, both quantitative and qualitative, is never innocent; numbers as well as stories that we tell and hear are both implicated in politics, and politics is influenced by research, which means that we need to pay attention to partiality as well as the quality of both outputs.

Ultimately, methods, like life, are messy; as Aradau and Huysmans (2014, 1) argue, we need "to understand methods as less pure, less formal, messier and more experimental, carrying substantive political visions." On the one hand, we need to approach methods pragmatically in terms of the questions that we wish to research—methods need to speak to the objects of our inquiry. On the other hand, methods, as noted above, are also political in terms of the competing modes of knowledge production, exchange, and legitimation that they engender and within which they are framed. So while they have the power to reproduce dominant narratives, they also can disrupt (Aradau and Huysmans 2014). The methodological form too, either quantitative or qualitative, matters less than we think—it is 'less important to its politics than the nature of the world it brings into being" (Davies 2020).

Finally, there is the question of the ethics of measurability itself. However accurate, should we, can we measure human relations? As

I argued in Chapter 1, active ignorance can mean that evidence remains always political in its reading. What, then, do we gain and lose by emphasizing measurability? Why do we need models at all? Can the model we developed (Rai, Hoskyns, and Thomas 2014) support the overall feminist argument about valuing unpaid domestic labor? As Sylvia Federici (1975, n.p.) has pointed out, there is a difference between measurements: "Many times the difficulties and ambiguities which women express in discussing wages for housework stem from the reduction of wages for housework to a thing, a lump of money, instead of viewing it as a political perspective. The difference between these two standpoints is enormous."

We hoped that we could find a way of representing depletion and giving it a value by calculating the costs of social reproductive work concretely to demonstrate its extensity as well as its intensity (Rai, Hoskyns, and Thomas 2014). Below, I outline the model that we proposed and reflect on the reasons we thought it important and useful to have a measure for depletion. I then discuss some methodological issues I faced when I sought to calculate DSR with the help of the model from the available data of the U.K. Household Satellite Account program (UK Office for National Statistics, 2018)—how working with existing quantitative data became difficult because of data gaps that reflect the nonrecognition of social reproductive work. In the book I use FEOT, a mixed-method approach inspired by time-use survey methodology, to understand depletion (see Chapters 3 and 4).

Federici (1975, n.p.) argues, "Our struggle for [better provision of] social services, i.e. for better working conditions, will always be frustrated if we do not first establish that our work is work." My argument on depletion is similar: that there is an urgent need to establish what this work costs, in terms of physical and mental health, self-worth and happiness, maintenance of households and communities, for which both quantitative and qualitative research is needed, as are different methodological approaches and data sets.

Measuring Depletion

Measuring depletion is not easy. Building on various theoretical and empirical attempts at measuring social reproductive labor time through time-use surveys, household satellite accounts, other measures of well-being, and environmental accounts, which I discuss below, we proposed a model for measuring depletion.

Depletion is a tipping point when individuals, households, and communities use up over *time* identifiable *resources*, such as health, earnings, and social networks, in carrying out social reproduction and where outflows exceed inflows (Rai, Hoskyns, and Thomas 2014). We developed a model to measure this depletion, $DSR = Rt < TH$, and explained it as follows:

"Individuals, households and communities use up identifiable gendered resources, such as health, earnings and social networks, in doing SR [social reproduction]" (89). We denoted the "stock of the resources available in each of these sites at a particular point in time (t) by Rt, the resource outflows (time spent on caring responsibilities, domestic chores, etc.) used up in the provision of SR as yt, and resource inflows (medical care, support networks, etc.) as xt" (89). We represented "Rt or the current stock of resources for each site in the following way:

$$Rt = (xt-yt) + Rt -1 \text{ where t} = 1, 2, 3 \ldots$$

Where Rt is the current stock of resources, $(xt-yt)$ is the difference between inflows (xt) and outflows (yt). This difference represents the net outflow of current stock Rt. In each site, Rt is sensitive to the existing stock of resources, denoted by $Rt-1$. Rt is also sensitive to the outflows expended towards normal wear and tear. However, if after accounting for normal wear and tear, the inflows that would otherwise replenish available stocks are reduced without a concomitant reduction in outflows used up in SR, there is a measurable deterioration in the sustainability of those engaged in SR. More specifically, when Rt deteriorates or falls below a threshold (TH) there is depletion of those engaged in SR." (89)

We represented it with the equation: DSR = Rt < TH (89). We acknowledged that the tipping point at which depletion can be measured will vary for individuals, households, and communities, and the consequences of DSR are nonlinear; as noted in Chapter 1, DSR in one site can and does affect the resources in other sites in different socioeconomic and historical contexts. Our concern was to identify the threshold at which social reproduction becomes harmful in the three sites—individuals, households, and communities—and to indicate how this harm might be measured as DSR (92). In addition, we noted that the inflows required to sustain individuals, households, and communities are different and we need to specify the correlations between them.

In measuring individual DSR the key variables might be issues of mental and physical health, stress and stress-related illness, anxiety, exhaustion, gendered violence, time spent on different forms of unpaid SR, and time available for rest, leisure, and maintaining the social networks that support individuals in their everyday lives. Overall, ways need to be found of measuring the costs of caring activities, taking account of mitigating factors which may exist. For the household, measuring DSR would mean measuring its viability as a site of social reproduction in the face of everyday economic and social pressures, including levels of income and the distribution of social reproductive work, the changing patterns of labor and consumption, decision-making, and intrahousehold bargaining. Some way also needs to be found to measure and assess the extent to which the household as a site of social reproduction mitigates or intensifies the consequences of individual DSR. In measuring DSR in communities, we would need to assess the "thickness" of social networks, the incentives and disincentives that people have to join these networks, the extent to which these are seen as strategies to mitigate individual and household DSR, their sustainability, and the interface of informal networks with formal institutionalized state structures and the private sector. The nature and levels of voluntary work also need to be measured.

Since the publication of Rai, Hoskyns, and Thomas (2014), I have found some difficulties in measuring DSR in the work that I have done. These include the following:

1. How to account for the irregular and uneven nature of depletion?
2. How to aggregate different forms of depletion at different levels and in different contexts?

3. The fact that the capacity to do social reproductive work involves renewable as well as finite resources, which complicates the criteria used to recognize and measure depletion.
4. How to devise methodologies and units of measurement which are valid across the different sites of depletion as well as North/South boundaries?
5. How to account for gendered desirability biases in existing data sets, in both questions posed and answers provided?

The issue of gendered desirability bias was particularly clear when, together with three colleagues who were well versed in statistical data analysis, I tried to work with the U.K. Time-Use Survey (UKTUS) data of the Office for National Statistics (ONS) to calculate depletion with the our model. To analyze the patterns of depletion we calculated a Personal Resources Scale by multiplying the time spent on a given activity by the standardized enjoyment scores for each respondent. To create the dependent variable, the Personal Resources Scale scores obtained were later summed for each respondent, with a value below 0 indicating overall depletion. My colleague, Piotr Bogdansky, constructed the Depletion Data Browser[2] to represent our calculations. Because the ONS was paying attention to the gender issues of care, it had introduced the element of "enjoyment" in its UKTUS questionnaire but did not consider the social desirability biases between women and men in the context of childcare. The means and standard deviation of enjoyment were simply calculated with omission of missing values and then multiplied by each individual's time spent on a given activity. We found it difficult to operationalize depletion as "proportion of time spent during outflow activities," given the limited number of feelings reported in the UKTUS diary (enjoyment and "rushedness") and their large missingness. We found that the figures for enjoyment for both men and women on care were high. However, we also know from other research that "[o]verall, men tend to devote more money, and women more direct care time, to the support of dependents" (Folbre 2006a, 195). Could it be, we wondered, that men say they enjoy childcare duties because they do these selectively and not as a matter of everyday routine, and women say that they enjoy childcare duties because they are socialized into not being able to complain about the burdens of childcare? For the model to work, we need appropriate data, revisions to time-use surveys already in operation, and attention to social and cultural norms as well as different locations that affect what is always a subjective measure of enjoyment or resentment influenced by social desirability biases.

These difficulties alerted me to the importance of critically assessing the potential of the model that we presented; in this book, I have not measured depletion using the model. Rather, I have disclosed its presence in different registers, argued for its recognition and compensation, and suggested ways of reversing it through individual strategies, collective struggles, and policy shifts. This builds on Ann Oakley's (1998, 707) argument that "rehabilitating quantitative methods and integrating a range of methods in the task of creating an emancipatory social science" needs the gendering of methodologies rather than focusing on gender and methodology (see also Macpherson, Taniguchi, and Froese 2021).[3]

In the rest of the chapter, I outline the various ways in which time as a measure of labor has been evaluated, theoretically and empirically, and how that, together with the difficulties in using the depletion model effectively, helped me to develop a new methodology for studying depletion.

Time, Value, and Measurability

I have been arguing that measurement can be important in valuing social reproduction and depletion as the costs of doing this work. A refusal to quantify women's labor has been justified by the history of gender relations—that the intensity with which women labor in the domestic sphere cannot be captured by units of measurement (Marazzi 2007). One way of addressing this criticism is to focus on the measurement of time (labor-time) and that of the value of the product (which reflects, in part, that labor-time) to understand the importance of measurement to debates on social reproduction.[4] Both are associated with the market as labor products/services.

In feminist debates on surplus value and wages for housework, time is a variable of value and is quantified as such—in exchange value in the market and in wages for housework; in both, the focus remains on socially required labor time and its value, the first in the process of production and the second as the price of labor (Elson 1979; Federici, James, and Dalla Costa 1975). In measuring value, while we might be able to calculate value independently of the market, this would have little purchase; fundamentally, as Elson (1979, 123) comments, in Marxist analysis value is political—a way to explore "why labour takes the forms it does and what the political consequences are" of particular forms of labor. The theory of value also "allows us to monitor the vital signs of a societal division of labor" and that "value was not about the content of an entity or action but about its significance for the social totality" (Collins 2016, 2), which produced the conditions in which labor was reproduced and surplus value extracted. However, value extraction takes place in a context of structural inequalities that are historically embedded in slavery and in colonization (Bhattacharyya 2018; Kundani 2023): "Blackness is a capacious category of surplus value extraction essential to an array of political-economic functions, including accumulation, disaccumulation, debt, planned obsolescence, and absorption of the burdens of economic crises. At the same time, Blackness is the quintessential condition of disposability, expendability, and devalorization" (Burden-Stelly 2020, 3).

Under capitalism, in the context of value extraction, time can be framed as hegemonic clock time—from slaves in the fields to wage slaves in the factories, and now also more flexibly wage earners in homes and hired spaces. Value extraction has attended to the ways time has been harnessed to racialized bodies; the history of struggle against the length of the working day has also been a struggle against levels of value extraction (see Chapter 1). While the discrepancy between value and worth is important to understand the racialized disposability of labor, it is equally important to frame the gendered relations of labor: social reproduction also provides capital with labor (birth time) and with a reserve army of labor (accumulated time) and maintenance of labour (care time) that is mobilized as a subsidy to capital. Further, clock time itself has expanded in post-Fordist production frames; it is now more flexible and fluid, while remaining "work time" (Harvey 1990). The technologies of surveillance allow for this time to be measured and mobilized for disciplining workers (Ajunwa, Crawford, and

Schultz 2017). Time, then, as we shall see in Chapter 3, while easily measurable in one way, is highly complex to measure historically and in terms of the tipping points leading to depletion. However, some feminists addressing the issue of measuring time in the context of social reproduction argue that even with the end of the dominance of the hegemony of clock time in post-Fordist production cycles, we cannot abandon improving attempts at measurement and calculation of time; rather we need to think about such methodologies differently (Adkins 2009, 334; see below and Chapter 3).

If Marxist theorists focused on surplus value extraction over time, then the Wages for Housework Campaign focused on time in terms of patriarchal exploitation:

> They say it is love. We say it is unwaged work.
> They call it frigidity. We call it absenteeism.
> Every miscarriage is a work accident.
> Homosexuality and heterosexuality are both working conditions . . .
> but homosexuality is workers' control of production, not the
> end of work.
> More smiles? More money. Nothing will be so powerful in
>   destroying
> the healing virtues of a smile.
> Neuroses, suicides, desexualisation: occupational diseases of the
> Housewife. (Federici, James, and Dalla Costa 1975, 1)

The reproduction of biological labor requires effort and time; reproduction of norms that validate a gendered division of labor makes housework the responsibility of the woman and waged work the input of the "male head of family"—both are trapped within capitalist social relations. As a result of this analysis, the Wages for Housework Campaign saw wages not as an accurate reflection of the value of this labor but as "the demand by which *our nature ends and our struggle begins* [italics mine] because just to want wages for housework means to refuse that work as the expression of our nature, and therefore to refuse precisely the female role that capital has invented for us" (Federici 1975, 4). Wages here were symbolic, on the one hand, of women's oppression and, on the other, of their subversion of family life.

While a wage symbolizes a social contract between capital and labor, housework is naturalized and as such is unwaged and unrecognized and therefore a subsidy to capital. Naturalization of gender roles also allows capital to insist, the campaigners argued, that housework remains unpaid—reproduction of labor, through naturalization of the biopolitics of gender relations, allows for the maintenance of labor through housework to remain outside the production boundary, and therefore unrecognized as work. Further, naturalization means that women's work is discursively framed by "love"—complaints about domestic labor are then cast as "unnatural." Federici (1975, 3) points out, "We are seen as nagging bitches, not workers in struggle" (see also Ahmad 2021 on the feminist politics of complaint). Nagging of course is often used as a justification for disciplining through domestic violence.

While the struggle for improved wages and conditions for work in the factory did not challenge the social role of the male head of household, demanding wages for housework did challenge the social role of women within the domestic sphere. These campaigners saw the demand for wages for housework as symbolic (challenging naturalization of social reproductive work) but also as a means for revolutionary change: "To say that we want money for housework is the first step towards refusing to do it, because the demand for a wage makes our work visible, which is the most indispensable condition to begin to struggle against it, both in its immediate aspect as housework and its more insidious character as femininity" (Federici 1975, 5). What was of course overlooked in this analysis was *who* would pay the wages and *how* wages would be paid and money transferred. Also not clarified was how the individualization of analysis of housework—women as individual wage earners through housework—would lead to collective bargaining, struggles, and transformations; by the 1980s this strand of feminist thinking on social reproduction declined. The point that I wish to underline here, however, was the clear thinking of this group of feminists about the importance of the symbolic value of the demand for wages (Rai 2016)—the fact that they wanted wages to stand in for recognition of social reproductive work.[5]

These debates found little reflection in mainstream economic understanding and measurement of work, however, which remained almost entirely focused on the labor market and waged work. The UNSNA, introduced in 1953 to measure economic growth of nations, and standardized globally in 1993, formalized the nonrecognition of nonmarket work in the domestic sphere as well as of social and environmental costs and depletion.

Accounting for Domestic Work: UNSNA

UNSNA is important to the debates on social reproduction and depletion because it sets the "production boundary" which establishes which activities are counted as "productive" and therefore as part of the market economy, and which are "not counted" because they are not deemed productive (Hoskyns and Rai 2007).[6]

The UNSNA (2009, 6.24) defines economic production "as an activity carried out under the control and responsibility of an institutional unit that uses inputs of labour, capital, and goods and services to produce outputs of goods or services." Here the production boundary includes the *marketized production* of all goods or services, "including the production of goods or services used up in the process of producing such goods or services" (UNSNA 1993, 2009, 6.27). It therefore explicitly excludes domestic unpaid labor as outside the production boundary because of its nonmarket nature.[7] However, the UNSNA does include the government sector in its calculations as well as owner-occupied housing, even though both belong to the nonmarket category. The argument here is that though nonmarket, these transactions have monetary value because of the wages and rent paid for work, which can then be accounted for, and that it is easy to impute a market value (rent) to owner-occupied homes. These sectors are also seen as "too important" to be omitted; the reproduction of life itself, social reproduction, is not therefore considered to be so important. Goods produced by households, including agricultural items for home consumption or for sale, have with some exceptions been included in the national accounts and in the measurement of GDP. Further, the UNSNA sets out by common agreement how national accounts of *all* countries should be constructed, standardizing the methodological exclusion of unpaid domestic labor globally.[8] This "not counting" is, of course, a form of nonrecognition of this work and its contribution to society.

As a result of feminist interventions in the debate about accounting for domestic work, in the 1993 revisions to the UNSNA two previously excluded categories of unpaid work were included: " (1) unpaid work in the 'difficult to measure sectors' within the market economy such as unpaid family helpers, home-based workers, etc., and (2) the unaccounted work of subsistence production—the output of which is meant for consumption." This relaxation of production boundary, however, extended only to "the own account production of housing services by owner-occupiers and of domestic and personal services produced by employing paid domestic staff" (Neetha 2010, 75; see also Hirway 2005; Hoskyns and Rai 2007). Important unpaid work such as production of meals, laundry, cleaning, shopping, voluntary work, and care of children, older people, and the disabled continues to be excluded from the production boundary.

As we saw in the introduction, Waring's (1988) aim in critiquing this approach to domestic labor was to initiate a campaign to persuade policymakers that the failure to count unpaid work both lay at the root of gender inequality and caused serious flaws in the way economic trends were evaluated (see also Waring and Carr 2011). Waring (1988, 49) also argued that the issue is political, not methodological: "When you are seeking out the most vicious tools of colonization, those that can obliterate a culture and a nation, a tribe or a people's value system, then rank the UNSNA among those tools."

The fact that unpaid service work in the home, such as care of children and adults, preparation of meals, and transportation of household members, is seen to be outside the production boundary is particularly important, since this renders these activities invisible and severs the link between domestic labor and other economic processes; this has been seen by some as a violation of human rights (Sepulveda Carmona 2013). Feminist economists and political economists developed robust methodological tools to measure the value of time and of unpaid labor more accurately; the household satellite accounts and time-use surveys in particular are important.[9]

Household Satellite Accounts

The idea of the household satellite accounts (HHSA) was that they would help to "a) give a more complete picture of what is going on in the economy, recognizing the value of unpaid work; b) track movement between unpaid domestic work and paid labour; c) understand the implications of policies which draw labour from the household sector, or require the availability of voluntary workers and d) assess the gender impact of policies" (Hoskyns and Rai 2007, 303; see also Varjonen, Hamunen, and Soinne 2014, 16). The HHSA are regarded as "experimental" additions to GDP, but are not included in it, and are thus not central to decisions about economic policymaking and spending (Eurostat 2019). The HHSA also provided an impetus for further work by feminist scholars on the calculation of unpaid domestic work.

The methodology developed to calculate HHSA is not the same across countries. Replacement costs, average costs, and opportunity costs have all been proposed for the valuation, as have input and output costs. For example, the United Kingdom uses the output method when calculating market production in national accounts, which makes the measurement of the productivity of household production possible (see Ironmonger and Soupourmas 2009; Holloway, Short, and Tamplin 2002; Harvey and Mukhopadhyay 2007). In practice, however, data collection for the output method is very expensive and therefore was not rolled out regularly; the first HHSA in the United Kingdom conducted in 2002, and the second in 2016. Many other OECD countries have used the input method, which relies on the availability of time-use data in many countries and has made it easy to value unpaid work time by a suitable wage or wages (Varjonen, Hamunen, and Soinne 2014, 9). However, scholars "were unanimous on the scope of the household satellite accounts: they should include all household production, goods and services, whether included in the SNA [System of National Accounts] or not. . . . [T]he accounts should [also] include [a] production account. This means that in addition to the value of labour also capital consumption and intermediate consumption should be estimated" (7).

While opportunity costs are not used very much in HHSA, it is important to note that women's labor force participation takes account of this—as an estimate of how much women could earn in a paid job if they were not doing unpaid housework. These estimates have led to policy concerns about women's labor force participation rates. For example, McKinsey Global Institute estimates that "global GDP growth could be $1 trillion lower in 2030 than it would be if women's unemployment simply tracked that of men in each sector" (Madgavkar et al. 2020, 2). However, as feminist scholars have argued, concern for women's employment has not led to shifts in social policy to connect labor force participation and the provision of adequate social infrastructure—the emphasis remains on building transport systems, for example, that support the "male breadwinner model" of employment; both are needed (WBG Commission on a Gender-Equal Economy 2020; Chapter 4). The unequal gendered division of labor means an increased depletion of women with their mobilization into the paid labor market, as domestic and care work and paid work lengthen women's working day and intensify extraction of their labor.

The momentum generated by feminist and environmental economists in challenging the UNSNA, however, led to some countries, such as Canada, India, South Africa, and the United Kingdom, to accept that these important elements of the economy need to be accounted for. HHSA came to be developed to account for the value contribution of unpaid domestic work to the economy (McDowall 2008).

As we can see, the ongoing marginalization of social reproductive labor and its continued exclusion from GDP is highly problematic but has not stopped feminist economists working to develop new measures such as the HHSA through methodologies like time-use surveys.

Time-Use Surveys

Time-use surveys (TUS) are now a well-developed methodology used to generate robust data for measuring social reproductive labor. This is done by measuring time spent on "paid work, household and family care, personal care, voluntary work, social life, travel, and leisure activities" (Eurostat 2019) using time-use diaries, observation, interviews by field workers, and group discussion. A clearer picture can then be mapped of who engages in social reproduction and for how long and where; this is important for measuring depletion both temporally and spatially. The claims for TUS are many: they can be "used to support equality, family, social, transport and cultural policies and to measure the value of household production and for international comparisons" (Eurostat 2019), which can "help in the attainment of SDGs [Sustainable Development Goals] 3 and 8, enabling governments to address them systematically" (Floro 2021,148). This methodology is variable across studies and institutions conducting TUS; Eurostat (2020) outlines methodology of Harmonised European Time Use Surveys as follows:

> The main classification system used . . . is the "Activity coding list" (ACL). The ACL assigns a code to the activities (primary and secondary) that the person is doing during the day. For that purpose the 24 hours of the day are split in 144 slots of 10-minutes and ACL codes are given to each of the 10-minutes slots. The activities described by the respondents themselves are coded according to the 108 category classification of activities that are reduced to 51 categories in the harmonisation processes of the data base. Other classifications used are the "Location" where the time is spent (including the modes of transport) and "With whom" the time is spent.

There have been important criticisms of this methodology—first, about the nature of time that it maps: clock or "task-oriented" time which "change[s] all time into money" rather than "social" time (Paolucci in Gershuny and Sullivan 1998, 71). Second, it focuses on individual time, while spending time is often enmeshed in household rhythms, which means that "locality and interaction" are not recorded, while "activity" is prioritized (As 1978, 140). Third, the diary method foregrounds some question and not others, skewing our understanding of patterns of time spent in a society (As 1978, 140; Cornwell, Gershuny, and Sullivan 2019). Fourth, the collecting of data via the diary method presumes the availability of time and education and statistical budgets to do so and therefore is biased toward the Global North (Esquivel et al. 2008); educational limitations and time poverty in many countries of the Global South and across class boundaries might mean diaries are inaccurately or only partially filled, skewing the results (Eurostat 2019; Rai and True 2020). Finally, the studies "performed are typically empirical, fact-finding surveys with little attention given to the theoretical issues involved" (As 1978, 125). So there is a need for more theoretical and analytical approaches to TUS to understand the constraints, trade-offs, and consequences of time expenditure (Stevano et al. 2019, 1; Cantillon, Mackett, and Stevano 2023), and therefore levels of depletion.

Instead of abandoning the idea of measuring time, however, scholars and researchers have both defended and tried to address these issues. For example, Gershuny and Sullivan (1998, 69) argue that clock time and social time and more sophisticated approaches to time-use measurement that include "the rhythm and sequencing of daily activities; the occurrence of multiple simultaneous activities; the duration of specific activities; the enjoyment of time spent in different activities and social contexts of activities" could be brought together for a more nuanced approach to TUS (see also Esquivel et al. 2008). They further argue that women are constantly having to reconcile these two very different scales of time—clock time and social time—and researchers should therefore find ways to measure what they call "scientific time," which is also imbued with sociological significance (Gershuny and Sullivan 1998, 69). Modeling time in this way can therefore demonstrate the interdependence of paid and unpaid work within the household (see also As 1978; Hirway and Jose 2011). Indeed, TUS have clearly shown that, as expected, being male tends to result in doing less unpaid care work across all countries (Esquivel et al. 2008; Budlender 2010a; UK Office for National Statistics 2016; TGNP 2009). They have also provided evidence of the effects of deficient social and physical infrastructure on the time devoted to sleep and rest, leisure and enjoyment, and other elements of replenishment such as food preparation and consumption.

Rai, Hoskyns, and Thomas (2014) discussed the example of a TUS in Tanzania which sought in 2006 to measure the extent and nature of unpaid care work (TGNP 2009) as a unit in the national-level Integrated

Labour Force Survey. It covered over 3,000 households and included both qualitative and quantitative data collection over several consecutive days (95–96, 92–93; also see Budlender 2010a).[10] The survey coded over 30 activities, which were then pared down to three: (1) SNA work, that is, work within the production boundary; (2) unpaid care work, including fuel and water collection; and (3) "non-productive work," which included activities that are "necessary for survival and well-being" (TGNP 2009, 18–19). The survey was able to address two complex issues: the first was multitasking within households,[11] where a distinction was made between the "24-hour minute" whereby multiple tasks carried out within the same time frame were given equal weight in a day, as opposed to the "full minute," whereby only one task was carried out in a period of time. Second was the underreporting of childcare, especially when there is no direct care taking place but "looking after" requires the carer to be present and alert, putting some stress on time (35. also see Chapter 3). This issue was addressed by asking three "reminder questions" in interviews with members of households. The overall results show that, in line with other countries where the value of social reproduction has been calculated, the value of unpaid care work in Tanzania is equal to "63% of the GDP" (TGNP 2009, 35; see also UK Office for National Statistics 2016).

The results were not surprising in gender terms—women overall spent the least amount of time on "non-productive work," most on unpaid care work, and only slightly less than men on SNA work (TGNP 2009, 18–19). The survey also suggested that hiring domestic workers mitigated depletion for households and that it is more likely that domestic workers will be hired where women in the household engage in paid work (22). This shows how the hiring of domestic workers increases inflows (xt) for those able to afford to buy in labor but may increase outflows (yt) and therefore intensify depletion for those who have to sell their labor as they have to do both paid and unpaid care work. What also becomes apparent through this survey is that overall women are bearing the burden of unpaid care work and are not able to offset this labor through "non-productive work" so essential for their well-being. Even though depletion is clearly occurring here, because the TUS did not ask questions about this, the extent and intensity of depletion remain unmapped.

Stress and Health

Measuring depletion through other surveys have taken on issues of work, stress, and health through analyzing time-use and health data[12] (Bird and Fremont 1991; Zuzanek 1998; Beaujot and Andersen 2004; Waring and Sumeo 2010) and qualitative data from public institutions.

In our article (Rai, Hoskyns, and Thomas 2014) we discussed a study from Canada based on mapping hours spent on paid and unpaid work from the 1998 Canadian General Social Survey on Time Use, which measured paid and unpaid work in different family settings (92–93).[13] The survey controlled for gender, age, income, numbers of dependents, types of work, and family composition. Stress was measured by the subjective assessments of those surveyed; of anxiety, time pressure, guilt, and health; by the number of conditions diagnosed and time taken off work over the previous 12 months. The study saw stress as fairly immediate, while ill health was seen as cumulative (see also Geronimus, Hicken et al. 2006). The findings of this study showed that the intensity of both paid and unpaid work increased over the period between 1986 and 1998, with casual paid work and long hours of full-time work (over 41 hours per week) being particularly stressful and consequently leading to poor health. Personal factors could mitigate the effects, particularly levels of income and a family structure where caring responsibilities are shared. This study suggests a clear case of depletion as the personal well-being of individuals and households falls below a threshold of normal wear and tear, especially where there are no replenishing inflows such as income and a supportive family structure. It is, therefore, not higher income that is replenishing per se but whether that income can be and *is* used to buy in help with social reproduction, such as domestic help or leisure that can reverse depletion. (This also chimes with the Tanzanian study.) Employment then can support social reproduction but can also contribute in the long run to depletion, which is visible as stress and poor health.[14] The equal weight given to paid and unpaid work in the survey made it possible to aggregate the work being done in ways that are not normally available. However, the study focused on the household, which means that we can assess the impact of the presence or lack of state support to families: What institutional mechanisms for replenishment are available to different groups of households that may decrease or increase stress related to paid and unpaid work? Further, this study asked about stress, but not about the impact of social discrimination, race in particular, on stress.

As I noted in Chapter 1, to account for high maternal mortality rates among Black women, Geronimus (1992) proposed the "weathering" hypothesis, "which posits that Blacks experience early health deterioration as a consequence of the cumulative impact of repeated experience with social or economic adversity and political marginalization" (Geronimus, Hicken, et al. 2006, 827). Based on quantitative data analysis—it uses the U.S. National Health and Nutrition Examination Survey data—the weathering hypothesis builds a multilayered analysis of the impact of stress on health and of race discrimination on stress by examining "gender and race differences in age-related allostatic load [the substances the body releases in response to stress] scóres" (827). Geronimus, Hicken, et al. were able to analyze this huge data set and control for poverty and for race in developing their weathering hypothesis, showing that the questions one seeks to answer are critical in mobilizing numerical data in contexts of social inequality and discrimination. Similarly, as Neetha and Palriwala (2010), commenting on the Report of the Time Use Survey (Indian Ministry of Statistics and Programme Implementation, Central Statistical Organisation 2000) , pointed out, in such surveys statistics are mainly used to provide robust data on economic production and workforce by measuring unpaid activities performed at home. This allows the studies to reflect more accurately the relationships between market and domestic labor in a context where work, "including market-oriented work and workers are grossly underestimated" (Neetha and Palriwala 2010, 76).

So, institutional contexts affect measurement tools, which can lead to different quantifications of issues under study (Buss 2015; Johnson 2015). And at the same time, the lack of attention to questions (of discrimination, marginalization, inequalities, and depletion) can lead to data collection and analysis being skewed; the question of data collection is therefore a political question and needs to be treated as such. Time-use methodologies are undergoing continuous revisions (see, for example, the work of Centre for Time Use Survey),[15] which hopefully will continue to refine our quantitative analyses of measuring time spent in terms of care and its effects.

The case studies discussed in this chapter also underline the importance of combining evidence gathering with political lobbying; it is necessary to understand all the economic and "non-economic" activities a person is engaged in, for which detailed TUS on a regular basis, contextualized with similar data, are the only way of encapsulating these dimensions in order to devise policy appropriately: "Those who are invisible as producers will be invisible in distribution" (Waring and Sumeo 2010, 93).[16] TUS are labor-intensive and expensive (the normal interval of TUS is 5 to 10 years); to be able to capture and develop policies to reverse depletion, the time frame might need to be shorter. Governments need to be convinced of the importance of TUS if this data is to be generated in a systematic manner over time and used to shift social policy. The same can be said about the HHSA that have been started and then abandoned by various countries.

As my work on care and social reproductive work developed, I took inspiration from TUS methodology but adapted it such that some of the issues raised above could be addressed (see Chapter 3). In part this was because when I discussed time-use diaries as a method with some of the respondents in my research program, the poorest of them did not have the time, literacy level, or confidence to record a time diary; the educated, professional, middle-class women were also time poor—work has to be stopped every 15 minutes to record in a timely and accurate way, and to do so over time, from two days up to a week, was not something they wanted to do. This method also raised the question of ethics of research: Is keeping a diary more work and less leisure time for my research participants? Lives are lived in spaces, in environments and atmospheres, which are also generated and altered through the labor of those who inhabit these. How do we capture these as researchers, and do so ethically? How can we factor in the spatial and the atmospheric elements of everyday life to develop a rich analysis of social reproduction and its costs?

In developing alternative strategies of researching depletion, I traded the scale of study for a focus on measuring time accurately, taking into account "social time" and reflexive time, location and context. I developed a method that also considered the time poverty of those engaged in both paid and unpaid work, as well as their educational levels. I worked with this methodology in 2016 (see Chapters 3 and 4) and used the experience to refine it further, together with my colleague Jacqui True; we called this method/ology the Feminist Everyday Observatory Tool (FEOT) (Rai and True 2020).

Methods for Researching Rhythms of the Everyday: FEOT

In developing FEOT, we identified and addressed the complexity of measuring time-use in everyday life through using a narrative ethnography that builds on both the epistemic histories of quantitative and qualitative research and one that pays attention to identities and subjectivities as well as structures of inequality and possibilities of change. While mapping time through a survey provides us with important insights, it does not allow us to explore the textures and rhythms of everyday life/work and their effects and how subjectivities are framed through this work, which in turn affect our sense of self.

Further, measuring time through a standard TUS and to factor in income does not show relationality: we need a sense of both time and space (where the time is spent) to understand the rhythms of the everyday (Felski 2000, 22). In terms of the home/work dynamic we need to understand both: the place of social reproduction inside and outside; Felski points out, the home is seen through modernist frames as regressive and the "outside" as full of surprises and movement, challenging us to progress (23; see also Chapter 4). Home is, of course, deeply gendered, attached in our imaginaries to the female figure—keeping home. The feminist impulse, then, to break the constraints of gendered social relations, includes getting away from this construct that allows a separation of property from care—the home, as in "house," is a property that continues to be largely controlled by men; home as a space of care continues to be the responsibility of women. So when we measure time, in the home and coming back home from work, how can we include the measure of space in our research? In terms of including income in contextualizing time-use, we also miss reflections on *how* class, familial, and social networks, ambitions, and aspirations shape the way social reproductive work is done and experienced. While a TUS will tell us how the hours of the day are spent, it will not be able to explain *why* this time is spent the way it is, and it will not be able to tell us *how* those who do social reproductive work reflect on the way they spend their time. How do they feel about the levels of fatigue and stress in doing their work, their position within their families and communities, the recognition of their labor, the systems of support they can rely on, and the subjectivities that develop over time that they can relate to? These are important questions that can help us understand the depletion of health, mental and physical; alert us to the depletion of self; and point us toward social and governance support systems that are important in the doing of social reproductive work.

FEOT[17] can have only a small sample size because it is labor-intensive and therefore does not provide the evidence at scale, but it can deepen our understanding of the everyday rhythms of life, the nuanced relationship between paid and unpaid labor, the social and familial networks that embed those performing social reproduction and insights into the subjectivities of those doing this work. As such, it not only provides us with time-use data—qualitative, thick description, reflexive—but also allows us to ask different questions about social reproduction and its costs. FEOT thus is a different sort of TUS, one that brings together TUS with "shadowing" (see McDonald 2018; Gill 2011; Quinlan 2008). Further, ethnographic research places the burden of recording on the researcher, not the respondent, and amalgamates observation and reflection, recording in both senses—recording the rhythms of everyday and recording reflections of the respondents through narrative interviews. How does this work? As outlined in the toolkit on FEOT, we (Rai and True 2020, 11–12) developed a Three-Step Method:

Step 1: Pre-questionnaire: this contextualizes the participant in their environs—cultural, social, and economic; it also allows us to avoid interfering with the participant's everyday routines during the TUS observation.

Step 2: Observation: shadowing or conducting the ethnographic observation through completing a time-use diary, every 15–20 minutes for one day consisting of 12–16 hours. Multitasking is recorded, as is the location, space, and environment where time is spent. As in many TUSs, also noted is the presence of and interaction with other household members. During this day, the participant and the researcher can also take photographs (with consent) as part of observation.

Step 3: Post-observation Narrative Interview: a post-observation interview/discussion with the research participant. Here, the time-use records of the observation and photographs can become prompts as well as memory aids. Interruptions for childcare, household chores, or work pressures are accommodated. The narrative approach to interviewing generates prompts for participants to reflect on their day in a way that suits them—what made them happy/tired/angry/sad on the day? When were they most/least stressed? what are their sources of support—family/friends/colleagues? Do they feel that they and their home-making work are valued—by the family? The community? Also important are reflections on who benefits from the/a particular activity that they engage in everyday? And what would make their lives better on an everyday basis? (Rai and True 2020, 11, 15)

FEOT allows us to treat domestic and paid work along the same time-space continuum, challenging the distinctions between productive/unproductive work, mapping both space and time, and bridging the gap between researchers and research participants. Triangulation of FEOT observations with existing data sets, policy literature, and secondary research on the available social infrastructure, state services, and responses of NGOs and nonstate actors is important to assess whether or not depletion through social reproduction is present, increasing without support, or decreasing with or without the support of social infrastructure (Rai and True 2020, 15).

FEOT is, of course, not without challenges: as a small-N study, it raises issues of generalizability and (as we have seen) therefore of authority; its methodology builds on time-use as well as intensive observation, which is time-consuming and tiring for the researchers; it is intrusive for the research participants to be observed for long periods of time; it requires considerable training for the researcher to build trust and carry out observations unobtrusively; it is expensive—more than one researcher might be needed to cover a long day's observation. Further, as Kahneman et al. (2006, 3) point out, "retrospective reports [memory work] are also susceptible to systematic biases." But as we have seen, biases are built into all research processes. The availability of "big data," which can now be seen as a byproduct of routine everyday operations of capitalism and which can be collected without "any special effort" (Savage and Burrows 2007, 887), might address issues of access and analysis but does not solve the political problem of what remains (in)visible in different contexts and what methodologies might be best suited to revealing it. The purpose of developing FEOT was to build on the strengths of TUS, to observe and understand the expenditure of social reproductive time (output) and its costs (depletion)—physical and emotional—as well as to respond to the gaps in TUSs in terms of reflexiveness about time and the costs of doing social reproductive work. This also emphasizes bridging the gap between research participants and researchers as they work together to map the everyday through carefully observing and recording as thick description the relational space and time in which it unfolds.

While FEOT needs further critical attention, the early results from research using this method are promising (Johnson and Lingham 2020, 2024; Lingham, Rai, and Akhter forthcoming). As Johnson and Lingham (2020, 79) note in their work on conflict and social reproduction in Myanmar and Sri Lanka, FEOT "yielded rich data, such as the extent to which women carry out multiple forms of social reproductive work at any one time. The combination of steps two and three of the FEOT enabled reflexive moments for some participants, who, during the post-observation interview, took the opportunity to reflect on and appreciate the extent of their labour, as it had been recorded in the time use diary. The method's feminist recognition of the importance of the everyday, and the overlapping dimensions of space, time and violence, resonated with participants' lived experiences and so was also valued by them." As we shall see in Chapter 3 and 4, this reflexive mapping of depletion is crucial to deduce the extent and intensity of depletion in contexts of stress, including lack of existing provision and support of social infrastructure.

Summary

In this chapter I have argued that measuring depletion can be challenging, but that both quantitative and qualitative methods can be used and are indeed needed to do this. Big-N studies like TUSs allow us to make claims about the length of working days, how and on what people in a society spend their time, and about the gender distribution of domestic labor. Other quantitative measures such as gender equality indices claim to put forward what is important to address in social policy. However, these methods do not capture the relations between time and space, the relationality between context and time spent, and the way concepts are used and abused in the surveys, skewing research. Therefore, Schmid (2022, 907) has argued that while gender equality indices are increasingly influential tools used for policymaking, their effectiveness can be increased by "complementing their findings with qualitative analyses." Data architecture is said to frame state policy; state policy is legitimized by data. As I have been arguing, there is an intimate relationship between expertise and the way numbers are used (Porter 1995), which is not written in stone and can be reworked and rethought; to intervene in this circuit of power we need to understand and use numbers differently.

Reflecting on the model Rai, Hoskyns, and Thomas (2014) proposed to calculate depletion, I have suggested, with others, that critical and reflexive improvements in measures, indices, and methodologies can help us overcome some of the technical as well as political gaps in measuring the costs of care (see also Berik 2018). As demonstrated by FEOT, a mixed-method approach could better reflect the intensity of and reflection on depletion. After all, as Caroline Criado Perez (2020, xiii) points out, "Statistics are a kind of information, yes, but so is human experience." The question I started with was whether the model we put forward—$DSR = Rt, TH$—is redundant. My answer has been that despite serious challenges to modeling social reproduction, we can develop new methodologies to "link narratives, numbers and images" (Savage and Burrows 2007, 896) to better describe our everyday labors of (re)producing life. FEOT, then, is an attempt to assess whether, if numbers are collected, analyzed, and challenged in conversation with stories, images, and experiences, we will be better able to understand depletion. In Chapters 3 and 4, I will demonstrate how FEOT helped me to understand better, although not quantify, depletion through social reproduction in the everyday lives of women in New Delhi.

3

A Day in the Life of . . .

Mapping Individual Depletion across Class Boundaries

Introduction

What did you do yesterday? This is the question that animates this chapter. Social reproductive work is marked with moments of both joy and of drudgery. It is relentless—everyday concerns dominate the rhythms of life. It connects the outside world of markets and public spaces with the inside spaces of households and communities. Social reproductive work is also therefore embedded in contemporary gender inequalities, socialities, and political economy. And it frames the shifting subjectivities of those engaged in this work—how they perceive themselves, how they think others value or not their work—within households, communities, and the wider society. How does this affect their self-worth, entitlement, and relationships within households? To answer these questions is also to more fully understand depletion.

Gendered regimes of work and leisure, of paid and unpaid labor, of temporalities and rhythms in spaces both domestic and public frame the everyday (Elias and Rai 2019). " 'Women' in general," Henri Lefebvre (1984, 11–12) wrote, "bear all the weight of everyday life; they are subjected to it much more than 'men,' in spite of very significant differences according to social classes and groups. Their situation sums up what the everyday is." In this chapter I approach social reproduction through an early version of FEOT (Chapter 2); I had not yet refined the method or given it a name, but the broad framework was there. To understand the labors and costs of social reproduction, I wanted to ask the following questions: How do women from different social classes organize their paid and unpaid work, and how is this work

Depletion. Shirin M. Rai, Oxford University Press. © Shirin M. Rai 2024.
DOI: 10.1093/oso/9780197535547.003.0004

narrated, valued, and translated into social goods and public policy? What narrative tropes are employed to describe this work as compared with waged work? What philosophical, gendered, political, and social histories are harnessed in these narratives on work? How do working people account for their time—to themselves, their families, and their peers—as they make sense of their lives? How do they manage their time? The focus, in this chapter, is on the costs of doing social reproductive work. Are women able to balance social reproductive work with waged labor? What satisfaction do they derive from one or the other or both? How tired do they feel? How stressful is the work inside and outside the domestic space? How valued do they feel by their peers, partners, themselves, the media/state?

In this chapter, I analyze depletion by revealing the everyday rhythms of doing social reproductive and paid labor by eight women, across time and space as well as class boundaries in one randomly chosen working/school day of their lives in New Delhi. I also analyze mitigation and replenishment through reflecting on the agency that they exercise to negotiate and subvert the challenges they face every day in the context of the structural violence of gender and class inequality (Chapter 1; Elias and Rai 2019).

Listening to individual stories can help us identify "what we can learn about the place and value of labour imposed upon very different women, from the kinds of conflicts and problems they articulate and find worth telling" (John 2013, 178–179). In their narratives of everyday lives, these eight women reflexively assess their labor, their stresses and strains, joys and challenges, their position within their families and communities, and their feelings about themselves in relation to others. As I read through the interviews, I was as aware of this self-reflection, as I was of the conversation between the researcher and the research participants. In this chapter, I focus on the lives of individuals and find that their strategies of mitigating depletion are very much focused on their familial and friendship networks; the state and even nonstate organizations are absent from their narratives. Of course, this does not mean that they don't access resources of/from these organizations. Indeed, one of them specifically mentions access to governmental health facilities. Others comment on the physical infrastructure provided by the state and that they make use themselves of, in particular transportation and street lighting and cleaning (see also Chapter 4). None of them mentions any engagement with NGOs and social movements; the focus of their reflections remains on their families and friends who provide the support they need. I am aware that this is a very small study—eight women do not provide a sample big enough to generalize from. Reflections on the state and non-state actors might have emerged more prominently in a bigger study. What emerges in this study is detailed reflections on their everyday experiences.

As I argued in Chapter 2, however, qualitative research can be situated in the wider literature that can include quantitative studies of time-use to get a better understanding of the issues raised. In India, for example, the National Statistics Office found that more than "90% of Indian women participated in unpaid domestic work at home in 2019 compared to 27% of men," which accounted for 3.1% of India's GDP (Oxfam 2020). "On the other hand, only 22% of women participated in employment and related activities compared to 71% of men" (Radhakrishnan and Singaravelu 2020). Social reproduction is then heavily dependent on the labor of women; they also bear most of the costs of this labor. Numbers and stories together help us understand how everyday life is reproduced, organized, and understood in different registers (see Bhowmick 2022 for a personal narrative, and Rao 2021 on the crisis of social reproduction).

Researching Everyday Rhythms in New Delhi: Introducing the Research Participants

The research was carried out by my research assistant, Pujya Gosh, in New Delhi over a period of four months in 2016[1]. Pujya Ghosh was doing her master's program, so it was important to agree on the time she could spend on the research and monetary compensation for her labors, which we did through the university. Pujya was totally engaged with the research and the questions that it sought to answer. It was her contacts that snowballed into the group we finally worked with. We saw each other regularly, discussing the various aspects of the work, such as selection criteria for identifying the women to be observed, occasional unforeseen rescheduling of observations, the gendered dynamics of the households concerned which affected Pujya's work, the levels of tiredness that Pujya experienced in doing this work, and how this affected her academic studies (see also Johnson and Lingham 2020). Recognition of the context in which Pujya was working was important for her as well as for me—I could reflect on the operational elements of FEOT as well as the few gaps that emerged or on the unexpectedly new aspects that were revealed through this research (Chapter 4).[2]

The sociopolitical context of the city of Greater Delhi is important in situating the research. Delhi is an urban mega-metropolitan city with a population projected to be around 22.1 million in 2025 (Government of NCT of Delhi 2019) and with a sex ratio at birth of 865 females and 1,000 males (Press Information Bureau 2022). Its women workforce participation rate (WPR) is below the national average and "has further recorded a significant decline of 10% between 2011–12 and 2017–18," with "women of the poorer households witness[ing] the larger decline in WPR when compared to women of rich households"; as a result we also witness increased levels of social reproductive work being done by women, "household chores such as cooking, cleaning, washing, shopping, caring for the elderly and children" (Chakraborty 2019, n.p.).

So what exactly did we do? First, we did a pilot for this research, which threw up the issue of the intensity of this research, and therefore the need for caution in terms of numbers. I was concerned to have a cross-class sample in order to understand the different ways that social reproductive labor impacts individuals engaged in it, the resources they can command, and the networks that are needed to support it. As this was the first time that I was working with FEOT, caution was required. Pujya and I decided that we would go for two people from each income level—upper-middle, middle, lower-middle, and working class—making a sample of eight women. All eight women were married, but their family life was varied, and they had different care responsibilities; some were living with their husband, others managed two households because their husband lived elsewhere for work, some had young children, others had parents and parents-in-law to look after as well as children[3]. Out of eight participants, three did not do paid work, and one had only recently started doing so. The anonymized details of the social and work profile of the research participants are shown in Table 3.1.

I decided to exclude men from this sample; the evidence that women do most of the social reproductive work in India is incontrovertible—in India, women spend around 297 minutes, whereas only 31 minutes are spent by men in domestic work (Addati et al. 2018; Samantroy 2022). Men are not entirely absent from this research, however; the reflections in the interviews of our respondents include their relations with their husbands/fathers/sons and the recognition of domestic work that they get (or not) from them . At the start of the research, Pujya explained what the project entailed, including the recording of their time-use every 15 to 20 minutes, and interviewing them the next day. Informed consent was obtained from each of them. Pujya and

Table 3.1 Profiles of Research Participants

Name	Profession/Class	Time taken to travel to work	Children
Respondent 1 SUNEETA	Lower-middle-class working woman. Age 34	30–40 minutes on a motorbike	One
Respondent 2 BINDU	Upper-class working woman. Age 48	Car—no driver	None
Respondent 3 MAMTA	Upper-class homemaker. Age 45	Driver-driven car + self-driving	Two
Respondent 4 MEERA	Working-class working woman. Age 28	Walks—22 or 26 minutes	Two
Respondent 5 NEELA	Middle-class homemaker. Age 28	Car, self-driving	One
Respondent 6 SANGEETA	Middle-class working woman. Age 43	15 minutes by car—self-driven	Two
Respondent 7 DEEPA	Working-class homemaker. Age 31	Walks	Two
Respondent 8 SABINA	Middle-class working woman. Age 38	Public transport, Uber	None

I carefully discussed what questions she would ask after the shadowing was complete; this typically happened the next day. I identified some main themes that Pujya would need to be alert to, based on the research questions for the project, but essentially, we wanted to know what the women feel about their daily routine as Pujya recorded it. Pujya asked of all the respondents questions about their networks and sources of support, issues of recognition of their work in the home by family and their wider networks, and their mode of transportation, their participation in public life . We agreed that as we were exploring sensitive issues, it was important that our research participants were aware of the purpose of our research, felt engaged with it, and thought it worthwhile. Consent was also obtained from the respondents to photograph them as they went about their daily life. These too were referred to in the interviews—as prompts and as records.

As the methodology involved shadowing, it was important that the participants as well as their families felt comfortable with Pujya being around for the whole day, taking notes, and recording their time use. Only one husband found her presence difficult on the day and asked her to leave earlier than she would have. Of course, most of the day the women were alone (if at home) or in their work environments. Once the consent of the eight participants was gained, Pujya fixed dates and times with them. She arrived at the homes in the morning around 6:00 a.m. and was with the women until they went to bed at night. This was of course really intensive and sensitive work; at one stage Pujya wrote to me, "The work is way more exhausting and complicated than one can imagine." As I noted in Chapter 2, the intensity of this work is important to take into account when setting up the research—the well-being of the researcher as well as that of the participants is important to consider (see also Johnson and Lingham 2020). Once there, Pujya started the recording process.

A typical recording notation by Pujya would look like this:

11:30: They all go out for their tea break. They walk to a nearby canteen and have tea and samosas. They come back after 20–25mins. Once back, she and her colleague (who is similar in age) spend some time on facebook and chat for a while. After 10–15mins of this she is back to work.

Or

9:15am: She does her yoga. She does that for exactly 20mins and then goes to the kitchen to drink a glass of lemonade with honey. She also has almonds, neem leaves and a small piece of whole turmeric. She makes dal for the servant's lunch and everybody's dinner. She puts food out for the boys, both breakfast and lunch. Then she goes to her room to ready and arrange her bags (work bag, gym bag etc).

And

8:30–8:40: Everyone is done eating. The kids retire to their rooms. She cleans up the table and puts the food away in the fridge. She does a few other chores like filling water bottles. Since the kids will wear casuals to school the next day, she doesn't have to iron their uniforms. She chats with me for a while. Usually she watches something on the TV or talks to one of her relatives. She goes to her room around 9:30–9:40. She would change, freshen up and go off to sleep. Usually she makes it a point to sleep off by 10:30.

Going over the post-shadowing interviews and the time-use records, I am struck by the openness, intelligence, and humor with which the respondents relate to Pujya. Inevitably, Pujya's presence would have affected their behavior to some extent, but we thought not for long. Their engagement with Pujya and their interviews show a generosity in exposing their everyday life to external scrutiny that is remarkable. Also remarkable is the sensitivity with which Pujya speaks with them, with gentle prompts and careful persistence. What emerges is a picture of eight lives of women along axes of class—homemakers, professionals, businesswomen, and domestic workers.

They all live in a relatively small area of Greater/New Delhi, considered to be wealthy, but with deep inequalities reflecting class, caste, and gender. The spatial locations of these lives are also different: living in small quarters provided by the employer, living near a cesspool in cramped quarters, living in a house with a garden in a crowded city. The spatiality also translates into traveling to paid work and for social reproductive work; as we will see in Chapter 4, commuting to work and making segmented journeys for care work can add appreciably to depletion. Reading through their diaries and interviews multiple times, several themes emerge as common to these narratives, despite enormous differences in the resources that each of them can muster. These commonalities are not consistent—some speak more of one issue than the other—but they are present in all the interviews. The inflows and outflows of life are also visible—moments of stress or humor or anger, of pain and joy, of anticipation and worry run as red threads through their narratives and diaries. The messiness of their lives is reflected in the complex ethnography of time-use that this chapter explores.

Social Reproduction and Depletion in a Megapolis

"The everyday establishes itself, creating hourly demands, systems of transport, in short, its repetitive organisation," writes Lefebvre (2004, 7). He could also have included, but doesn't, the everyday establishing itself through demands of care—of children, of the old, the adults, of the household itself. Methodologically, a key aspect of feminist work has been to acknowledge the importance of everyday experiences. According to Sandra Harding (1987, 9), "If we want to understand how our daily experience arrives in the forms it does, it makes sense to examine critically the sources of social power." Feminists have also underscored the importance of different experiences of the everyday, indicating intersectional identities of class, race, ethnicity, and sexuality of women as well as of those who research their experiences (Elias and Rai 2019, 6). The research with eight participants in Delhi was an attempt to understand the everyday rhythms of their lives as they cope with social reproductive work, with consequent inflows and outflows, and understand the levels of depletion that they experience in doing this work, taking into account their ability to mitigate and even replenish.

We find that social reproduction generates a volume and intensity of work that defines the lives of these women. Depending upon their class positioning and whether or not they do paid work outside of the home, this work is often done with the help of others—both paid and unpaid—but remains stressful for those who consider themselves to be primarily responsible for it. Care work is relentless; most women interviewed during this research do not see it as something that they can choose to do or not do—they just get on with it, not challenging gender norms directly: "We have to do this work . . . send children to school, cook, clean, keep house. . . . [I]f this is the situation then why worry [*ghabrana kya*]? There is no choice," says Deepa. Upper-class educated women tend to reflect on what they want done differently—by their partners and sometimes by their children. For working-class and lower-middle-class women there is little time for self-care and reflection; what there is, is spent largely in front of the television, a pause from the hectic everyday; middle- and upper-class women try to look after themselves by going to the gym or out with friends. The ability of women to organize social reproduction depends on their access to care networks and their ability to buy in labor of others and to redistribute this work within the home—education and higher income helps. It also depends on state policies—the decreasing women's labor force participation and the education of girls in India are areas of state concern resulting in some, not sufficient, support through local and national support initiatives (Samantroy 2022). Finally, the research shows that women who are in paid employment value their work, and all women wish to be valued within the home.

Speaking about these issues was not always easy for our participants, and some found it difficult to speak of the burdens of care/housework. "When a wife becomes a mother, her world revolves around her child, husband and home, so you need appreciation, otherwise you get irritated. Some people don't admit this but I do, so I ask for [appreciation]," Neela, one of our research participants, tells us shyly. Social vocabularies make "naturalized" links between mothers and caring, between women and nurture, between homemaking and a woman's role.[4] However, these social vocabularies can be loosened; reading the scripts, I find that reflections on specific moments in the day when the women felt tired, stressed, or joyful can give us clues to other rhythms that might be welcome but are not easy to reimagine in the hurly-burly of the everyday.

Negotiating Time and Space across Class Boundaries

As will become clear in this chapter, resources supporting social reproductive work include gendered and generational time—the importance of the labor of mothers, mothers-in-law, and sometimes friends and neighbors; the ability to minimize "dead time" or what is deemed nonproductive time—the queues, waiting for expensive, poorly funded, and inefficient public or private transport to go to work (see Chapter 4 for more on this). Impinging on support for social reproduction is also the relationship between time and the state's role in maintaining particular gender orders—the lack of work-based childcare, maternity/paternity leave, and healthcare services. Time is a resource that women in well-paid work can buy in; as a commodity it can and does reduce the burden of everyday labor for some women at the expense of increasing it for others. A strategic focus on time as a commodity in the context of the everyday allows us to see how depletion through social reproduction is built into the social economy of individuals, households, and communities .

Further, as will become clear in the narratives below, time connects different spaces of the everyday—daily routines traverse time and space through travel, work, and care regimes. Simple matters such as taking children to school means that not only do the children need to be overseen in order that they are ready in time, but also that they reach school safely—by school bus, by driving them to school or walking with them. The spaces of home and work are thus connected with timely repetitions. Negotiating space in New Delhi is not easy and the lack of secure and timely public transport or access to private vehicles increases depletion (Figure 3.1; see also Chapter 4).

In all this, class matters. As bell hooks (2007) writes, "It is impossible to talk meaningfully about ending [gender exploitation] without talking about class." Cheap domestic labor in India means that many middle-class and upper-class women can afford help to do the hard chores such as cleaning and cooking. Some have drivers; others have cars that they drive themselves. As Bindu says, her life would improve "outside if I had a driver; I drive myself. I feel I would then be able to use that time to make my phone calls [for work]." But what of those who cannot afford help? Those who work for others and within their own homes? Those who work to keep the household running with a minimum of state and familial support? Deepa is a working-class homemaker. She is 31 years old. She studied till class 10. She has been

Figure 3.1 Class matters—cooking after a day at work. Photographs by Pujya Ghosh.

married for 12 years. She has two daughters: 10 years and 6 years. She has never done paid work. Her husband works as a part-time domestic worker and is also a *peon* [orderly] in Indian Oil. This is her everyday that Pujya records:

5:30–5:45am: She wakes up. She freshens up and goes for a 10–15mins walk. Once back she wakes her kids up. She then makes tea for her husband and gets the elder daughter ready for school. She also makes their lunch for school.

6:30am: She leaves with her daughter to go to school. They walk to the school. It takes about 15mins to reach.

By 7am she is back. Then she gets the younger one ready. Both the times she gives them a bath and gives them glass of milk and a fruit (banana or apple). She leaves with her by 7:30. She walks to the school and back. This time it takes her 40–45mins to do the trip.

8:15am: She is back. She makes breakfast and packs lunch for her husband. Her husband is at his employer's house downstairs since 6:30am and just comes back. After he gets ready they eat their breakfast together and by 8:45 he leaves for work. Once the house is empty, she gets to her other chores. She cleans the house, washes utensils, soaks

Figure 3.2 Washing clothes for the family. Photographs by Pujya Ghosh.

clothes, arranges the washed utensils, heats milk, cleans the fridge, and puts in the vegetables she bought last night.

——————- Every Wednesday there is a temporary market (Haat) that sets up near their house. At around 10–10:30pm when the vendors are packing up and the police have already started harassing them, they start selling off the remaining things for very cheap, that's when she and her husband go and buy groceries for the entire week.

9:30am: She goes for her bath. Once out she does her puja (prayer). Then she makes tea and sits with it for 15minutes with that.

10:15am: She goes to get her elder daughter from school. She is back by 10:50am. The elder daughter is having her exams and therefore her school got over at 10:30. Otherwise it gets over at 12:30. So usually she finishes her cooking and washing clothes before going to pick her up. Then she gives milk and fruits to her kid. After that she gets to washing clothes. This is her everyday chore. In fact, over the weekend she gives washing clothes a miss.

Around 12pm she starts cooking lunch. She also cleans up the place as soon as she is done cooking.

1:30pm: She leaves again to pick up the younger one from school.

2:20pm: She is back. She helps her kid freshen up. Then she makes lassi.

Once we all have that, nobody wanted to eat lunch right away so she decided to do some knitting work. There is a centre near her house which employs women to knit for them and they get paid per piece. This is something she has started very recently and says it is more of a recreation than an income opportunity. It gives her a chance to step out for a couple of hours at least two–three days a week and also meet new people.

Around 3:45 she served lunch to everyone. She cleared up things by 4:30. Then she rested for a while.

Around 5:30pm she steps out with her kids to the colony park. The kids play there and she takes her walk. They spend about an hour there. Once back, she takes the clothes off the line and folds them and puts them aside. In case there is anything that needs ironing then she does that as well.

——————- Sometimes she needs to take the elder daughter to her tuition classes and again go back after an hour to pick her up. She also watches TV for an hour or hour and a half in the evening.

Around 7pm she makes tea. Her husband walks in around that time. She gives him tea once he settles down. He has bought some sweets from work so she serves them up. Then she sits with the kids and their homework. The elder one mostly manages on her own but the younger one still needs her help with work. Her husband goes downstairs again by 8pm.

9pm: She goes to cook dinner. She cleans up after and washes utensils again. She fills bottles and keeps everything ready. The younger one falls asleep in the meantime so she somehow drags her out and feeds her something.

Her husband is back by 10:30 and after a little while she serves dinner to everyone.

She wraps things up by 11:30–11:45.

——————— Tomorrow is a holiday so there is no school and office. Therefore the evening was spent in a casual way.

The recording of rhythms of Deepa's life underlines the relentlessness of social reproduction. Given her socioeconomic position, levels of inflow are low and outflow high; she has a long working day that stretches across the lives of her children and husband, leaving little time for herself, other than praying and an occasional cup of tea. Depletion can be read off this diary of a day.

Outflows: Exhaustion, Stress, and Health

Unsurprisingly, care work takes up a lot of energy and time. The rhythm of school time dictates the lives of those with young children; responsibility for elderly parents means the workday stretches at the beginning or the end; adult children too need to be supported in different ways—emotionally, sometimes financially—which can be a cause of worry. The insistent persistence of work comes through in the interviews, in acceptance of the way things are, even as desires for more recognition, help, and time for self-care disrupt the narrative of smooth running of everyday life. Mamta's day begins early, records Pujya:

> *6:40: Kids are woken up. She helps them get ready especially her son. Then she makes banana milkshake for them. They leave [for school] at 7:30 sharp. She goes to drop them. They have a driver. . . . Once she drops them off, she visits her parents who live close to the school. She stays there for 10–15mins. She usually checks on them once a day. Today she came because her father isn't too well. She also picks up some sheets from there for laundry.*

Sangeeta's day is also busy:

> *6:30am: She wakes up. Today is Saturday so she woke up a little late. She is usually up by 5:30. But she can't wake up any later than this because she has to go to her school in any case but an hour later than usual. After she freshens up and takes a bath, she does her puja. Then she fills the cooler, waters her plants and does her bed. Her mother who is visiting them is also up by then. Then she takes her dog out for a walk. She is back by 7:30. Then she makes tea and prepares breakfast. She serves tea to her mother and her mother-in-law and sits down with her cup of coffee.*
> *——————[If this were a weekday, then instead of breakfast she would be making tiffin for school.]* (Diary: 20)

Figure 3.3 Elder care. Photographs by Pujya Ghosh.

What strikes one reading these notations of morning rhythms is that the day starts busy; that children and parents (sometimes neighbors and in-laws too) need time; that there is a relentlessness of household work that has no name but that occupies these women. If sending the household to school/work is busy, the responsibility of being there for them at the end of the day is also stressful. As an upper-class woman, Mamta experiences stress but also has the resources to address this, as she explains: "Earlier I used to feel so stressed. . . . I went to a physio in Max [hospital]. . . . I almost cried . . . my head hurt so much! He . . . said it was because I was so stressed and that out of twenty-four hours give yourself at least one hour. . . . [T]hat is when I joined my art class and that relaxed me."

For those in paid employment, the urgency of this work is greater—the schedules of lives of other members of the household need to be combined with their own needs for being at work. Suneeta, a lower-middle-class mother, says: "I run around in the morning. . . . I have to make breakfast, pack our lunch, bathe my daughter, get her ready, feed her and give her milk. . . . [T]he stress in the morning is great . . . it is like I sit in a fast train, which stops only when I get to office."

Later she adds: "[E]ven during working days, I do *jharoo pocha* [sweep and mop] the house before leaving. . . . [A]t the weekends I do all the washing and deep clean; I have no maid to help me." This adds to physical and mental depletion before Suneeta goes to do paid work, when "clock time" takes over. The lines between the two are of course blurred; time in its many forms is ever present in these lives, ruling their sleep, rushing them to and from work, through different parts of their homes—bathrooms, kitchens, bedrooms—to arrive at the bus stop, the workplace, rushing to pick up or meet children from school. Rushing is an integral feature of their everyday.

As Lefebvre (2004, 9) writes, "Rhythm appears as regulated time, governed by rational laws, but in contact with what is least **rational** in human beings: the lived, the carnal, the body. Rational, numerical, quantitative and qualitative rhythms superimpose themselves on the multiple **natural** rhythms of the body (respiration, the heart, hunger and thirst, etc.), though not without changing them. The bundle of natural rhythms wraps itself in rhythms of social or mental function." (bold in original).

What is interesting in the narratives of these eight women is that for most, time is at a premium. The time "for what you will," which we discussed in Chapter 1, is squeezed between the paid and unpaid work and outside the rhythm of the everyday social reproductive work. What self-time there is depends on the support systems around them—the wealthier go to the gym, the lower-middle-class employed have access to the internet at work and so can go to their Facebook page, most watch television in the evening, but all of them are aware of the "rushness" of their lives.

Inflows: Familialization of Social Reproduction

As outlined in Chapter 1, inflows include leisure time, pleasure derived from social reproductive work—playing with children, for example, access to healthcare and support networks that help mitigate the depletion through social reproduction. Buying in labor is an important element of mitigation for the wealthier. To say this is not, however, to say all about this issue. There are significant differences in the nature, amount, and time of bought in labor: some women have full-time live-in help; others employ a cleaner once a day; the upper classes have live in domestic help, many have more than one, with drivers to chauffer them to and from work and with ferrying children and the elders in the family. These considerable bought-in resources do not redistribute responsibilities of social reproduction within the household, but they do make the drudgery of everyday chores easier.

Cutting across class, others in the family and neighborhood are important to the everyday doing of both paid and unpaid work; mothers/in-law, sisters, husbands, children also help to mitigate the depletion experienced by some women. Parents/in-law pick up the children from playschools, for example, or ensure that someone is at home when the children return. They are there at the beginning or the end of the day to help dress children for school or to put them to bed. They help with the cooking and cleaning and watering the garden and sometimes walking the dog.

Friends and friendships are strongly present in this narrative of the everyday. Suneeta, a lower-middle-class office worker, depends on her older sister and her friends for support: I share everything with *didi* [elder sister], which makes me feel relaxed. . . . [W]e don't have the time to meet every weekend, even every other weekend, but now we have phones so we talk. . . . [S]ometimes I see her with my daughter, sometimes with my husband. . . . [W]e meet every other month. . . . I meet my friends in the mall . . . we have a WhatsApp group and we fix place and time to meet. . . . [When I go with my friends] I leave my daughter with my husband [giggles]."

Neela, a middle-class homemaker, longs for friendships: "I am sailing my own boat just now; I am on my own these days; honestly I am not in touch with my friends any more; they are busy and timings don't match so I don't have any one to share with. . . . I speak to my mom, Anshu's mom [Neela's mother-in-law] about daily details about Ananya [daughter], that is all."

For Meera (a domestic worker) friendships are memories of a time when she earned a wage for paid work, before she was married and had responsibilities of running a home and looking after her children. Pujya writes:

She really enjoyed herself in Dubai. She shows me photographs of herself there with friends, because she says that was one of the happiest days of her life. She occasionally gets in touch with them because none of them live in Delhi; they are mostly still in Dubai. These women were the only friends she really ever had. The memories of her work-based journey to Dubai remain important to Meera. (PG Notes: 16)

Carving out space for oneself often means watching TV, with or without the family. Suneeta watches TV everyday:

> *9.00pm: She usually serves her husband food and feeds her daughter at the same time. Once they are done, she changes into her home clothes, freshens up and then eats while watching TV.* (Diary)

Almost all of the eight respondents referred to this as a restful period but other than Mamta, who likes watching *Grey's Anatomy*, no one refers to any specific program they watch; one gets the feeling that TV is the pause button in a hectic life, a mode of transitioning from time for others to time for oneself, to sit down and not be on call. Other spaces carved out—reading, art class, yoga—are marked by class; middle-class women refer to these activities, but working-class women do not. Mamta looks forward to her art class: "Number one, I get to meet Shikha; she is a very good friend, she is like a sister to me. . . . I can share everything with her. . . . [S]he and my brother-in-law are my twenty-four-seven confidants." But apart from this, she doesn't get much time for herself: "I can't even get a pedicure."

Neela, a middle-class homemaker, says, "Maximum two hours I spend on myself a day; I like doing crochet and reading books when I get time. Yoga, I won't count because Ananya is always around, and that is too distracting; anyway it doesn't happen on a daily basis." Pujya notes that Bindu, an upper-class working woman, does yoga:

> *9:15am: She does her yoga. She does that for exactly 20mins. (Diary: 4)*

Bindu explains, I spend quite a bit of time on myself; I do yoga every morning for half an hour and spend two hours at my gym everyday and at the end of the day I watch TV; but mostly I am running around for others.

Pujya notes Sabina's leisure time in this way:

Sometimes she goes to her mother's place, or they [she and her husband] go out somewhere like a movie, or to a friend's house or sometimes friends come over. If they are not eating out then she does the cooking. Usually there is no set plan. (PG Notes: 8)

Even though this is much more leisure time than, say, what Meera, who is a domestic worker, has, Sabina reflects that she doesn't do as many things for herself as she would like to. For instance, she would like to go for a walk, but that usually doesn't happen because there is no time. She tries to do yoga three times a week. She reads on the metro, so that's something she does for herself. On weekends, she gets a chance to meet her friends and unwind, but through the week there is no such option.

Playing with children features in the everyday of these women less than I expected. This is partly because of the age of the children—some are adults and others are teenagers—but also because the children themselves are under pressure of school work. Spending time with children is often not play but helping with their homework. Suneeta has a small child; Pujya's diary about Suneeta's day reflects the juggling with work and play:

> *By 6:30 we are home. She washes up and goes to make tea and some snack for the kid. Her husband freshens up too and switches on the T.V. to watch the news. She plays with the kids as she makes tea . . . .*
> *————We all sit and drink tea and she plays with the kid. The child fusses over the food so [she]breastfeeds her. She usually does that, twice or thrice a day.* (Diary 2)

Neela has more time with her daughter, who is only one year old:

> *9am: She wakes up. She comes out of her room with her kid after half an hour. Then she makes tea and breakfast. Once done she drinks tea and also plays with her daughter.* (Diary 16)

The diaries and the notes of the day show that the lines between work and play are fine; women cross over these frequently—cooking and playing, folding clothes and playing, supervising their children's play with a neighbor's child, multitasking (see Chapter 2).

Healthcare is an important inflow. However, "[despite the] growing economy and technology in India, only 36% of the women have access to a sanitary pad or go and visit a doctor to discuss their health issue[s]" (Bhattacharya and Sachdev 2021, 113). I was interested in understanding not only the research participants' access to healthcare but their attitudes toward their own health; like time for "what you will," do they make time for keeping healthy? For some, exercise is part of their daily routine—they do yoga, meditate, and go to the gym. For others, such stepping out of the daily routine is impossible because they lack money to invest in themselves and they lack time as they do the household chores and often paid employment. For some, access to private healthcare is not an issue; others depend on government hospitals, which are overcrowded and difficult to access. Most are more aware of the health of their families but do not necessarily prioritize their own. Suneeta, for example, uses the state-supported Employees State Insurance (ESI) card for health issues:

Generic medicines they buy from a chemist near by, otherwise they make it a point to pick it up from an ESI dispensary. For check ups also they go to an ESI hospital. She is very prompt about her daughter's health care needs but tends to slacken off when it comes to her [own] because she is tired and there are always things to do. Thankfully nothing serious has ever happened and she believes that she wouldn't let things go out of hand really. (PG Notes: 4)

Bindu, on the other hand, is wealthy and is careful of her health:

She takes a lot of care to maintain her body and energy. She does not ignore any physical discomfort and because of her husband she has access to the biggest doctors in the best facilities. (PG Notes: 8)

Mamta, can also afford to be

very particular with her family's health. She doesn't like delaying attending to health issues on any count. There is an annual check up for everyone, including thyroid and hormone profiles for her daughter, and she is always on top of it. (PG Notes: 12)

Unsurprisingly, healthcare and class are intimately connected: access, information, and focus on health is far more visible in middle- and upper-class women.

Inflow/Outflow: Employment, Self-Worth and the Double Burden

Of course, many aspects of everyday life cannot be neatly slotted into inflow/outflow boxes—they overlap. As we saw in Chapter 2, inflows can be undermined by outflows and outflows mitigated by inflows that are both tangible and intangible. For example, lack of recognition of social reproductive labor can erode confidence even in contexts of class privilege, and inflow from increased self-esteem through recognition can mitigate the considerable burdens of doing both paid labor outside and unpaid work in the home. This does not mean that there is no physical depletion—tiredness from long hours of paid and unpaid work—but appreciation of this work is often a mitigatory aspect of everyday life.

One of the surprising findings of this research was the reflexive value placed on paid employment—by those who do it as well as those who did but do not do so now. Despite the double burden of social reproductive and productive work, the employed women Pujya interviewed took pride in the fact that they had an income, were aware of the social benefits of their employment, and wanted recognition of their contribution to the family income and well-being. This is particularly interesting (and open to question) given the falling labor force rates for women, referred to above, which is in part because of gender-unfriendly workspaces, displacement by men in jobs during economic shocks such as COVID-19, and, as everywhere, women carrying the primary responsibility of social reproduction (Deshpande and Singh 2021). Bindu notes the difference in attitudes toward her once she started working: "One more thing is definitely there; because of my professional life my relationship with others has definitely improved a lot. They started giving me value which earlier they didn't; which they should give to everyone anyway."

Bindu believes that staying at home isn't respected in society: "Women need financial independence. The person who doesn't go out [homemaker] she only hears from her husband and children about what goes on outside and how she is. When she starts going out for work then she meets so many other people and realises how she is. . . . [O]nce I started working I didn't have to say I am so-and-so's wife or mother; I could be just me." She says that by the end of her day, "I am physically exhausted, but mentally I am not tired at all." Of course, she has domestic help at home to mitigate this tiredness, but it is important to note both her tiredness and her valuing of her paid work. Balancing paid work with care responsibilities is part of these women's everyday routine—most of them did not reflect on any significant redistribution of social reproductive work within the domestic sphere. Employment is also a site of both income and sociality. Take, for example, Suneeta's [from a lower-middle class family] day at work:

9:45: She reaches office. Before setting out to work, she has to clean, make breakfast, pack lunch, get her daughter ready, feed her, make her food and get ready herself, drop the daughter off at the crèche and reach work. This is late for her. She is in her office by 9:30 most days . . . .

10:15: The attendant (who sits there) comes in with two big stacks of files from the cash section, to be computed . . . .

————-People working here are very friendly to each other. They have their inside jokes. People refer to her as "Badi Madam" (Big Madam)! . . .

————She also calls up the crèche to check on the kid.

Around 11:30: They all go out for their tea break. They walk to a nearby canteen and have tea and samosas. They come back after 20–25mins. Once back, she and her colleague (who is similar in age) spend some time on facebook and chat for a while. After 10–15mins of this she is back to work.

—————Though they have a computer at home, they don't have internet. So office is the only place she can access facebook etc.

By 2:30 everybody settles down with their work.

—————-The scene in the office is the same as morning. There are no more tea breaks.

5:15: Her husband comes to pick her up and they leave.

Around 5:45: They reach the crèche. She alone goes up to get the kid. She takes an update from the lady there and her son as he packs the bag. (PG Diary: 1-2)

When interviewed about her day, Suneeta says that she thinks of her housework as a hobby: "Make a hobby out of housework because you have to do it anyway. . . . [Y]ou should work if you can, of course, it will help you financially, but also use your knowledge. Sitting at home can make your knowledge dull." For Meera, a domestic worker, working is not an option but a necessity. When combined with the pressures of work at home, this becomes intolerable at times: "What I do in the morning is fine, and of course, my job [as a domestic worker] is important, but then when I go home and have to do all the dishes and wash all the clothes, that is terrible, and I hate that." Working for her is important to support her family, her husband: "I only help; my husband earns. . . . [H]is salary comes on the seventh; if we need money on the first then my money helps; even without that, I can help the children I have opened accounts for five hundred rupees for the girl and the boy. . . . [T]his way we don't have to ask others." The conflicted emotions that she expresses here about paid work are deeply felt; she is miserable and feels depleted at the end of the day, and yet there is no way out for her—she has to work and do the everyday drudgery of domestic labor. Her escape into the future is that of her children's lives—their escape from her world of drudgery may yet be her escape too; pride in seeing them economically secure and with an improved status in life would be a reward for her.

As a journalist Sabina is aware of not only her own situation but also of women more broadly. In her interview she tells Pujya that she believes she is good at her job so she feels comfortable, which she wouldn't if she could not do justice to the work given to her:

> It's not a burden to her in any way. There are days when she feels really depressed; she questions her choices, the fact that she spends half her life in the train. There are days when she is so tired she doesn't feel like walking to the metro station or take the train back etc. There are difficult work days . . . but on overall, she likes it. . . . [W]ork broadens people's mind, gives them a chance to exchange ideas, ones gets to learn from experience. But that doesn't mean that women who are not working are not living their life to the fullest. That is a choice that they have made, and they should not be made to feel sorry for their choices. (PG Notes: 22–23)

As we will see in Chapter 4, commuting to work is particularly tiring:

> [Sabina] thinks it's the physical exhaustion that gets to her; there are days when she falls asleep in the metro and she doesn't feel good about it. (PG Notes: 23)

So, while physical exhaustion and mental and emotional fatigue are a thread that ties together these three narratives, there are different subjectivities at play here. It is, then, difficult to say what is an inflow and what is an outflow. For Meera, doing domestic chores is more palatable in paid employment than at home; Suneeta needs a transcendence of domestic work into a hobby to cope with the drudgery; for Sabina, paid work is empowering and domestic labor is shared with her husband, but traveling to work is exhausting and stressful.

I have been arguing that recognition is a measure of value; the desire for recognition of caring and social reproductive work is present even though it is not always met. Of course, in the intimacy of familial relationships, recognition takes many forms—spoken and unspoken. However, these eight women were acutely aware of their status in the family, the sources of this and at times the lack of recognition and their need for it. As Deepa reflected, "Sometimes when there is an argument he [her husband] tells me, 'You sit at home all day, what *do* you do? Why couldn't you get this done?' Then I feel all husbands are like this; I feel like saying you stay at home one day, then you will know what is what! . . . [W]hen I speak to other [women] they say their husbands also say the same—you stay at home all day, what do you do." As far as recognition of her work is concerned, she says, "He [her husband] is an introvert. . . . [H]is nature is that the doesn't express himself at all. . . . I wish he would; I do want to know what place I have in his life. . . . I have girls, so they are close to me and I hope will appreciate me when they grow up." Sangeeta, a nursery teacher, started working after being a homemaker for 10 years after marriage: "My husband's attitude is the same as before I was working. . . . [H]e tells the children to help me out, now that I am working, and he handles them when they complain about me. . . . [I]t is really important to me that he understands [her pressures of work] and I like that he notices if I have done something special [for the family]."

One of the important inflows is that of support from the family, and from the husband in particular—both practical help and valuing the social reproductive work of the women. Not all get this support, but some do. This support is also not the same as redistribution of social reproductive work—the responsibility remains the woman's; the husband provides specific and occasional help. Suneeta giggles when she speaks of her husband helping her; here we find acceptance of the work and resistance to norms that make it *her* work:

> He is okay. . . . [O]bviously I do all the housework. . . . [W]omen have to do this okay. . . . [H]e is supportive though . . . helps me in the house . . . goes to the market to get all the groceries [*saaman*]; he does all the outside work, pays the bills. . . . [T]hat is his responsibility, and will help if the child is crying. . . . He has never said [he appreciates me]. . . . [D]on't they say that boys don't express their feelings? [giggles] But I can make out that he does appreciate me."

Mamta's husband is a big support. He takes care of things when she is out with friends: "He never stops me . . . not that I take his permission [giggles]; I just tell him; but even then, he never says don't go."

> "She participates in car rallies and goes away for two days and her husband would work from home and let her enjoy" (PG Notes: 11).

Sabina's diary records:

> *Around 10:10, her husband comes back. He walks in with vegetables and some groceries. He freshens up and straight heads to the kitchen. It is his job to prepare dinner.*
>
> *While the husband cooks, we chat in the living room. He joins us sometimes. They also squabble a little bit over some of the responses she was giving to my questions.*
>
> *11pm: They sit to eat their dinner. Once done, she clears up the table and settles the kitchen, though her husband did clean up after cooking.* (Diary: 28)

There are of course those husbands who don't help at all; Neela's husband, for example: "He is not much of a help; he is the father of my child but he is not a father who looks after her.... [H]e won't change his lifestyle." Pujya notes.

> Even with the kid, he constantly keeps calling her [Neela] for help. For instance, the kid had peed in her pants; she had to leave her cooking to come clean the place up and ensure if the kid has been changed properly (PG Notes: 24).

Education, gender awareness, and class can impact the division of labor in the household, but often the social norms and gendered expectations get in the way. Bindu reflects: "He [her husband] doesn't think anything of me ... he only thinks of me as a housewife, nothing else.... [H]e is constantly pulling me behind; where I can walk ten steps, I actually am able to walk only six.... I don't want to entertain people at home without prior notice I could be double successful if he would be supportive.... [O]nce a week he comes home and says "oh! Such and such are coming for dinner." ... I feel I am just a slave at home."
Other sources of support are mothers, mothers-in-law, and friends; this network is critically important for both those engaged in paid work and those who are not, and it is nurtured in different ways, adding to domestic responsibilities and often reproduction of gendered hierarchies within the home. Mamta's diary reveals the emotion-work for which she also feels responsible; this is also the quid pro quo for the wider family labor that she relies on:

> *8.30am: In the meanwhile, her husband gets ready for work. He does the puja and waters the plants etc. She also makes her husband call different people in the family (her dad, his mother, her eldest sister) to take update on things and their lives. It was primarily to check if they need something.* (Diary: 9)

Sabina's mother-in-law and sister-in-law are very supportive of her:

> The strongest support system in her life is her parents, especially her mother. She talks to her mother everyday.... She is also grateful for

her maid and shares a connection with her. They chat quite a bit and she gives her suggestions etc. because she thinks it's her duty as the privileged one. She also helps with her maid's studies. She thinks her life would be very stressful without these support systems. (PG Notes: 29)

Her mother-in-law is also Sangeeta's biggest support system. "She cannot imagine her life without her mother-in-law. The next person she relies on is her new friend/neighbour. She thinks her life will be very different if her support system isn't there any more" (PG Notes: 22).

Similarly, Mamta leans on her mother and mother-in-law: "Whenever I feel overwhelmed, I say quietly to [my husband] that I will go to either my mom or mother-in-law for a night." Meera's mother-in-law, on the other hand, doesn't help but adds to her work: whenever it's a holiday her mother-in-law (also a domestic worker) comes to visit: "She is otherwise nice to me but when she is there all she does is play cards with her friends. She hosts a kitty party[5] and I have to do everything. You would think that a grandmother [would want] to spend time with her grandchildren when she visits. But she barely spends any time with the children."

Summary

Through reading the narration of the everyday life of eight women in New Delhi, I have been arguing that depletion is the residue of social reproduction, especially where public and private support for this work is minimally recognized and outflows outstrip inflows. Through time-use diaries, shadowing/observation, and interviews we find that depletion takes the form of physical exhaustion, mental stress, and social isolation in a context of patriarchal, gendered distribution of social reproductive work. Depletion is affected by the social positionality of those doing this work—buying in labor to mitigate depletion is a strategy available to those who can afford it. Depletion then gets passed down the labor chain. Meera's story is a case in point. She is a domestic worker and works to contribute to the household economy and support her children's education; she works as a domestic laborer mitigating the social reproductive labor of others; she also does housework at her own home. Her days are long, stressful, and exhausting; depletion is more visible here than in the case of Mamta, an upper-class homemaker who has a cook and two maids who help with the housework. We witness Mamta as busy and responsible for the efficient running of the home—the routines of getting children to school, organizing their daily lives—which includes looking to the needs of her extended family and neighbors and supervising home improvements and the help in the home keeps her busy, but of course the levels of depletion that she experiences are very different from what Meera experiences. Class is an important element of not only the experience of depletion but also its intensity and the possibilities of mitigation to reverse it. What brings these two women in the same frame is their social reproductive labor; what keeps them apart is how this labor is organized and resourced.

As I read through these narratives I am struck by the agency and coping strategies of these women as they bridge their public and private lives; other than Sabina, most are primary carers of the home, even though some are employed outside the home, which creates a "double burden" of paid and unpaid work. Their agency is also visible in the way they approach this work—there is a sense that they have to just get on with it. Some are aware that change is needed, but there is also much acceptance of things as they are; they have to accept and make do. Humor is deployed to resist social norms of the gendered division of labor. All this reflects what Felski (2000, 31) calls the need for making "peace with the ordinariness of daily life" even as they actively negotiate their everyday. While we get glimpses of joyful moments in their lives, the shadowing reveals the relentlessness of social reproduction that washes over their everyday; the one day that we recorded in the life of these eight women is busy—the routines of everyday life that Lefebvre writes about enmesh them. Routines rule their everyday, depleting them but also enabling them to keep some control over their life; routines also make the work manageable—the women are able to parse themselves through the completion of their everyday tasks. There are few highs and lows in this recording of these eight lives; for most it is a day like any other, with its rhythms dictated by clock time: family going to school and work, cleaning, shopping, cooking, working, the humdrum but necessary tasks of keeping life going. And yet finding an opportunity to reflect on their everyday lives, they are able to articulate their hopes, fears, frustrations, and sources of strength and support—what makes their lives what they are. Speaking out also helps them to identify their sources of strength, their hopes and aspirations—for themselves and for their children.

Depletion is a red thread that goes through this everyday landscape—tiredness, exhaustion, lack of recognition, the relentlessness of their work are all mentioned by each and every one of them in different contexts. Even before Pujya finishes her question "What is your typical day?" Neela jumps in: "My day is tiring; it is just very tiring." Some of them are acutely aware of the need for recognition of their labors, the status that paid work can bring to a woman, and the importance of developing networks of friends and family to help in delivering care. Some are conscious of the need for redistribution of social reproductive labor, but most accept the gendered division of labor as given and try to negotiate it by seeking occasional help from husbands or family members or friends. While these mitigatory aspects are important, we are less aware of how they are able to connect the public domain as a source of support—the familialization of social reproduction in the everyday means that the demands on the state for provision of support are largely absent from their narratives. Through these narratives, we get glimpses of healthcare needs being delayed, issues of access to public healthcare, and the limits of public insurance medicine, and we notice the impact of poor public transportation on physical tiredness and stress (see also Chapter 4). However, and because of this lack of state provision, largely the everyday support systems are familial. The dependence on family also of course means that transformative discourses of redistribution of social reproduction only occasionally disrupt this gendered distribution of work.

These are not the "total women" of Lefebvre—their lives may be framed by an unequal and burdensome gender regime, but they negotiate this actively, thoughtfully, and with awareness of their own positionality in society and in their families and worksites. They do not seem to participate in collective action to change their lives; instead they mobilize the resources to hand. They are not, therefore, as Redden (2018, 160) seeks to invoke, "transformational women," agents that have the potential (rather like Lefebvre's "transitional man") to transform the everyday. As Heller (1984, 129) argues, "[W]e would simply not be able to survive in the multiplicity of everyday demands and everyday activities if all of them required inventive thinking. . . . Disengagement is an indispensable precondition for . . . continued activity." The women in these stories are instead socially embedded but self-aware and engaged subjects who accept and carry the responsibilities of social reproduction with limited resources that they nurture, to stretch and to add to as they try to mitigate the depleting effects of social reproductive work. Of course, it is because they cope as they go through their everyday that also allows their work to be overlooked—there is no crisis of social reproduction leading to collapse of the system here; neither is there any attempt by them to transform their everyday. What we witness rather is coping with their everyday challenges at the cost of depletion, variously mitigated, of their lives. This coping is not indicative of domination, as Lefebvre would see it; rather it is about negotiating life—through consenting to particular roles, complaining about them (sometimes), and also reshaping them within the social structures that frame them (see Felski 2000). No cost-benefit analysis or inflow-outflow calculus can directly capture this depletion, but by shadowing their lives for one day we can become aware of the differential and depleting costs of the caring.

4

Depletion on the Move

Commuting and Social Reproduction

Introduction

Virginia Woolf (2014 [1930]) takes a walk and comments, "That is true: to escape is the greatest of pleasures; street haunting in winter the greatest of adventures. Still as we approach our own doorstep again, it is comforting to feel the old possessions, the old prejudices, fold us round; and the self, which has been blown about at so many street corners, which has battered like a moth at the flame of so many inaccessible lanterns, sheltered and enclosed."

For Woolf, a walk underscores both an escape from the rhythms of everyday life and the return to the safety and familiarity of life. For Sangeeta, one of our research participants (see Chapter 3), short distances are exhausting because of poor public transport accessibility as she copes with her children's needs and her domestic work: "I used to get exhausted last year a lot. My children were going to coaching classes, evening classes. . . . [B]uses are really crowded; I had to go to get one then the other. . . . The distance is not much but because of traffic I used to get exhausted." And then there is Meera, combining work and social reproduction in difficult circumstances, cutting through a jungle to save time; anxious about her safety and aware of the filth of the environment, and starting paid work after experiencing the physical and mental stress of walking to work; she tells us, "[Walking to work] on the main road, it takes more than half an hour, through the jungle it is half the time, but it is not very nice—many people do potty there . . . because we don't have toilets at home. . . . I go in the morning, it is foggy and I feel anxious in case someone bad turns up."

In this chapter, three women—Sangeeta, Meera, and Sabina, whom we met in the previous chapter—with very different lives, experience

Depletion. Shirin M. Rai, Oxford University Press. © Shirin M. Rai 2024.
DOI: 10.1093/oso/9780197535547.003.0005

contrasting rhythms of movement in public spaces, but all feel depleted through these. As always, gender and class are entwined here—for Virginia Woolf, the key is the freedom to roam, to wander in the city, to live other lives while doing so. In other contexts, walking in public places can carry the threat of caste-, sexuality-, and race-based violence that routinely traumatizes, injures, and can even end the lives of those thus marginalized. The experiences of Sangeeta, Meera, and Sabina also reveal what Sánchez de Madariaga and Zucchini (2019) call "mobility of care"—travel for reasons of social reproduction.

In this chapter, I conceptualize commuting as a form of *liminal labor*—an in-between state, between the spheres of production and social reproduction. I see it as the extra time taken for and to do paid and unpaid work, time that is overlooked, unrecognized, and therefore not taken into account. I then map its costs as depletion. To do so, I build on the discussion of commuting and everyday life and map the commutes of the three women in New Delhi, by focusing on the arc of travel that connects their public and private worlds. Depletion because of commuting is a feature of all their lives, affecting their approach to their employment, their domestic responsibilities, their travel, and their level of well-being. I "travel" with them,[1] among others, on their everyday journeys to uncover how commuting increases depletion that marks their everyday, in greater and lesser forms.

As we saw in Chapter 3, class divides the experience of commuting to work for these women and the resources that they can mobilize to mitigate their depletion. I first map the field of study of commuting and social reproduction, and then examine the costs of commuting in different frames—time, timeliness, temporality, health costs, economic costs—and also issues of sociality and solidarity that get attached to commuting. Finally, I identify some policy gaps that arise as a result of overlooking the mobilities of care and of depletion through social reproduction.

Commuting and Its Multiple Affects

In mainstream literature commuting is largely referred to in the context of traveling for paid work to the site of employment. "Commuting" is defined as "the activity of travelling regularly between work and home" (Cambridge University Dictionary); of course, "work" here means paid work, and there is an assumption of regular work. Similarly, when we think of conditions of employment we think of conditions in the *sites of work* (SDG 8) that are stable; as commuting falls between the spaces of home and work, it is not, with few exceptions, regarded as work related and a responsibility of the employers. Unsurprisingly, then, debates and policies about "work-life balance" focus only on commuting to do paid work, not on precarious and/or social reproductive work. This framing has consequences—in terms of human well-being and depletion as well as in terms of social policies and state investment in infrastructure (transport, flexible working hours, health and safety). Public spaces and infrastructure are the state's responsibility, but commuting is not high on the agenda; often the issues of transportation ease for market access take precedence (see Chattopadhyay and Duflo 2004). In India, for example, commuting was one of the biggest problems reported by women in relation to their working life, but this is largely overlooked in the policy frameworks that wish to increase women's labor force participation (Jagori 2010).[2]

Commuting time adds to work time, lengthening days, increasing stress, and affecting well-being differentially; disabled workers in New York, for example, "generally seek higher wages in exchange for longer commute times [and earn 17.1% less], but the results differ by race/ethnicity and gender. Compared to white men, minority workers earn much less, and white and Hispanic women have significantly shorter commute times" (Wong et al. 2020, 1) constraining their job options. As I will show, traveling to work, both paid and unpaid, can significantly increase depletion; commuting from home to work and back affects the inflows and outflows that in turn increases the intensity of physical as well as mental depletion and adversely impacts both paid work and social reproduction.

Care Mobility

So what about traveling to perform social reproductive duties? Figure 4.1) In their paper, Sánchez de Madariaga and Zucchini (2019,

Figure 4.1 Segmented journeys. Photographs by Pujya Ghosh.

143) outline mobility for care activities as "escorting children to school, to sports and to other extra-curricular activities; doing non-leisure shopping; errands in public offices; visiting and escorting sick and elderly relatives, and so on. Such mostly unpaid activities imply travelling to specific locations in the city, at specific times during the day, using the available transport systems, under certain conditions of price, ergonomics and safety. Importantly, they need to be combined and made compatible with work in paid employment." They argue that mobility surveys do not measure this travel, leading to an undervaluation of care-based travel, and consequently of transport infrastructure needed for doing this travel. Based on their research in Madrid, they find that the total trips made for paid employment are almost the same as trips made for care: 33% and 29%. If the valuing of social reproduction is important for addressing depletion, as I have been arguing, so surely is the recognition of travel for social reproduction. In this chapter, I will therefore address both—travel to paid work and daily travel related to social reproduction—and show that both are intertwined and affect the levels and intensity of depletion. Depletion, as I have been arguing, is the arc that connects the public and the private worlds of those engaged in social reproduction.

Research shows that men commute longer distances than women, which has been attributed to the gendered and "the spatial segmentation of labour markets and constraints of residential choice behaviour. . . . [It] is particularly affected by the presence of children in the household" (Schwanen, Dijst, and Dieleman 2002, 1490). In Sweden, for example, "if there were young children in the household the disutility was higher for female commuters than their male counterparts" (Sandow, Westerlund, and Lindgren 2014, 1499). In Spain, the gender gap in who makes care trips is considerable: women do 40% of their travel for care-related responsibilities, and men only 9% (Sánchez de Madariaga and Zucchini 2019, 158–159). In terms of mobility for care, having children is a key distinguishing factor between the lives of men and women: "For women [in Madrid], trips of less than 10 min represent 54% of the total, and 75% of these trips are made by women who have dependent children. By contrast, for men trips of less than 10 min make up only 21% of the total, and men with dependent children make only 10% of these trips" (Sánchez de Madariaga and Zucchinni 2019, 162).

The U.K. Harmonised European Time Use Surveys data on travel, when put through the Depletion Data Browser (see Chapter 2),[3] clearly shows differential patterns of travel by women and men on the basis of time spent on everyday activities. Travel related to shopping, escorting children to and from education, and escorting children to places other than education (social reproductive work, in other words) is done more by women than men, while men do more traveling for commuting and social activities; slightly more than women on "travel related to education" and to "social activities" and for "day trip/just walk" (see Figure 4.2).

Added to this, a sense of insecurity affects commuting: traveling through ill-lit and conflict-ridden spaces has the threat of violence (Johnson and Lingham 2020); reputations are at stake if waiting for public transport is misconstrued as loitering, and family status is adversely affected if going out to work provides public visibility that being a home worker does not. As Buck-Morss (1986, 119) writes, "[T]he flaneur was simply the name of a man who loitered; but all women who loitered risked being seen as whores, as the term 'street-walker' or 'tramp' applied to women makes clear" (see also Phadke, Ranade, and Khan 2009). In this chapter I treat depletion through commuting as much about traveling long distances to work through varied and at

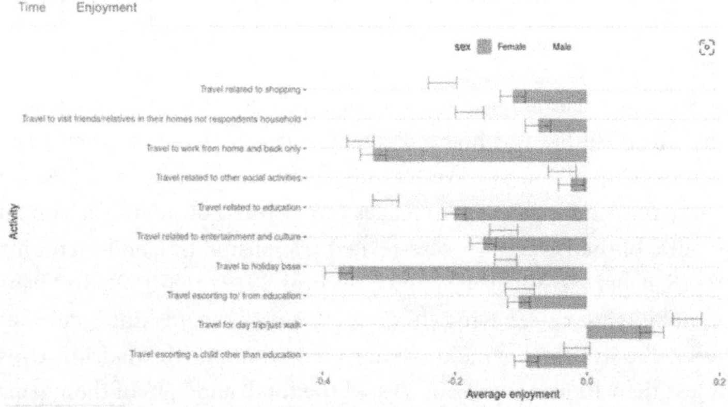

Figure 4.2 Depletion Data Browser: Travel/Time.

times inhospitable landscapes, as making many short journeys to carry out social reproductive work. This helps us to challenge the divide between paid and unpaid work, to take into account work-life balance, and to understand the time, health, and economic costs of commuting for both paid and social reproductive work and therefore the depletion that accompanies it.

Commuting is largely an outflow—it negatively affects health and sense of well-being. It is also an outflow in time costs, lengthening the working day, and an economic cost. As Datta (2020, 12) notes, "Free time was not 'free' per se; rather, it was the time in between two different timelines—between commuting and working, between family routines of cooking and childcare." And yet, as we will see, there are also inflows of commuting for some, which help to prepare for work, maintain life-work balance, or simply allow for pausing time in a busy life. The liminality of commuting is therefore important to recognize.

Next I map and analyze the commuting stories of women, for whom traveling to work is an essential part of their everyday life, to outline the different aspects of commuting that contribute to depletion. In Chapter 3, we saw how everyday rhythms of work frame depletion and how temporal and spatial landscapes are negotiated, with what costs in terms of depletion. Here, I discuss how the effects of commuting map onto everyday life.

Experiencing Commuting

Commuting is experienced differently.

Sangeeta, Meera, and Sabina all live and work in New Delhi, the capital of India. New Delhi has an area of 1,483 square kilometers and had a population of 29.59 million in 2019, and it is considered one of the fastest growing cities in the world. Its temperature varies, from long, hot summers (40C to 45C) to cool, dry winters (7C to 25C); weather plays an important part in commuting experiences. According to a report by Jagori (2010, 33), an NGO working with domestic workers in New Delhi, "Most [domestic] workers [in India] used public transport to commute to work. Even if they worked in the most adjacent residential area, the distance was too long to walk . . . 44 percent of the sample walked for about half an hour every day and 32 percent walk for more than 30 minutes. The remaining 24 percent walked for less than half an hour. Most workers also spent at least 30 minutes waiting for transport. The [monetary] cost of commuting was high and domestic workers spent an average of 14 percent of their wages in commuting." Korzhenevych and Jain (2018, 735) note, "Income disparities mean that women commuting to jobs outside home use public transport more often and private cars less often than men. . . . [O]n average, women make fewer and shorter trips than men . . . [and] only 21% of women, as opposed to 47% of men, use private motorized vehicles, more than 95% of which are two-wheelers. Cycling is unpopular with Indian women."[4]

Meera has regular work with one family as a domestic worker,[5] which includes sweeping and mopping the flat and cleaning the kitchen and washing up; she also has a temporary replacement position with another family, doing the same work. Like most domestic workers in her area, Meera walks to work every day. She works in a gated community, where the boundary to the residential area is walled off and secured and where gates, staffed by private security guards, regulate entry and exit. This is not unusual in New Delhi; spatial demarcation of class underscores the neoliberal city's approach to security—fences, gates and *chowkidars* (watchmen) mark the privatized boundaries for the rich (see Biswas 2021). Closing off routes into the "colony," as a residential area is called in India, affects the workers entering on foot;

walls and fences prevent them from taking the shortest route into the colony and their work.

Depending upon the route she chooses, it can take Meera between 22 and 27 minutes to reach work. Given her household responsibilities, she chooses the shortest route to the apartments where she and many other domestic workers work. Google (Figure 4.3) cautions that the route "may involve errors or sections not suited for walking" because the shortest route involves both sectioned-off areas and areas that are a health hazard.

Still, saving five minutes each way can be useful, so Meera often climbs over the fence that sections off the apartment block from the surrounding working-class areas on the fringe of the city. Pujya Ghosh makes this notation in Meera's time-use diary:

> *8am: She starts her walk to her workplace. It is especially hard today because of the rain and there is water logging and slippery mud everywhere.*
>
> *————She doesn't carry an umbrella. On asking she says that her brother-in-law keeps losing them so she's stopped buying new ones. Walking together under the same umbrella was getting difficult. So she was pretty much drenched by the time we reach her workplace . . . .*
>
> *Around 12:45: she starts back home. On her way back she picks up her daughter from school. . . . There is a makeshift place at her*

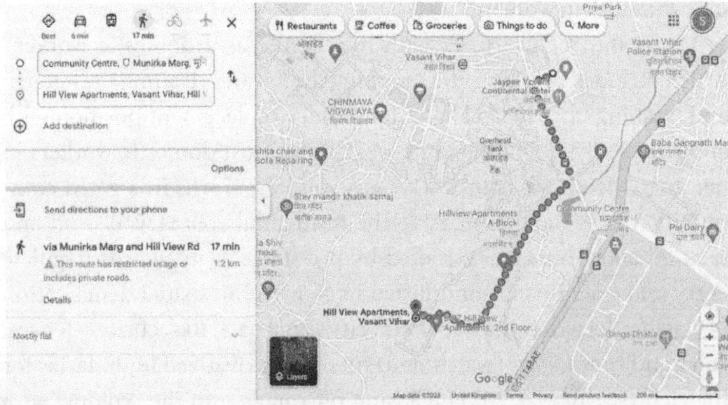

Figure 4.3 Meera's journey to work.
Source: Google Maps.

home where they can take a bath and pee. But to defecate they all go to the nearby hilly/forested area. There are sections divided for men and women there. That is the same area she crosses when she comes to work. It's a short cut and takes 15–20mins to walk. She then scales the wall and goes into the colony. This is apparently the route everyone living in that area takes to go to their place of work. Very soon her son will be going to school and he'll get over at 11:30am. This will just make her schedule tighter. (Diary)

Meera works close to home so that she can manage both her paid and unpaid work. "She looks tired and anxious; she hardly smiles," Pujya writes in her notes. Meera's story reveals the daily reality of depletion: the walk to work through inhospitable landscapes, arriving at work already tired and/or distressed (soaked from the rain on this particular day), and rushing back home, picking up her daughter on the way, to then more domestic chores in the home, which she hates (see Chapter 3). In its report on domestic workers in Delhi, Jagori (2010, 32) concluded that "the time and money taken to reach work . . . left them with less time at home and increased their fatigue levels. Further, to cover the commuting expenses, some of them were forced to increase the number of households. On the other hand, those with young children were forced to reduce work as they had to get back to care for them."

Sabina has the privilege of being middle class; she lives in New Delhi and works as a journalist in Gurgaon, a satellite town of New Delhi,

Figure 4.4 Meera's commute. Photographs by Pujya Ghosh.

which has attracted many businesses and corporate residences, and which is poorly connected to New Delhi by public transport. When we contacted her, she had just moved jobs from a magazine to a publishing house so that she could have more predictable working hours and had also moved house so that she could be closer to her work. This is her commuter story:

> From 2015–16 I lived in GK2 [Greater Kailash] and worked at [X], on KG [Kasturba Gandhi] Marg. I took the Violet [metro] line to work; the metro station was close to my office but I had to take an auto from my house to the metro—a 10 minutes ride, from there it was 25 minutes metro ride to my work; from there I used to walk or if too hot, take an auto to work. . . . On the way back I used to get done pretty late—around 9pm, so couldn't walk to the metro so took an auto [scooter taxi]. . . . [R]elying on autos was very tough, especially in really hot summer months. . . . I felt unsafe, especially at night . . . and they overcharged me all the time. . . . From GK2 to Gurgaon was longer, the toughest year . . . I would take an Uber Pool, get late to work because the Delhi people would be dropped first; I would be constantly checking the App hoping he [Uber driver] would not pick up others; it was very stressful . . . travelling with unknown people was also difficult. The metro option was no good—it took a very long time and I had to change twice. For both it took 2 hours. . . . Once we moved to Vasant Vihar I started taking Uber Go as the fare from there was affordable and takes me only half an hour.

We can see her three different journeys on the maps in Figure 4.5.

Sabina's journeys to and from work alert us to the importance of class-based resources for mitigation of depletion: money, confidence, access to transport and choice. They also tell us something about the way in which commuting affects her work; when traveling by public transport, she feels anxious, gets to work tired, her productivity is adversely affected, and she cannot present herself to her colleagues as professionally as she would like to—she feels "dirty," her clothes wrinkled and not "fresh." Unlike Meera, she does not have children to drop off at school and pick up on the way back, but long hours traveling

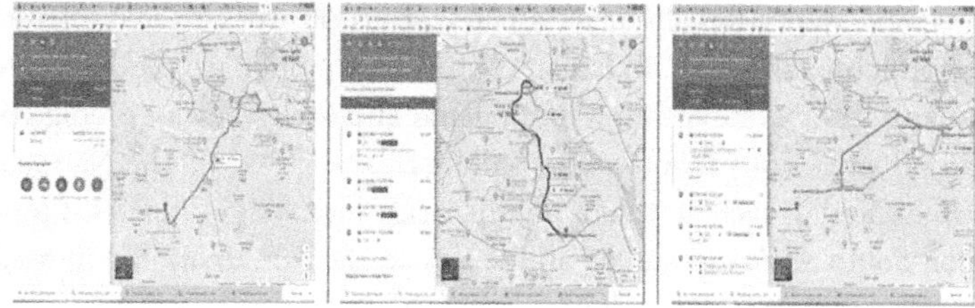

Figure 4.5 Journey 1: GK2 to KG. Marg. Journey 2: GK2 to Gurgaon. Journey 3: Vasant Vihar to Gurgaon.
Source: Google Maps.

to and after work are nevertheless exhausting—she feels "really dead" by the time she gets home.

We learn about many aspects of depletion from the experience of these two women's journeys to and from and in between work. Next I map the literature on commuting and in conversation with the narratives of our respondents discuss its depleting effects .

Commuting Effects: Mapping the Field

Commuting is context bound.

There is considerable literature that deals with commuting and its effects in everyday life in its different dimensions. In the Global North, walking to work is often depicted as a way of keeping healthy as well as changing the rhythm of the day. In most Global South cities, given the distances, lack of pavements or walkways, high levels of traffic, and pollution, walking to work is a last resort and often a marker of poverty. In both situations, walking to work presupposes that work and life spaces are relatively close. Walking can of course be built into traveling to work by public transport—from home to the metro station, from the metro station to work, for example. Globally, "Indians spend more time in daily office commute than people in most countries in the world, with more than 2 hours on the road every day, according to a report by office commute platform MoveInSync" (*Economic Times* 2019). In the United States "workers spend, on average, twenty-four minutes traveling to work each day, which means they spend nearly a week of twenty-four-hour days per year just in work-related transit" (Hofmeister 2005, 60). In England, "[o]ver 24 million people commute to and from work each day in England and Wales, for an average of 56 minutes" (Royal Society for Public Health 2016, 3). The National Household Travel Survey in South Africa revealed, "About 17,4 million South Africans walked all the way to their destination, followed by 10,7 million individuals who made use of taxis and 6,2 million who used a car/truck as a driver. . . . [M]ost workers used private transport (43,5%) as their main mode of travel to work, while 35,0% used public transport. . . . In 2020, travel cost (30,8%) surpassed travel time (23,3%) as the biggest factor influencing modal choice of households" (South Africa, Department of Statistics 2021).

State investment in physical infrastructure is therefore needed together with investment in social infrastructure to allow carers to access the world of work with the least depletion, including through commuting. However, compared to repairing potholes in roads, less attention is paid in transport policy to issues of safety such as lighting on dark streets and cheap, safe, and regular public transportation so that women, racially minoritized people, and those with disabilities might feel secure and not harassed (see also Martin 2022 on women commuters in South Africa; DNA India 2013). State investment in public infrastructure and provision of reliable and safe public transport, costs, and access to private cars or trucks and length of travel are therefore important factors in decisions that households make about education and jobs. Of course, choice is not something that everyone can exercise in equal measure. The fact that Indian workers travel longest, and that 20% of South African workers walk all the way to work and back, alerts us to issues of disparities of wealth across nations as well as of class within countries.

There is an assumption that there is a trade-off between better employment and schools and lower house prices with longer commutes to work (UK Office for National Statistics 2014); however, more men than women do the long commutes because of pressures of social reproduction responsibilities: "Improved infrastructure and new technology, [especially in richer counties] . . . make it possible for people to accept job offers further from their place of residence, which is believed to facilitate the skill-matching needed for sustained economic development" (Sandow, Westerlund, and Lindgren 2014, 1497). Gendered analyses of commuting show care and the health effects—both physical and mental—of commuting. Roberts, Hodgson, and Dolan (2011) suggest that in the United Kingdom women were more sensitive to commuting stress than men, even when working hours and occupations were controlled for, and that the stress came from a gendered division of everyday household-related activities (in Sandow, Westerlund, and Lindgren 2014, 1499). Stress and caring responsibilities also affect gendered mortality rates for commuters. Sandow, Westerlund, and Lindgren, for example, conclude that "women who have experienced long-distance commuting face a significantly higher mortality risk compared with women with short commutes to work" (1499). Of course, class matters here, as do social values of families: "[F]or women with long distance commuting experience, substantially lower survival rates are found among those with low education and low income. A very different picture emerges for men, for whom mortality risks do not seem to be associated with long-distance commuting' (1496).

Negative effects on the health of women who commute are not just physical; their mental health is also depleted: "commuting has an important detrimental effect on the psychological health of women, but not men" (Roberts, Hodgson, and Dolan 2011, 1064). Women's commuting time is entangled with their larger responsibility for everyday household care tasks. Think of a woman who needs to use public transport to commute, and also for taking her children to the creche before leaving for work and picking them up in time after work. The physical tiredness of the work commute can then be compounded by the anxiety about getting to the creche in time, getting to work in time, and then leaving work to pick up the children on time; depletion becomes a state of the everyday. Transport policies do not take these segmented journeys into account (Sánchez de Madariaga and Zucchini. 2019).

Bissell (2018) notes the liminality of *transition life*; he argues that commuters can experience transformations of the self as they travel, including developing skills to map and negotiate space and time. However, as I have been arguing, women and men experience commuting differently, as do the poor and the rich; transformations of self or otherwise are then tethered to these different experiences. Sabina's experience does not reflect a positive transformation of the self, for example. The daily commute can indeed provide precious "me-time" to work, read or think, listen to music or podcasts, or simply to wind down from the working day (Bissell 2018). This, of course, depends on the form of transport (metro or car or walking, for example), anxiety to reach the next chain in the trip (to pick up children, for example), and the number of changes to transport needed to complete the journey (short segments of a long journey that will interrupt time needed for relaxing, whether transport is crowded or not), and of course the element of choice, and whether the person can afford better or worse transportation if it is available (see Sangeeta's story).

Commuting can also affect personal relationships, which can often be tarred by commuting time or distance, by who has access to and makes use of better transport, who travels longest with what effects (tiredness, anxiety about balancing paid and unpaid work or assuming less responsibility of domestic work because of longer commute). " 'Discrete event history models show that long-distance commuting between home and work significantly enhances the risk of separation for couples if the woman commutes but not if the man commutes. . . . In the East German sample, though, it is not the full-time employment of women but the necessity to commute over long distances that enhances the risk of separation significantly" (Kley 2015, 139). Typically, people who commute for work increase their wages (Manning 2003), but Friberg (2006 in Sandow, Westerlund, and Lindgren 2014) shows more time spent on commuting can also reinforce traditional gender roles because it is usually men who engage in long-distance journeys to work. "Absent men cannot participate in everyday family activities, which affects the life situation of all members of the family" (Sandow, Westerlund, and Lindgren 2014, 1497). Commuting also affects familial and marital relations. Sandow (2014, 526) has shown that in Sweden "separation rates are higher among long-distance commuting couples compared with non-commuting couples." As Bindu tells us her story:

My husband moved to Jaipur when our kids were very small so I ended up being at home for the first ten years. . . . I don't even end up going to Jaipur that often; my husband comes over. He also gets busier during the holidays and festive seasons because that's when the major selling happens so we don't even get a chance to go for a holiday." The depletion of households is then often a result of the absence of one person from sharing the joys and burdens of family life and the increased burden of another in coping with everyday care work.

Well-Being Costs

In a major study, the UK Office for National Statistics (2014, 5) found, "The effects of commuting on personal well-being were greatest for anxiety and happiness, suggesting that commuting affects day to day emotions more than overall evaluations of satisfaction with life or the sense that daily activities are worthwhile." We have seen how Meera and Sabina also highlight the erosion of their well-being because of their segmented (short and long) commutes.

Commuting is an embodied practice. For those engaged in paid work, depletion intensifies tiredness and physical discomfort and adds an extra length to the working day and can restrict the kind of jobs they undertake. Sandow, Westerlund, and Lindgren (2014, 1498) note that commuting is "'a major cause of stress impacting on the individual's physical and psychological health and well-being. . . . Longer commutes are also associated with other negative health outcomes, such as higher blood pressure, obesity, poor sleep quality, fatigue and low self-rated health" (see also UK Office for National Statistics 2014) They also find that poor women commuting long distances have a higher mortality rate than poor men (Sandow, Westerlund, and Lindgren 2014, 1509). Further, health is affected as long commutes can lead to irregular sleeping arrangements, tiredness, and stress. The Royal Society for Public Health (2016, 3) reports that "the factors seen as most detrimental to health and wellbeing by commuters themselves are: 1) Journey delays, 2) Overcrowding, 3) Anti-social behaviour, 4) Uncomfortable temperature, 5) Long commute." These generate stress and physical discomfort and erode well-being, all of which can be seen as outflows resulting in depletion. The environment of commuting is both physical and cultural. The fumes that clog the atmosphere in urban areas, for example, the rubbish that goes uncollected, and the lack of toilet facilities (which can mean dirty streets) all affect the health of those who commute (Doron and Raja 2015; see also Meera's story above).

Many of these factors affect those going to work as well as those engaged in mobility of care; escorting children to school, elders to hospitals, going to public offices for household errands, for example, set up inflexible "chained trips" during rush hours, causing increased exposure to pollution and infections, bodily exhaustion, and worry. Women do more of these chained trips than men do: Lyons and Chatterjee (2008, 188) find that "women [in the United Kingdom] . . . are more likely to follow a commute/business journey with a shopping, escort or social trip (21%) than men (12%)."

Commuting-related depletion affects the life choices that women can make in the context of travel:

> Women [in India] limit the colleges they could attend primarily because of safety issues. So they won't have to venture beyond a certain distance and in that sense, women have to constantly strategize in terms of how they can safely move around the city and also rely on their family members to reach their destination safely. However, men take the more direct and cheaper mode of shared public transport to get from one place to the other. Women have to bear the additional burden of worrying about sexual harassment in order to find a route that is safer than others and incur more cost. In many other cases, they may limit their opportunities by not travelling far so as to stay in close proximity to their neighbourhood. (Gupta 2018)

Of course, such depletion is differential—most upper-middle-class women in urban India would have a car and a driver; middle-class women take taxis or drive their own cars; lower-middle-class and poor workers tend to either travel by foot or rely on public transport.

If we see embodiment as connected to our emotions, then commuting is also an emotional practice—it elicits a wide range of feelings such as fear and anxiety, debilitation and enjoyment; as Sheller (2004, 221) writes, mobility "is implicated in a deep context of affective and embodied relations between people, machines and spaces of mobility and dwelling, in which emotions and the senses play a key part." "Feeling dead" or "feeling dirty" or exhausted, as Sabina says she does, or being rested and having some "me-time," which she also speaks of, are outflows and inflows of commuting. Both Sabina and Meera feel the bodily depleting effects of commuting—tiredness, exhaustion, stress are everyday features of their lives as they travel to and from work. Meera comments on the filth that she has to walk past, the fear that she feels as she sees defecating people in the morning on her way to work; Sabina speaks of the anxiety she feels as she gets to work "not fresh," feeling exhausted even before she reaches work. Finally, the mode of transport makes a difference to levels of anxiety; in the United Kingdom " 'those who travel to work by bus or coach had lower levels of life satisfaction and a lower sense that their daily activities are worthwhile on average than those who travelled to work in a private vehicle . . . [and] people who walk to work had lower life satisfaction and a lower sense that their activities are worthwhile on average than those who commute to work in a private vehicle" (UK Office for National Statistics 2014, 10).

These findings are of course contrary to the freedom that Woolf found as a flaneur, "street haunting." Sabina speaks of the heat, the crush of people on the metro, especially in rush hour, or traffic jams between Delhi and Gurgaon that might mean a much longer journey than expected, affecting her level of anxiety about reaching work in good time and in a good frame of mind. Some argue that crowding is a subjective perception of commuter density, which can then lead to passenger stress (Cox, Houdmont, and Griffiths, 2006). In analyzing the British Household Panel Survey data, Kunn-Nellen (2015, n.p.) finds that "whereas objective health and health behaviour are barely affected by commuting time, subjective health measures are clearly lower for people who commute longer." And that these effects are more pronounced for women and for commuters driving a car. Commuting also negatively affects regular exercise for women and positively affects calling in sick. Clark et al. (2020, 2777) conclude that "longer commute times are associated with lower job and leisure time satisfaction, increased strain and poorer mental health. The strongest association is found for leisure time satisfaction."

It is thus not surprising that, if we measure travel by enjoyment, with all its problems as discussed in Chapter 2, women in the United

Kingdom enjoy travel less than men, on all but a single measure—"travel for day trip/just walk"—and even on this, they enjoy walking/traveling less than men do (Figure 4.6). This must also be seen in the context of commitments to household work, which can limit *when* women can travel to work and for *how long* they can stay away. Everyday travels for care are depleting for women.

Commuting by public transport versus car or public transport versus private taxi also raises issues of time and timeliness, levels of anxiety, physical exhaustion, financial resources and the cost of travel, and increasingly guilt regarding contributing to environmental pollution.

Time, Timeliness, and Temporalities of Commuting

Sabina worries about the time it took her to travel to her workplace, the exhaustion that she felt at the end of the journey, about price surges in taxi fares at night, and the lack of cheap but safe transport to travel after work, but also about the effects on her subjectivity; she felt unprofessional: "I would feel that my day was over when I got in to work; I was so tired! There was such a crush on the metro, then walk to work in the

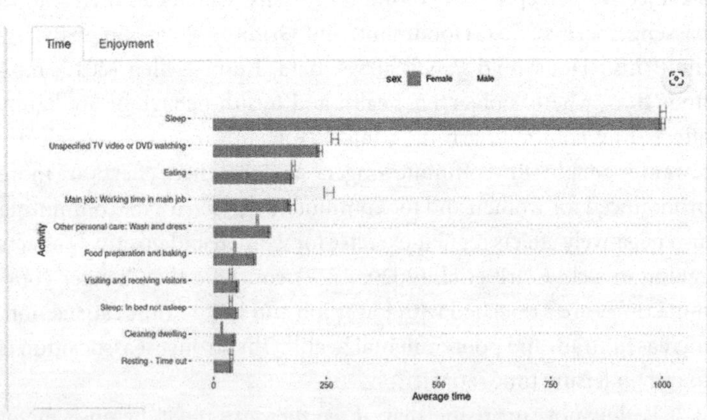

Figure 4.6 Depletion Data Browser: Travel/Enjoyment.

heat, I felt as if I had not bathed, felt dirty. You want to present yourself well at work, no?" And, of course, she also felt that she was unable to be herself when she reached home: "I felt really dead when I got home." Commuting time marks her day.

Commuting to paid work is driven by "clock time," "the commodified time of the capitalist economy, in which time is equated with money and [in which] the time needed to develop human relationships has no place" (Bryson 2007, 2–3; see also Davies 2001 Middleton 2009). In this context commuting reveals the pressures of clock time imposed by class, race, disability, and of course by paid work and mobility of care. Together with others, I have been arguing that we need to understand time and temporality as "a relational construction . . . that lies at the heart of (women's) everyday life as shaped by . . . caring" (Davies 2001, 133). This also allows us to reflect upon the aspirations for relational time of those who care—time for self, "time-out" (133), and "time pass" or loitering (Phadke, Ranade, and Khan 2009). We can then assess how clock time and paid work and insecurity affect the gap between everyday aspirations and the levels of depletion through modes of commuting. Time—night rather than day—also makes a difference to experiencing walking back from work: " [the road] is not well lit. There are some street lights, but they are placed far apart. There are dogs everywhere and they bark. Theft and purse snatching is also common. Last week, one of my friends was robbed. Her purse was stolen. We are also harassed by men on the street as we walk home from work," says an H&M factory worker in Cambodia (Newell 2019, n.d.; see also Siddiqui and Ashraf 2022; Ruwanpura 2022); this is not an uncommon experience for women who work in factories across the world. After a long shift at work, gendered violence and anxiety and fear accompany the worker home. Walking in this context is not something to be enjoyed; it is to be endured and done quickly and efficiently, with as little contact with the hostile environment surrounding her. The H&M worker probably keeps her head down, not making eye contact with anyone on the street; she walks as fast as she can to cover the distance to home or to the bus or metro stand, all the time hoping that she is left alone and is able to reach her destination without harassment.

A sense of being in danger restricts women's mobility, adds to stress and depletion, and stops them from enjoying their time in public spaces. This is also why most of the work done on women and travel focuses on safety rather than enjoyment; as Phadke, Ranade, and Khan (2009) have argued, public spaces should not just be spaces that women negotiate to get from A to B but should be spaces they are able to enjoy being in. Occupying spaces with confidence can strengthen the fight against violence against women, lessen the anxiety of travel, and reduce the stress levels of individual women traveling to and from work, mobilities of care, and traveling for social reasons. Clock time and relational time are intertwined; they cannot be separated out. The clock time of our public lives as well as the lives of others (children's school time, for example) affect our relational time directly.

As Sabina's story tells us, time and travel are also *segmented*—in her case, through mode of travel—walking from home to the gates of the colony, from there looking for an autorickshaw,[6] the auto journey to the metro station, the metro journey, itself segmented into two changes (which can itself be stressful during rush hour), then either walking or taking the auto to work. These segmented journeys underline the lack of control over each element: Will she be able to get an auto in time? Will it be too hot to walk? Will it be raining? Will she start too late from work because of a deadline and miss the last fast train? So many variables affect commuting every day. These segmented journeys also add up to long days—early starts, late returns—full of anxious moments which do not allow her to relax and enjoy her work.

These chained trips are an issue not only for those in paid employment; those engaged in mobility of care are also affected. The responsibility of care of children and of older or disabled members of the family increases depletion through commuting. Take, for example Deepa, the working-class homemaker we met in Chapter 3. As we saw through her time-use diary, her day revolves around doing housework and ensuring that her children can go to school and to after school activities in safety. Commuting is also segmented by dropping children off at school on the way to work, for example, and ensuring that one is back from work in time so that a child doesn't come home to an empty house. Looking in on an ill parent on the way back from work also forms part of some of these chained trips (Sánchez de Madariaga and Zucchini 2019, 148; Schwanen, Dijst, and Dieleman 2002; Chapter 3); any break in the chain—a missed or canceled bus, having to leave work later than expected—can lead to anxiety and stress or decisions that may cost more than one can afford (having to take a taxi instead of a bus, for example), leaving one exhausted and depleted at the end of the journey.

Of course, class matters here too; Sangeeta, the middle-class schoolteacher, owns a car. However, she is not protected from the stress and exhaustion of the horrendous New Delhi traffic, and combining a paid workday with mobility of care, even though her commute and chained trips look quite different from Deepa's:

> *Around 8:20: . . . heads to her school. It is quite close and takes about 15mins to reach. She drives herself and picks up a colleague on the way.*
> *9am: She reaches the school.*
> *[Her workplace is quite close] and takes about 15mins to reach. She drives herself and picks up a colleague on the way. . . . She picks up her kids from school on her way back. . . . Last year when her kids where going for tuition classes, she had to go pick them up from two different places and at different times. They should go by bus but on the way back it would be too crowded. So doing that every other evening in bad traffic used to get her very exhausted. . . . She travels to most places, for work, shopping etc by car. Even when they travel, they go by car which means they don't go to too far away places. She does most of the driving herself. It has almost become that they only go to places where the car goes.* (Diary)

Chained trips made for social reproductive work therefore intensify depletion.

Economies of Travel

Commuting has economic consequences.

Men earn more and hold more secure jobs than women, and transport policy reflects this by operating a "male-breadwinner model" (Christensen 2019, 251). Everyday travel to work can be more stressful, risky, and violent for women. Yet this is not a tension that can be simply resolved by living close to work. In his study of domestic workers in Delhi, Sonal Sharma (2016. 7) writes, "[W]hile geographic proximity allows women workers to do both paid and unpaid work, they constantly struggle to balance the home and workplace, a physically and psychologically strenuous task," as we have seen in Meera's story. The distance between home and work can also limit the jobs they seek, often taking on more insecure and poorly paid jobs. Furthermore, Wong et al. (2020, n.p.) find that in the United States, "substantial employment and wage gaps persist between workers with and without disabilities," as a result of inadequate transportation availability. Liedberg and Hendriksson (2002, 270) add, "Several of the [disabled] women could not use public transportation and were unable to walk even fairly short distances. They used private cars. However, this entails financial expenditures that add to an already taxed budget."[7]

Economic costs of commuting therefore come in different forms. There is the cost of the commute in terms of money spent—on petrol and on transport fares. This can impose considerable costs on individuals and households and force alternative spending cuts. As Vishwanath, founder of Safetipin (an Indian NGO for safe travel for women), noted, " 'In late hours the prices of cabs also shoot up and for young women, they aren't earning that much and if half their salary goes into transport, then it becomes a problem. Then the families also start showing concern and continue working is not easy. So, if we have such extra worries for women, we know that is why female workforce participation in India is going down" (Gupta 2018). Further, the cost in terms of *time spent* traveling can be wasteful for the economy: "[a] car driver[costs]—£26.43/h [to the economy]; bus passenger—£20.22/h; and rail passenger—£36.96" (Lyons and Chatterjee 2008, 185). Travel time unreliability can impose "additional costs on travellers and employers beyond costs from travel time alone. Currently, however, travel time unreliability is not taken into account in calculating monetary costs of congestion" (185).

Economic costs can also include the rents or mortgages in particular areas of the city that take into account daily commutes of household members; there is often a trade-off between long commutes and rents/mortgages. Further, problems of housing affordability can and do often restrict labor market flexibility, especially for those who have young children, "leading to longer commuting times affecting individuals' quality of life and environment" (Barker 2004, 123). Sabina moved to Vasant Vihar from CR Park[8] or Alakhnanda in New Delhi; rents in Vasant Vihar are much more expensive than in the other two areas, but the commute for Sabina (to Gurgaon) is far shorter. So commuting and its costs are an important factor in making decisions about where to live; even higher rent or property prices are accepted to shorten the commute. This is particularly so for families with children; as mothers are seen to be the primary carers, the father does the longer commute so that the mother can be available for the care work.

Decisions about where to live are "influenced not only by length of commute but also by life stage, education, income, managerial and professional status, job prestige, hours spent at work, gender ideologies, and the ages of the youngest children" (Hofmeister 2005, 77–78) and by race, gender, and the physical needs of the able and differently abled. They are also fundamentally affected by the resources available to the household: a poor household may have few options but to live in poorer suburbs that necessitate a long commute; aspirational middle-class households may wish to live in leafy gated communities that may also necessitate long commutes; dual-employment households may need to take decisions based on who is seen as the primary carer and therefore needs to work closer to home. Class, gender, and transport infrastructure all affect commutes to work. As McLafferty and Preston (1991, 4) noted in the context of gender, race, and commuting in the United States, "Residential segregation of racial groups means that minority women and men often live in areas distant from and poorly connected to major centers of employment growth" (see also McLafferty 1997; Preston, McLafferty, and Liu 1998; Ibipo 1995) They also note that racialized and segregated lives of minorities means that, contrary to assumptions, Black and Hispanic women commute as far as the men of their communities and white men and women (McLafferty and Preston 1991, 1). Without adequate investment in public transportation and radical redistribution of social reproductive work between men and women, levels of depletion among women of racialized minorities are high. As a result, African American women are less able to take advantage of employment opportunities that urban centers provide. Studies have shown that if we analyze the patterns of commuting, racial segregation is also reflected in workplace (see Dannemann, Sotomayor-Gómez, and Samaniego 2018; Farber et al.

2015). A focus on commuting, then, allows us to better understand inequalities that are both gendered and raced and how these affect opportunities, costs, and everyday depletion.

Sabina is conscious of the different travel costs of her commute—there is the human costs (anxiety, physical tiredness) and then there are financial costs (Uber Pool vs. Uber Go; metro). She outlines for us her costs of the long commute: from GK2 to Gurgaon, the cost is INR 60 for the auto plus 80 for the metro, totaling INR 140 each way. For the Uber Pool it was the same. "I spend 220 rupees each way. . . . [I]t does pinch me a bit, but that is better than being exhausted."

In terms of paid employment, then, the cost of commuting most often comes directly out of workers' pockets. For example, workers in the United Kingdom spend an average of £42,000 on commuting during their working lives (Bissell 2018, xiv). While in many countries the highest paid employees often get their travel to work paid for—the car, the chauffer, the petrol—for most workers this is not the case. The unpaid time of travel to paid work can thus be seen as a subsidy to the employer since it brings workers to their door for free.

Mobility of care also costs—in terms of transport quality and fares adding to household expenditures and affecting family resource distribution decisions. Compared to white parents in the United States, more single parents, who carry the sole burden of care responsibilities, belong to racialized minority groups, which means, as studies cited above show, that they might travel longer to get any job to support their families (McLafferty and Preston 1998, 537).[9] Further, more women than men work in the paid care sector, which presents its own challenges in terms of travel and work. In a recent class action in the United Kingdom against Sevacare, a service provider, one carer complained that she "visited all of her clients by bus. But there were some days . . . when she spent more time trying to get to her clients than caring for them—she could spend seven hours travelling each day and not be paid for it" (Conway 2016). The U.K. PSA Commission on Care concluded, "Precariousness of jobs—not just zero hour contracts but also an irregular work pattern . . . and work in multiple locations that can lead to greater travel (30% of CC Survey respondents work in more than 5 locations and 10% in 2–5 locations) can adversely affect the well-being of care workers. Long travel time can lead to the extension of the working day, greater tiredness and vulnerability to illness" (Elias et al. 2016, 35). Commuting for work or for care is not, however, entirely depleting; significant outflows are mitigated through some inflows.

Sociality and/of Commuting

On most journeys on trains and metros we see people reading, talking, listening to music/podcasts, watching programs on their phones or tablets, and even playing games. Although commuting adds to the stresses and strains of the everyday, this in-between time can, under certain conditions, provide moments of pause, of rest, of "me-time." Sabina makes phone calls in the Uber Go, which she couldn't when traveling by metro or by Uber Pool: "I sometimes talk to my mother, my parents . . . usually I just chill; I enjoy the morning cab ride going to work. . . . I reach office fresh," she tells Pujya. Smartphones are a constant feature of the everyday life of women in India. The mobile phone "enabled them to dwell in a parallel time of 'leisure' in ways that had not been possible earlier" (Datta 2020, 12).

Sabina also enjoyed reading on the metro when she had a shorter commute; that was her "me-time." I too remember this time. I commuted from Coventry to London for three years by train, a journey of three hours (one and a half on the train and the rest from home to and from the transport hub). The relief of catching the train after my own segmented journey—walk, tube, train, bus—meant that I could relax and either catch up on work (on the way to work) or on reading novels (on the way back). The routine provided the pause time for taking stock of work/life, of catching up on work, or reading or just being. The contrast with these times and when I was rushing to catch a train, or unable to get a seat because of the crush on the train and the frustration that caused remains vivid in my memory. The inflow of "me-time" when available can mean the difference between reaching home somewhat de-stressed and rested or "feeling dead," as Sabina felt. Bissell (2018, n.p.) notes, "Another woman bemoaned how her lengthy commute by car and then train took away from time she could otherwise be spending at home. Yet she spoke very affectionately about the sense of community that had built up over years in her train carriage, and how people looked out for each other, making sure they hadn't slept beyond their stop."

And yet, as Sabina told us, commuting from Gurgaon to Delhi affects sociality negatively too:

> I think if I have a drink with colleagues after work I still have to make it back to Delhi . . . that is at the back of my mind; I don't want to be a party pooper. . . . [I]t is not something I can do easily. . . . [I]f you leave at eight-thirty or so then you think that a cab is not safe and after having a few drinks it is not nice to go by metro."

Distance and time contract her social circle, not allowing Sabina to get to know her colleagues better. Friendships and collegiality therefore suffer in long commutes; physical tiredness and emotional and mental anxieties associated with travel mean that Sabina curtails her social life after work in favor of going home and "to bed."

Summary

Virginia Woolf (2014 [1930]) walks and writes about it as a flaneur; de Certeau (1988) makes a distinction between walking as a style or use, or synecdoche (when a part is made to represent the whole or vice versa) and asyndeton (the disconnection of the place/space from its physical surroundings). "[P]aths run through people as surely as they run through places," writes Robert Macfarlane (2013, 26), who then goes on to discuss walkers who are largely men, traversing the British "green and pleasant land." However pleasant and liberating, I see little relevance of these distinctions or "rhetorics" to the everyday lives of women like Meera, for whom walking is work, work that is depleting, underlining the compulsion and lack of resources that makes them walk, undermining their health and well-being.

As we have seen, Meera's, Sangeeta's, and Sabina's stories show how chained and segmented commutes intensify depletion: walking through inhospitable landscapes, making several walking trips to and from children's schools, arriving at work already distressed (soaked from the rain, feeling dirty and tired), and going back home exhausted. Commuting is work that affects both paid and unpaid work; it includes the mobilities of care and of paid work. It affects our everyday choices and our life choices.

However, commuting is not counted as work—you certainly won't see nonmonetary commutes (walking long or repeated distances) registered in GDP figures, for instance. As we saw in Chapter 1, the System of National Accounts (SNA) production boundary excludes social reproductive work; it also excludes commuting to work through a concept of "hours actually worked" (ILO 2008, 16). So, while both SDG 5.4 and the ILO challenge some of the assumptions built into this time, the concept of productive time remains central: "Working time comprises the time associated with *productive activities* [my italics] and the arrangement of this time during a specified reference period" (ILO 2008, 46). However, feminist work—academic and activist—has led the ILO to collect data that is sensitive to and would improve the measurement of hours actually worked "for certain jobs and groups of persons in employment," "such as work at home, commuting time, short breaks, overtime and absence from work" (51). This could and needs to feed into policy frameworks for transport, work, and welfare.

The evidence also shows that although there are some inflow elements to commuting—me-time, making connections with fellow commuters—it is largely depleting. Commuting depletes those who stretch their day to accommodate its paid and unpaid variants. Social relations—of gender, race, and class—are inscribed in the sweat and exhaustion, in the anxiety and occasional terror of commuting, which can be seen as another element in the equation of social reproduction. Yet it is different from most other tasks insofar as it is considered neither labor nor not-labor. Traveling to work is the in-between space and time of exploitation, a liminal labor.

COVID-19 brought about the contraction of commuting and its total cessation for many for a time.[10] If commuting increases depletion, is regarded adversely by most, has economic and welfare costs, then would this pause in commuting teach us new ways of thinking about work and about depletion? During the pandemic, the stresses and strains of commuting might have ebbed (Tapper 2023),[11] but the burden of reshaped home rhythms continued to be largely borne by women. As families stayed at home, women found the burdens of increased housework fall on them. What COVID-19 showed us was both the possibilities of reshaping work but also the continuing burdens of social reproduction, carried unequally, increasing depletion.

Addressing issues of commuting and gender inequalities cannot, therefore, be seen in isolation from the issues that I have been highlighting: the recognition of the value of social reproduction and its costs. Commuting is one factor that increases these costs and is therefore important for us to consider, especially in the context of the pressures by the state and on families to increase women's labor force participation.

We have seen three major issues related to commuting and depletion:

1. Commuting is an embodied practice, with different methods of commuting having differing positive and negative impacts on the body and wellbeing: active commuting may strengthen muscles and bones in the context of adequate nourishment, or may increase exhaustion; public transport can cause physical discomfort and exposure to infectious diseases through shared confined space; air pollution and road traffic accidents are exposures that vary with mode of transport.[12]

2. The time taken to commute is additional to normal working hours. This needs to be recognized and compensated by employers as well as the state in different ways: providing cheap and safe transportation, planning transportation systems that are gender aware to increase the sustainability of travel over periods of space and time for those who have to combine paid and unpaid work.

3. Commuting has economic costs, which inevitably are more difficult to meet for working-class people than for upper-class people, affecting their decisions about living, choice of transport, and vulnerability to poor commuting experience. Like social reproduction, commuting and its physical, mental, and economic costs (depletion) can be said to subsidize capital. Community transport schemes to offset economic costs for the economically vulnerable would help both paid workers' and unpaid carers' travel.

Building on the literature and the empirical evidence that I have presented, I would suggest that recognizing the liminal value of commuting in understanding both paid and unpaid work can also help us democratize mobility frameworks. Commuting is framed by gendered power structures; mobility is a precondition of connecting "different kinds of subjects, spaces, and scales" (Sheller 2018, 9). Further, "the liberal subject is essentially a moving subject, and her first and most fundamental freedom is freedom of movement" (Kotef 2015, 58), even though this freedom is played out in differing landscapes—both spatial and temporal—for different subjects (men, women, Black, white, upper and lower castes, able and differently abled), which affect their everyday lives as well as their subjectivities. To decenter and democratize mainstream mobility frameworks that often underpin state policies, we need to address the social inequalities that "extend from bodily restrictions and disabling environments to transport exclusions and uneven infrastructure to unequal access to resources and energy, and unequal exposures to harms and pollution" (Sheller 2018, 24).

Recognition of value is an important, although not sufficient, condition for addressing inequalities and injustices; recognition of commuting as a cost of both paid and unpaid caring is important if we are to understand the levels of depletion. Reshaping and democratizing mobilities frameworks requires recognition of both paid and unpaid, long and short, frequent and infrequent, chained and segmented journeys that people make across boundaries of class, caste, race, and gender every day.

This approach to commuting thus politicizes what is often seen as a technical issue: more or different transport networks, for example, for individual commuters to access work further and further away from home. Given that commuting is embedded in social inequalities and connects private and public worlds of life-making and maintenance, we need to develop an approach to commuting that allows for the recognition and responsibility of addressing the costs of commuting not only by individuals (with all the caveats placed on them by class, race, and gender) but by the state and the market (employers). Commuting can then become part of the social infrastructure that is necessary for delivering social reproduction without intensifying depletion (see Sandow 2014). This approach means that delivery of equitable transport resources can be seen as "activities that are essential for meeting basic needs, such as food stores, education, health services and employment opportunities" (Pereira, Schwanen, and Banister 2017, 182), as well as for social reproduction. Capitalist social relations are, as I have shown, often inscribed in the depleting affects of commuting for both paid and unpaid work. In this chapter, commuting emerges as an important element in the equation of depletion through social reproduction.

5

Depleting Futures

Children Who Care

Introduction

Children also care.

The literature on social reproduction focuses largely on the burdens of paid and unpaid work done by adult women and men in the maintenance of life. However, children are not only recipients of care but also do social reproductive work: they participate in housework, help with family businesses, and care for younger siblings and ill family members (Joseph et al. 2020), and in so doing they contribute to the capitalist economy within which their households are embedded. They are also entangled with capitalist productive relations as both future labor and ongoing consumers. Historically, the labor of children in homes, fields, and factories has supported the growth of capitalism, but even now, when children and childhoods have been disassociated from formal labor regimes, children continue to work in different contexts and locations. In the Global South, there is evidence of many children doing both paid and unpaid work to contribute to family incomes; in the Global North, while paid labor is largely performed by adults, children's contribution to care work continues, albeit often overlooked or malrecognized. This latter is the subject of this chapter.

In many countries, children work as domestic workers—with long hours, deprivation of education, and often under cruel conditions of work, with consequences for their health and well-being (Ebrahim 2023). A focus on this kind of work takes our attention from the expansive approach of social reproduction as reproduction of life; children take part in this labor and in so doing present us with—as we will see below—alternative ways of thinking about labor (Ferguson

Depletion. Shirin M. Rai, Oxford University Press. © Shirin M. Rai 2024.
DOI: 10.1093/oso/9780197535547.003.0006

2017). Initially, it was assumed that care work by children occurs only in "exceptional" circumstances, such as when parents are seriously ill (Aldridge and Becker 1993a; Becker, Dearden and Aldridge 2000). However, we see children taking on huge caring responsibilities in different contexts, for example, during pandemics, such as HIV/AIDS-affected contexts in Sub-Saharan Africa (Robson et al. 2006; Becker 2007; Bray 2009; Evans 2010). They provide support to household members when "left behind" by a migrating parent (see Mahon 2020). Children also migrate to help their families: "Often they are sent abroad by parents desperate to keep them safe and they arrive in strange countries unaccompanied and feeling totally alone; they must look after themselves and worry about their families left behind" (Children's Society). Further, children support their families when they are displaced by conflict; there are an estimated 13 million child refugees in the world, and "around a million refugee children in Europe" (Children's Society), contributing to their families on the move through dangerous terrains by helping with everyday chores and care needs.

Children therefore negotiate care in different economic, political, and social contexts—at an individual/family level they may be rich or poor or just making do; they may be growing up in a context of austerity, as in the United Kingdom in the past decade or so or in countries with well-resourced state provisions or in countries where families are unable to access welfare safety nets and where educational and health opportunities for children are minimal. Children are affected by gender norms in the contexts in which they care—sons may do different care tasks than daughters, for example (Wihstutz 2011, 448). And, as Susan Ferguson (2017, 113) argues, "they are also agents of their own self-transformation into capitalist subjects . . . who are able and willing to both sell their labor power for a wage, *and* who over time take increasing responsibility for their own social reproduction" and, as we shall see in this chapter, of others' too. So there is a spectrum of contexts in which children do care work, which does not fit neatly into analytical categories of care recipients and caregivers. In this chapter I explore how and at what costs social reproductive work is done by children and with what consequences—depleting as well as empowering—for their everyday lives, their growth and development.

Changing social understandings and constructions of childhoods are most often built on a Western model of childhood, which is then promoted by international organizations (Qamar 2022). This resulted in their care work being seen as problematic (for a review of this literature, see Aldridge and Becker 2003, 4; Joseph, Sempik, and Leu 2020). Pushing back against this approach and viewing children as individuals with agency allowed children to be seen as benefiting from their caring roles through participating in family life as equals, or at least as self-aware contributors (Aldridge and Becker 2003; Luttrell 2020; Svanberg, Stott, and Spector 2010); the argument was that overlooking children's care work ignores the rewards that children experience through care work—their self-worth in supporting their families. This approach also sought to disrupt Western imagery of ideal family life and childhood innocence.

I argue that this valorization, like the valorization that adult women get for their care work, does not necessarily translate into valuing the work of children; that, as with adult carers, the costs of care work on the lives of children are various and can deplete their everyday lives. Here, I want to address depletion by recognizing the important work of care that children do and by arguing for better, more appropriate, and greater provision of support for children as they negotiate the multiple challenges of working, caring, and playing.[1] This support (Chikhradze, Knecht, and Metzing 2017), can be in the form of provision of schooling, education, healthcare—both physical and mental—and supporting their depleting households through improved conditions of life and work. As we shall see, children also let us see alternative ways of thinking about work. Depletion through social reproduction is not, then, just a concern for adults who care, but is also a concern for children who perform social reproductive labor. This is not only a concern for children in the Global South, where state regulation might be weak in this regard, but also in the Global North, where countries like the United Kingdom have been operating under regimes of austerity imposed by care/less capitalist states.

In this chapter I study unpaid care work of children and their depletion in the context of one of the richest countries in the world: the United Kingdom. I do not wish to claim that the lens of depletion on the care work of children and adults can simply be seen in the same frame. Children are embedded in a gendered and racialized society differently from adults, have different (one could argue fewer) economic and social resources they can mobilize, and while they are subject to similar pressures of consumption-led subjectivities in a capitalist society, they are also exposed to different routes to and out of their condition. As Becker, Dearden, and Aldridge (2001, 2) note, "[W]hen children undertake significant care work within the home, and where they and their families lack appropriate health and social care support and adequate income, then many young carers experience impaired well-being." I argue that despite the positive effects of participating in care work, children experience depletion, which takes different forms and leads to distinct social harms, which need to be understood in order to reverse them.

First, there is bodily harm—physical and mental health adversely affected by responsibility for care. As Joseph et al. (2020, 78) write, "[Y]oung people who care for individuals may carry out the same tasks as paid and trained health and social care practitioners. But they are unpaid and untrained." That lack of training and support can lead to physical injury in doing the care work. Second, there is discursive harm, which either doesn't recognize their work or frames their work as "abnormal," leading to the disapprobation and the fear of disciplining of children who labor and of their families (see Nunn and Teppe-Belfrage 2019). Third, we also see evidence of emotional harm—as in anxiety and worry experienced by child carers through bullying at school and stigma attached to their care responsibilities. And finally, harms of citizenship (or children's rights) are evident—the discourse of "the normal family" generates the invisibility of child carers whose situation is not readily articulated in the language of children's rights (beyond process rights) and the practices of child welfare professionals. In all these different forms of depletion, class, race, and gender remain critically important. A focus on children's agency, therefore, I argue, needs to be complemented by acknowledgment of the harms that child carers may also experience. This is important for the recognition of the work of young carers.

Approaches to Child Carers

In this chapter, per Becker (2007, 25–26), I understand child carers[2] as "children and young persons under 18 who provide or intend to provide care, assistance or support to another family member. They carry out, often on a regular basis, significant or substantial caring tasks and assume a level of responsibility that would usually be associated with an adult." Children do this care work, often willingly, as part of their duties to keep the family going, often in circumstances not of their choosing, with different resources at their disposal, many in contexts of scarcity or sometimes of violence, which affects their lives. This labor goes toward filling the gap between household income, needs, and state provision. Of course, children not only care but are simultaneously cared for; their needs are more or less met by family and through the state provision of healthcare and education—again variably, depending upon the state provision. They gain from being a carer (emotional rewards and recognition); many existing studies of child carers emphasize their resilience, which identifies the potential of child carers to construct positive social identities and develop competence through work (Skovdal et al. 2009; Evans 2010; Svanberg, Stott, and Spector 2010). However, as we shall see in this chapter, they also experience caring as exhausting and depleting.

There are several lacunae in the research on children's work. First, the focus is mostly on the paid work of children, which, though an important issue, does not cover the extent of care labor that children do that is unpaid and which could sometimes be in addition to paid work. Second, children and paid work literature largely focuses on children in the Global South,[3] which does not capture the complexity of relations between paid and unpaid work. Third, the literature on children doing social reproductive work focuses largely on "the girl child" (an odd singular category that erases so many distinctions of class, race, and sexuality). Therefore, while there is now considerable research on the largely adverse impact of paid labor by children outside the home and its impact on their physical and mental health (Grugel and Poley 2012; Grugel and Fontana 2015; Hughes et al. 2017) there is limited scholarship on children's unpaid care work (Grugel, Macias, and Rai

2020; Camilletti, Banati, and Cook 2018; Chikhradze, Knecht, and Metzing 2017).

An exception is Wendy Luttrell's (2020, 22–23) work, which highlights what she calls the "choreographies of care" "made visible by the kids as a means to shine a light on the inter-related and coordinated elements—people, time, feelings, intimacies, values, and dynamics of power—that the young people invoke to frame their childhoods, learning, and growth." Such a choreography can allow for "an alternative social orientation in which care and care work take their rightful place at the center of everyday life—highly visible and highly regarded not only in the spheres of family and school, but in the very fabric of democratic society and in our fundamental understanding of freedom and social justice itself" (204).

Children Who Care and the Costs of Caring

Depending upon the methodology, we have different estimates for children and young carers; for example, in advanced industrialized capitalist societies, between 2% and 8% of all children, young people, and young adults are carers (Leu and Becker 2019); based on the U.K. Census of 2011, it is estimated that "there are almost 166,000 young carers aged 5–17 in England" (Clay, Connors, Day, et al. 2016, 2). The England Children's Commissioner's Office estimate, however, was 102,000 in 2019 (Public Health England 2020, 9). In Canada, Stamatopolos (2015) calculated for 2006 just over 1 million unpaid young carers, though she takes a more expansive age definition of 15–24. Figures for countries in the Global South are less accurately known; it is estimated that 55% of Argentinian and 64% of Indian 7- to 14-year-olds participate in household work (Lyon, Ranzani, and Rosati 2013, 8–9), a substantial number of whom will also provide some level of care, but we do not know how many. Patchy public service provision for working-class and poor parents and the chronically ill and disabled, along with growing numbers of women in formal and informal labor markets, would suggest that poor children in low- and middle-income countries are even more likely to provide care work, even in circumstances when they do so at a cost to themselves. As Chopra and

Zambelli (2017) observe, there is, in practice, a high prevalence of intergenerational transfer of care to children, especially sibling care, as our research here also suggests.

As with adults, social reproductive work by children is also done on a terrain of capitalist productive and social reproduction relations, which frame childhoods; poverty, inequality, and exclusions based on gender and race are reproduced and also challenged in schools, playgrounds, houses/homes, and state and nonstate institutions of care (Duryea and Arends-Kuenning 2003; Edmonds and Pavcnik 2005). The crises of capitalism and the resulting austerity policies insinuate themselves into and leave their traces in everyday life "weaving together biography and history, the private and the public" (Nolas, Varvantakis, and Aruldoss 2017; Bywaters et al. 2017). Poverty and inequality then frame care of and by children. And yet there is little child-focused, intersectional literature that considers the ways in which age, income, gender, race, and other factors might intersect with gender in the doing of social reproductive work and the experience of depletion.

Gender inequalities are important to study in the context of what Parliwal and Neetha (2011, 1049) have called "gendered familialism," which they define as stratification of care practices that are also reflected "in public discourse and policy, which reiterates care as a familial and female responsibility and works to devalue and diminish the dimensions of care." This stratification plays a role in the allocation, distribution, and acceptance of children's care work (Aldridge and Becker 1993b; Cass et al. 2009). However, there is little firm evidence of how care work depletes children, girls and boys, despite an assumption that the costs of unpaid care are generally mediated by income. Households' social reproductive strategies (Nunn and Tepe-Belfrage 2019) include the distribution of labor within the home; the fewer the resources, the greater the need for children's labor to fill the care gaps in the home. Finally, there is limited literature that brings into one frame childhoods across the Global South and North and the "push and pulls into caring" in different locations (Becker 2007, 33). The flows of migration of adults as well as children, the demands of labor in global production and care chains, and the gaps in social reproduction, all of which have important effects on the everyday lives of children, make it imperative that we understand and study children's roles in social reproduction and study "the intra-household and intergenerational distribution of care and domestic responsibilities, its determinants and effects on child wellbeing" (Camilletti, Banati, and Cook 2018, 1).

What we know about child carers has generally been framed by the sociology of childhood and some public health literature, which has identified, above all, the agency and capacities of children (James and James 2004; Chikhradze, Knecht, and Metzing 2017). Researchers have identified not only the adverse effects of care labor on children but also the empowering aspects. They have argued that the provision of care by children is not necessarily an intrinsically harmful practice; rather it enables them to make a contribution to their households (Cass 2009; Skovdal et al. 2009), and it can foster a sense of self-esteem (Robson et al. 2006; Abebe and Kjørholt 2009; Evans 2010). Further, that by participating in care work, children can come to understand the collective responsibility for care, pushing back against the individualized, neoliberal framings of society (Luttrell 2013). This literature serves to remind us that research and policy should regard children as independent rights-bearing people. The significance of children's agency in providing unpaid care within their family is important—though we should be alert to the fact that children's agency in deciding to take on unpaid care, how much of it they deliver, and how they do so may in practice be highly constrained (Chopra and Zambelli 2017).

Perhaps because of the focus on children's agency, few studies have asked whether children and young people are being harmed or depleted in the process of doing unpaid care work. Those who do, present worrying evidence; Stamatopolous (2018, 182; see also Chikhradze, Knecht, and Metzing 2017) identifies a "care penalty" that affects young carers in the future as well as the present. As noted, there is also some evidence that care work by children leads to lower rates of schooling (Robson, Ansell, Huber, et al. 2006), and that these children may also experience depression, stress, anxiety, and stigma (Boyden, Porter, and Zharkevich 2016; Camilletti, Banati, and Cook 2018). In terms of education in the United Kingdom, several studies have shown that young carers and young adult carers may experience various economic and social disadvantages and difficulties, including restricted educational opportunities and employment (Joseph, Sempik, and Leu 2020, 78; see also Kaiser and Schulze 2015), difficulties in meeting the demands of university education (e.g., Kettell 2018), reduced social capital (e.g., Barry 2011), and experience of stigma leading to secrecy and social withdrawal (e.g., Bolas, Van Wersch, and Flynn, 2007). Lloyd (2013, 67) discovered that children who were carers "had poorer health and well-being, reported less happiness with their lives, were more likely to be bullied at school and had poorer educational aspirations and outcomes than their peers who were not carers."

Further, children may not be listened to in the home if they complain about tiredness, or their school may not recognize the importance of care work in their lives. According to the Children's Commissioner, "39% of young carers said nobody in their school was aware of their caring responsibilities", and therefore that school's disciplinary regime adds significantly to children's' anxieties and stress (Children's Commissioner, 2022; np). Research indicates that professionals in healthcare and social care often were either unaware of or did not take into account the contributions that children make to caring and household management where a parent or other household member has a chronic illness or disability (Joseph, Sempik, and Leu 2020; Aldridge and Becker 1993a, 1993b, 2003; Warhurst, Bayless, and Maynard 2022). The disciplinary role of social services may lead children to hide their work if state support might separate them from their families, such as when social services label the family as being unable to care for the child (Clay, Connors, and Day 2016; Metzing-Blau and Schnepp 2008). This fear, of course, adversely affects the ability of families to seek support, even if it is available (DfE 2018). But neither the severity of these costs nor the point on "the caregiving continuum" (Becker 2007) at which costs kick in is clear; nor is there much research as to whether more imaginative social policies could help mitigate these costs (see Joseph et al. 2020).

Therefore, the agency-centered focus found in sociology of childhood approaches needs to enter into more systematic dialogue with feminist research on depletion through social reproduction (Grugel, Macias, and Rai 2020). In this way, we can identify whether and how far the harms caused by depletion are similar to or different from those experienced by adult women, and the impact of age and children's status in the household on their well-being.

Children need recognition for what they do as carers (see Aldridge and Wates 2005). A study that used photographic participation techniques with young carers whose parents had serious mental health problems shows emphatically that children are competent social agents both as carers and in research processes, and that recognition for the roles that they undertake as carers is a vital component in their coping strategies (see Aldridge and Sharpe 2007; Luttrell 2020). Such recognition requires professionals to understand the young caring experience and include children in discussions wherever possible, accepting that they are competent and capable, while also recognizing that they may have additional or specific support needs. Ongoing awareness-raising about the needs and rights of young carers, and recognizing their contributions, is therefore critical (Dearden and Aldrich 2010, 222).

Social Policy Landscape in the United Kingdom for Children Who Care

To understand children's costs of caring, it is important to situate their caring practices in the wider socioeconomic and social policy landscape of the United Kingdom. The United Kingdom is a signatory to the UN Convention on the Rights of the Child (UNCRC 1989), which emphasizes the need to see children as "the holders of their own rights and not passive recipients of charity but empowered actors in their own development" (Buckley and Budzyna 2023, 15) and that state policy should be shaped accordingly. The UNCRC also recognizes that all children should enjoy the same rights, including the right to protection from harmful work, quality education, and leisure time, and that these too should be actively promoted. On ratification of the UNCRC, governments undertake to deliver the progressive implementation of these rights and recognition of children's agency. They have obligations, therefore, to respond to the children's needs through social policies and a process of recognition and support, as well support for their families; otherwise, there is likely to be continued tacit acceptance that there are significant numbers of children who live without protection because they are regarded as "outside" actors.[4] The UNCRC obliges states to ensure not only the individual rights of the child but also to address broader issues of poverty and discrimination.

In 2010 the U.K. government gave an assurance that "the Government will give due consideration to the UNCRC articles when making new policy and legislation . . . but recognise that, like other state signatories, the U.K. Government and the UN committee may at times disagree on what compliance with certain articles entails" (House of Lords and House of Commons Joint Committee on Human Rights 2015, 9).

The austerity years in the United Kingdom have increased poverty and inequality levels. Child poverty rates among young carers were higher than among other children (Vizard, Obolenskaya, and Burchardt 2019). "The average annual income for families with a young carer is £5000 less than families who do not have a young carer" (Children's Society 2013, 5). The social profile of children who care thus reflects social inequalities in wider society, leaving them vulnerable to the ongoing effects of poverty along the axes of gender, class, and race. Poverty also affects the "weathering" (Geronimus et al. 2006) of children, who can then more easily fall sick and take longer to recover, with clear impact on their education and well-being: "Young carers' physical and mental health and psychosocial outcomes were significantly poorer, and they were significantly less likely to see themselves entering further or higher education," conclude Robison, Inglis, and Egan (2020, 139) in the context of Glasgow.

Poverty intersects with race and ethnicity to further adversely affect children who care and their families. In the United Kingdom, it was found that "[c]hildren in Asian households were 2.5 times as likely, compared with the national average, to be in persistent low income during the period from 2013 to 2017," and "[c]hildren in Bangladeshi and Pakistani households were the most likely to live in low income and material deprivation out of all ethnic groups" (Khaliq 2020, 2). Thirty percent of Black children "live in low-income households, and 22% live in low income and material deprivation" (12). The Children's Society (2013, 5) found that "[y]oung carers are 1.5 times more likely than their peers to be from black, Asian or minority ethnic communities, and are twice as likely to not speak English as their first language." While care work is gendered, both girls and boys participate in caring within the family. Social and economic factors thus affect the lives of children who care and the levels of need that they experience.

The social care regime that is in place in the United Kingdom mainly focuses on poor families and those from racially minoritized groups; these families are more dependent upon the state for help. The increasing levels of poverty and inequality in the United Kingdom and the Universal Credit system introduced by the Conservative government in 2013 were condemned by Philip Alston (2018), UN special rapporteur on extreme poverty and human rights in 2018: "[L]ocal authorities, especially in England, which perform vital roles in providing a real social safety net have been gutted by a series of government policies. . . . The widely respected Institute for Fiscal Studies predicts a 7% rise in child poverty between 2015 and 2022, and various sources predict child poverty rates of as high as 40%."[5] The COVID-19 pandemic has put further pressure on local social and healthcare services, intensified by the government's fiscal policies that directly and adversely affect the poorest families; as Human Rights Watch observed (2019), "the budget allocated for welfare for children and families has borne the brunt of public expenditure cuts, falling by 44 percent between 2010 and 2018."[6] This has led local authorities, especially those in the more deprived areas of the country, to focus their work on statutorily mandatory adult social care and child protection services rather than improving the social infrastructure needed by child carers, who then are largely dependent on charities working in this area. This has led to increased poverty, lack of educational facilities, and falling rates of health of poor families in a rich country (Kelly et al. 2018; see also BMA 2018; UK National Audit Office 2018).

In England, under the Children and Families Act of 2014, "A young carer's needs assessment must include an assessment[7] of whether it is appropriate for the young carer to provide, or continue to provide, care for the person in question, in the light of the young carer's needs for support, other needs and wishes" (UK Government 2014, 96). The Carers Allowance can provide financial support to young carers, but only if the carer meets all three of the following criteria:

1. They are over 16 years of age.
2. They spend "over 35 hours a week caring for someone who is accessing a disability living support benefit (such as Personal

Independence Payments, Disability Living Allowance, Armed Forces Independence Payments or Attendance Allowance)."

3. They are not in full-time education. (UK Government n.d.)

However, claiming Carers Allowance may reduce other benefits that the carer or the person they care for receives. The benefits regime of the U.K. government has become increasing complex and punitive since the Coalition (May 2010–2015) and successive Conservative governments (2015–), which adversely affects the everyday lives of child carers and their families, adding further anxiety and deprivation to their lives. This punitive social support landscape frames the care work of children and young carers that form part of my study.

Children, Families, Care, and Caring: The Study

My analysis of child carers and depletion builds on a small qualitative study of 20 unpaid child carers, both boys and girls, of different ethnic (British Indian, White British, British Polish) and class backgrounds, undertaken in 2018. The research was done with the help of Anni Piiroinen, who worked as my research assistant on this project, who was empathetic, responsible, and rigorous as she gained the trust of the children as well as the carers. The study took place in the Midlands, United Kingdom, at an NGO working with child carers called YCS.[8] Mark Graham was our contact at YCS, and we gained enormously from his commitment to the cause and his understanding of the issues involved.

In the study, we understood unpaid care work as three or more hours per week of regular or irregular care or other household work, which included helping with the paid work of adults, shopping, cleaning, and washing. We spoke with children as young as 8 and as old as 16. We took into account age, gender, race, and class during this research. In preparation for the study, Anni participated in and observed several activity sessions as a volunteer at YCS, after which she conducted one-on-one interviews with children who used the service. (The names of all the children we interviewed have been changed, reflecting their ethnicity, to anonymize them.)[9] This was done after getting their consent and in the presence of Mark as the responsible adult at YCS. Anni also interviewed three staff members of YCS. Anni and I also joined 19 families on a YCS-organized day trip to Bournemouth, a seaside town in the south of England, for some respite and time together for the whole family. On the way, we conducted a parents' survey on their perceptions of the impact of their children's care work on their well-being. After the research was completed, I took the children out for a day at the local bowling alley and lunch to say thank you and to talk to them about what they felt about the project and about their contributions to their families. So the information upon which I build my analysis is multilayered and multisited, with many conversations in different geographical and affective locations.

The research was carried out in the city of Coventry, a historic city with a population of 355,600, (Centre for Cities, 2024) of which 24.1% are those born outside the United Kingdom (The Migration Observatory 2018) According to the Coventry City Council (2019, 4), there are 3,100 young and young adult carers under the age of 25. The Council is worried that "[i]nstead of seeing friends, enjoying hobbies and doing homework, children as young as ten are cooking, cleaning, managing medication, shopping and looking after brothers and sisters" (4).

Coventry City Council (2019, 22) has established a Carers' Response Emergency Support Service, which provides practical support if a carer has an emergency and needs support; around 1,000 families with carers are registered with this service. The Young Carers (Needs Assessment) Regulations, 2015, section 4(h) specifically requires the local authority, when carrying out a young carer's assessment, to determine whether the carer is a child in need; how this assessment is carried out remains moot. In the case of Coventry City Council, the assessment of needs of child carers has been outsourced to YCS, which I discuss below. The information on the web pages dedicated to addressing the needs of young carers is sparse; the funding for supporting child carers seems largely to come from the charitable sector rather than core Council funding. Further, a lack of understanding of the family situations across different contexts means that the responsibility for establishing and addressing need is often put on the child carer; the Coventry City Council (n.d.) website advises the child carers, "Make sure your teacher or year head is aware that you are a young carer. They can help you if your caring role begins to affect you at school or if you have any problems, for example getting homework done or revising for exams. Your school may have a link worker or a school nurse that supports young carers." But if the family is wary of social services, and the children do not feel able to share their experience with the teachers, and if the teachers and the school are not well enough resourced to help identify these children, then how can we depend on the children themselves to look after their own interests? Self-care also needs time, confidence, and contexts of care, which are often not available because of lack of public funding of schools and of care.

The 24 households we worked with are not entirely representative of the Coventry population, but present us with valuable insights about care, caring, and depletion of children (Table 5.1). They are self-selecting in that they are registered with YCS as families where children care for a family member and attend sessions at the NGO we worked with; there will be many who could be more in need of the support that YCS provides but do not have access to it for various reasons of marginalization. The families are varied in size, form (extended, not just nuclear), class, and social location, and some are headed by a single parent. These varying family forms

Table 5.1 Family Profiles

Family member: 2-4	9
Family member:	7
Family member:	3
Severity of care needs (out of 5): 1-2	3
Severity of care needs: 3	10
Severity of care needs: 4-5	7
Families with short-term care needs (<3 months)	0
Families with long-term care needs (>4 months)	19
Daily pattern of caring: help needed continuously	19

were introduced to us by the children, who often included their grandparents in the family:

ANNI: How many people are there in your family?
MATT: Just close family or sort of everyone? My close family is four.
ANNI: Okay, and then who's everyone else? Your uncles and . . .
MATT: Uncles and aunties . . . about thirteen, fourteen.

Similarly, Henry says, "I've got two sisters, a brother and my mum and dad, obviously, and I've got a nephew and I think I've got like a few cousins as well and aunties and uncles and that."

The care needs of the family, described to us by the children we interviewed and by the parents who participated in our survey, are varied too: brain hemorrhage, strokes, autism, short and long term, with less or more severity. However, these households do not just require care, they provide it too; a disabled parent would provide a home, sometimes pocket money, love and affection and praise for the child who cares for them. The extended network of family members—grandparents, uncles and aunts, cousins, nephews and nieces—differentially contribute toward respite and financial and emotional support; as Molly told us, "[S]ometimes we go to stay at our Aunt Hayley's house."

Stereotyping on grounds of social class can often reinforce inequality and frame policymaking (Durante and Fiske 2017). Highly gendered and idealized notions of the (middle-class) family and childhood can prevent policymakers from responding to the needs of poor children who care. There are often gendered and judgmental perceptions of parents who are poor and of racialized minorities, which add to the worry that parents have about social services "taking away their children" (see below). As Mark, the YCS worker/coordinator, pointed out, "[T]hat's the problem: people aren't identifying themselves as carers because you're making it worst case scenario. People need to see the regular kids, the massive percentage of kids who are carers but don't necessarily have crap lives. . . . But the government won't do that because it costs money."

Care work done by children attending YCS's sessions spans a wide spectrum of responsibilities, from standard household chores such as

Table 5.2 Children's Caring Jobs in Households

Cooking	5
Cleaning	5
Tidying	2
Washing up, loading/unloading dishwasher	2
Washing clothes, loading/unloading washing machine	1
Medical—finger pricks	1
Play with sibling	4
Bathing	0
Dressing	4
Reading	1
Fetching and carrying	1
Personal care	1
Company/attention	4
Feeding	2
Everything	2

cleaning, cooking, and washing dishes, to mundane activities such as making someone breakfast, to more personal or intimate forms of care such as help with dressing and medical help, such as finger pricking for diabetic tests. Piotr, an 11-year-old Polish boy, outlined some of his responsibilities: "The jobs I do mostly is washing up the dishes and sorting out the clothes to go into the washing machine and vacuuming the house. And also tidying my room." Children also help with providing emotional support to the family member requiring care, including keeping them company, calming them down, or distracting them from their worries. Table 5.2 shows the various jobs done by the child carer, as identified by the various number of parents in our survey.

The children spent variable time on caring, from less than an hour every day to more than five. When asked about the time spent on care work by the child, the most common answer by parents was one to two hours per day. All parents said that the pattern of care was continuous through the year. Temporalities of everyday care (see also Chapters 3 and 4) are an important issue for the children; they have to learn to time-manage at an early age, not only their schoolwork but also care work. Luttrell (2020, 200) notes that the children in her study are aware of "'ordinary' vs. 'extraordinary' (that is, interesting) time; school and homework time; work time; family care time; and personal 'free-time' that is subdivided into me-time and being-with-others-time. . . . [T]he young people seem compelled to account for what they want to do, what they need to do, and what they think they are supposed to be doing with their time."

Child carers have to negotiate this temporal landscape. We saw in Chapter 3 how the mornings can be a particularly pressurized time for mothers; they can be for children also. Adil, a child carer, explained his routine: "In the morning, I wake up early and then they'll [parents] be asleep. 'Cause my dad comes back from work at midnight, like two a.m. . . . So I pull him [sibling] downstairs and give him . . . cereals." Matt stays up late to do his homework:

I do tend to end up sort of up at midnight doing my homework. I mean, there is a part of it that's me; I can't be bothered to do it and then I leave [it] and then I end up doing it later. And then I realize, actually I should've done it earlier, oh well. And then I never learn from that. But I know we stop helping mum around seven and then it's normally, she'll just sit there for a little while and then go to bed. So, the rest of that time is sort of mine. And then I go to sleep and then I wake up at six in the morning for school, to get ready.

There is a lack of freedom and spontaneity that the children feel, shuttling between school work and care work (Table 5.3). Asked why she liked coming to YCS, Anna said simply, "Freedom, I guess." But Matt responded:

As long as I still help with the lunches I can go and do what I want. I do have to sort of arrange it. I can't just go Saturday morning "Oh yeah mum I'm going out with my friends." I have to arrange it with

Table 5.3 Children's Caring Time per Day

Time spent by child on caring per day: <1 hour	1
Time spent by child on caring per day: 1–2 hours	7
Time spent by child on caring per day: 2–3 hours	1
Time spent by child on caring per day: 4–5 hours	1
Time spent by child on caring per day: >5 hours	4
Time spent by child on caring per day: random time/varies	3

her early in the week and then we'll sort of prepare for me to go. . . . This weekend will be the second time I've ever gone out without my mum or dad or family member. So it'll just be with my friends. So last time and this time we went to Sector 7 bowling.

Parents worry too—about the effects of care work on their children even as most parents surveyed felt that this work was also beneficial for their children. About half of the parents in the survey worried that their child's caring responsibilities were affecting their schoolwork and their friendships. The majority of parents also worried that their child was more grown up than their peers due to their caring responsibilities (Table 5.4).

The YCS staff found the conventional portrayal of caring as a set of practical chores quite problematic, criticizing what they saw as the stereotypic portrayal of a young carer as a child pushing their mother in a wheelchair. It became clear during the research process that there is a vast range of different caring experiences, which should discourage sweeping generalizations about the well-being of carers. The staff emphasized that there were a lot of children and families that were coping well with their caring responsibilities, even if these took up a lot of their time. On the other hand, there were some carers who were struggling, and experienced their caring responsibilities as overwhelming.

Often the children we spoke with did not see their care work as work. This is very different from Lutterell's findings (2020, 203): "Perhaps the most essential of the young people's insights in this project is their profound basic understanding that *care is work*: it requires time, effort,

Table 5.4 Parental Concerns for Caring Children

Parent thinks care work is beneficial for child	17
Parent thinks care work is sometime beneficial for child	2
Parent thinks care work is not beneficial for child	0
Parent thinks care work is affecting child's school work	9
Parent does not worry care work is affecting child's school work	10
Parent worries care work is affecting child's friendships	10
Parent does not worry care work is affecting child's friendships	9
Parent worries child is more grown up than their age because of caring responsibilities	14
Parent does not worry child is more grown up than their age because of caring responsibilities	5
Parent worries that child gets physically tired looking after family member	6
Parent does not worry child gets physically tired looking after family member	11

resources, and coordination; it demands attention and investment; it is mundane, necessary, and arduous. Its operations (its choreographies) are often complex, intricate and interdependent." In our cohort of child carers, we often encountered denial of the word "work" in association with care. Instead, they used terms such as "help" and "helping" and "looking after" and "worrying." This was underlined in response to whether they get any money for the work they do: there was surprise, puzzlement, even outrage about this; pocket money, yes, but transactional payment, no! So recognition of their own work is something that the children frame as altruism and empathy or as simply a part of their life—as Piotr says, "Just do it!"

Emotional Costs of Caring

The goal of our research project was to better understand the costs of social reproductive work to children and the possibilities of depletion that might accrue as a result. Costs of caring that the children identified included feelings of worry about a family member, which could impact their concentration at school, and missing out on other activities due to caring responsibilities, such as spending time with friends or pursuing hobbies. It also included coping with the stigma of being a carer.

Depletion and caring, as well as valorization, go hand in hand. The children experience the benefits of helping their families. Greg, a 12-year-old white English boy, told us, "Emotionally, it's kind of like, I feel like it makes me more empathetic, is that the right word? Because I see what she [his mother, whom he cares for] goes through on a daily basis. So, when other people, I see when they're stressed out, I know how they feel in a way 'cause I live with someone with it everyday. You kind of feel bad for the people 'cause you're dealing with someone with it." James, who is 13 and helps his two brothers with special needs, replied to the question "Do you like helping them?" this way: "Yeah. 'Cause you know that you're helping someone else that like, actually needs your help so I put them first, before me." And nine-year-old Kunal, who is Indian British, loves helping his mother, who has to look after his grandmother:

ANNI: You like [helping] your mother?
KUNAL: I like it!
ANNI: . . . Why do you like it?
KUNAL: Because she's nice! And she's cool!
ANNI: Yeah, so you get to hang out with your mother?
KUNAL: And she's beautiful.[10]
ANNI: You never get tired of it?
KUNAL: No.

While the children saw themselves just getting on with caring, this did not mean, however, that they always like it or never feel resentful or upset, as Adil told us:

ANNI: So looking after your little brother, does it sometimes stop you from playing like PS3?
ADIL: Yeah.

ANNI: How does that make you feel?

ADIL: Depressed.

ANNI: Yeah? Have you told your mum or your dad?

ADIL: Yeah, sometimes.

ANNI: Have you said like, "I don't want to do it"?

ADIL: Yeah, I've said that sometimes.

ANNI: What did they tell you?

ADIL: They say that you still have to look after your little brother. . . . I
have to play with him on his Nintendo Wee.

Young carers' experience is marked by worry—for those for whom they care and for themselves, which makes it difficult to distinguish time apart from caring. Here we also see the spectrum of "caring about" and "caring for" (Becker 2007), on a continuum. YCS staff pointed out that constantly worrying—"non-practical aspects of caring"—about a family member can be at times more exhausting than doing practical care chores. Here "caring about" includes tasks like cleaning and tidying and carrying out basic domestic chores, while "caring for" is a state of taking on responsibility for caring, which affects children's time, and takes up much of their attention. The worrying children do for their family member spreads the caring activity far beyond any physical act of caring, making it a constant activity. One YCS staff member emphasized the persistent presence of caring: "I would say [the] majority of carers care all the time. I think that's what it comes down to. Whether you're doing anything physically, whether you're doing cooking, cleaning, anything like that, or whether it's just emotional support, it's always there. The caring role never really goes away."

Constant worrying can be invisible and thus easily ignored, but it is depleting. Children worry particularly when they are at school and unable to know what is going on at home. As 10-year-old Anne-Marie told us:

ANNI: Do you ever worry about your mum being okay?

ANNE-MARIE: Yes.

ANNI: When?

ANNE-MARIE: Practically all the time.

ANNI: All the time, why?

ANNE-MARIE: I just worry about things.

Worrying can also prevent children from going out with friends or moving away to university, not necessarily because they are forbidden to do so but out of concern for their family member.

Some children are bullied at school about their different "normal." Gendered roles perhaps play a part in this. Eight-year-old Adil is bullied and has reported it to his teacher: "I tell her . . . I tell her that sometimes I get bullied. Sometimes [it is] not nice." Mark, the YCS coordinator, pointed out, "There's also the bullying that happens to a lot of young carers: 'your mum's in a wheelchair' or 'your mum always . . . smells like alcohol.' That kind of stuff. So, they have to deal with all of that within school" (see also Bird 2018, 26).

Children also feel guilty if they take time out from caring. Greg says, "She [mother] sort of has anxiety, if I'm allowed to say that. She worries about me going to school . . . coming here [to YCS]. It's one of those things; I kind of feel bad in a way that I'm here and I'm having a good time but she's at home, pulling her hair out . . . 'cause its stressful."

Children feel isolated. Other children in their neighborhoods, families, and schools do not feel the same pressures of managing care; communications with these peers can be difficult:

ANNI: Do they know about the fact that you care for your mum, and about your situation?

GREG: Not a lot of people do. I kind of keep it to myself, really. . . . I don't feel the need to tell people. . . . So I leave it as it is.

ANNI: You said sometimes schedules clash because of like your care duties and so on. Do you feel the need that people don't understand you when you say you cannot make it. . . ?

GREG: Yeah, I do; they do just get confused and in the end I just say "Well my mum is ill, I can't really make it." That happens with a lot of [people]. . . . [A] lot of things clash but I do still sort it out.

Friendships need nurturing (see also Chapter 3), and time and perhaps a socially level playing field to thrive. Most of the children we interviewed did not share much about their home life with their friends; some did not have friends or had them at a distance. Rachel, who is 12 years old and home-schooled, explained:

ANNI: Do your friends know that you're taking care of your mother?
RACHEL: Well, not really because they're on the internet . . . in America.
ANNI: Yeah? So do you ever talk about what's going on in your life?
RACHEL: No.

Similarly, Anne-Marie is reticent about sharing her concerns with her friend Emily:

ANNI: Does your friend Emily know about your mum, that you help to take care of her?
ANNE-MARIE: Yeah. . . . Well I mean she comes here [to YCS] so . . .
ANNI: Do you ever talk about who she's taking care of and who you're taking care of?
ANNE-MARIE: No. We are normally just playing.

James, who is 12 years old and looks after his father, said, "Yeah, there's been a few weekends where it's just me and my dad and I can't really play out with my friends. But in the week 'cause my mum's there, I can play out with my friends. . . . Sometimes it does [bother me] 'cause I'm like inside all day."

Friendships are affected when children feel that the difference between their and their peers' lives is considerable and unbridgeable, even though their peers cannot see it. Twelve-year-old Matt said, "[M]ost of the time it's easier just not to think about it. But sometimes it is very hard 'cause you see all these kids whinging 'Oh yeah it's not fair, my mum made me do the washing up, it not fair.' And I'm sat there like, 'I do a lot more than that; stop whinging!' So, sometimes I think about it but it's easier not think about it and just get on with it. Whinging's not going to do anything to help me."

Emotional harm is often also experienced as stigma of care work; this combined with a general fear of social care involvement can prevent families from seeking help as they fear that it portrays them as bad parents and creates the risk of their children being taken away.

A worker at YCS explained, "People just panic. And the fact that their child is doing things at home that other children aren't, they're worried that people are gonna think that they're not good parents, that they can't cope as a family, and that's not always the case." The stigma of care work is connected to a larger misunderstanding of care work, according to YCS staff, who emphasized that care work done by children is quite common and usually takes much less dramatic forms than people assume. It was specifically stressed by a staff member that care work is not comparable to other kinds of labor: "[I]t's not like their jobs, it's not like they're sending kids down the mines or sweeping the chimneys." Rather than seeking to eradicate care work done by children, the approach of the organization was to support children and families in doing their care work. Replenishment could build on such an approach.

Caring and Depletion of Households

Depletion, of course, occurs on a household level as well as an individual level. Often, within the family, the care work provided by the parent for one family member can infringe on their ability to provide care for others, as caring duties limit the time and energy parents can give to their children. One parent said that caring for a family member "affects us as a family as I am constantly tired due to being up all-night testing blood sugars. We have one to two hours a day as a family together." The care provided to children can also be affected by the illness of the parent. A mother was worried that she was "always in pain and tired . . . irritable and drained or asleep so children try to just leave me alone." The YCS worker Mark reported, "[A] lot of families do feel guilty when there's like siblings with autism or disabilities, they feel bad for the young carer because they feel they don't give them all the attention that they should be getting because they have to focus on the other young person. . . . But then there's other families where it's just normal for them and they just get on with it." As Table 5.3 shows, a majority of parents worry that their children are growing up too soon, that their schoolwork, health, and friendships are being adversely affected. To the question "Do you worry that this [care] work is affecting [the child's] schoolwork?" one parent responded, "No. But lack of sleep is, as her brother is not a good sleeper [because of his care needs], and they have to share a room." Sharing a room was not something I had considered to be an issue for child carers, but space, matters, especially in the context of caring.

In response to the question "What impact do the care needs of your family member have on the time you spend with your children?," a parent said, "I have very little time for my other children and when I do, I'm often tired." Another answered, "[I]t is impacting my mental well-being; I get very stressed; younger son always get ignored." Further, the relational character of care also means that the stress and anxiety, well-being and time pressures experienced by the parents affect the children who do care work.

ANNI: What does your dad do?
KUNAL: Shouting. At my mum's face and Rahul's face!
ANNI: Why?
KUNAL: 'Cause that means he getting angry.
ANNI: Do you know why he's getting angry?
KUNAL: No!!

Families also fear social services' approach to children who care; "their caring roles silence them in many ways through the fear of coming to the attention of professionals and the associated fear of being separated from their families—a response all too often applied in the past (Aldridge and Becker 1993b, 377; see also DfE 2016). Mark at YCS told us:

We do have some young carers who have parents with mental health problems or drug and alcohol problems, where they don't want their parents to know that they have spoken to someone about it, [be-cause] they've been told by their parents that they are not allowed to talk about it. . . . There's been a couple of cases . . . they've [the parents] found out, and then . . . they've been in trouble and we've never seen them since. . . . There's a fear of social services, the fear of having their kids taken off them or the fear of being told they're not good parents.

Three percent of children in England—up to 400,000—are in the social care system (Ofsted 2021). We also find that the "proportion of young people taken into the care of the state has increased" (Benaton et al. 2020, 1). There is also the public political discourse supported by the Conservative government of "troubled families," which can be seen as blaming poor families for the social conditions in which they find themselves, including their children's truancy or behavior in school (Hargreaves et al. 2018). As we will see in Chapter 6, anticipating harm to the family increases depletion of the household and its members. In this context, fear is a powerful driver of familial distrust of the state and underlines the lack of trust of government; replenishment then becomes difficult.

Caring, Depletion, and Replenishment

As we have seen, the care work of children raises important issues of depletion, of recognition and agency, of familial need and support, of poverty, social inequalities, state policies, and neoliberal governance, and of individual circumstance. These issues are not easy to deal with, especially under conditions of austerity, which adversely affects social policy. However, without attempting to do so—through recognition, state policy at national and local levels, and through investment in social infrastructure framing the children's lives—it is inevitable that the depletion of children who do care work will intensify, affecting their life chances and everyday life. YCS plays an important role in supporting the children who care through a range of services providing replenishment.

The Role of the Nonstate Sector: YCS and Schools

YCS staff visit schools, carry out one-to-one and family advice visits, and offer activity sessions on their premises, where children play on their own and with other children, learn some everyday skills, and often receive a hot meal. Anni was initially struck by how "normal" the activity sessions were, as they did not really differ from standard afterschool clubs. Mark explained, "[M]ost of the time when [children] walk through the door to do the activities, anything that they've got to do with a caring role or responsibility they just leave at the door." Care work is not explicitly mentioned by the children or by the staff, nor are the activities organized by the YCS strictly tailored toward their care duties. Anni noticed that children would come in, usually dropped off by their parents, and most often start playing pool or go on the Xbox or PlayStation. Some children would stay chatting with the activity coordinator and volunteers about everyday topics unrelated to their caring roles.

Several children we spoke with mentioned cooking as something they do as part of their caring. For YCS, letting children cook fulfilled a dual role: as a recreational activity but also as a way of encouraging healthier eating. Many of the children came from poor backgrounds, which affects their diet. "A lot of people eat a lot of crap, a lot of junk food," said Mark, "so [there is] weight gain and the lack of physical activity because they're at home all the time. . . . So with regards to vegetables and things, we've had kids who didn't even know chips were made of potatoes." Many children said that the activity sessions provided by the organization allowed them to have a break from their everyday life and caring responsibilities. James said, "I get a lot of help from here. Mainly a lot of motivation and stuff and like tips that kind of help me . . . 'cause sometimes I do get quite frustrated sometimes with my brother. And they help me to not get frustrated, to like kind of get a grip and look after them."

YCS is not a counseling service but an advice, information, and support service and is solution-focused rather than providing psychological support. Replenishment and respite *is* what YCS provides to children who do care work. William told us, "I find it's like a break. I don't have to worry 'cause I always have something to do, instead of just sitting at home. . . . But here I'm thinking about other things, like playing with friends, making new friends, helping people, like, play games."

The need for a "one-stop shop" for young carers is referred to by both the Coventry Council website and members of YCS; as Mark pointed out, "[T]he more [different] services there are, the more people involved, the more confusing it gets for families and young people. . . .

We feel it should be like a one-stop shop for young carers: a service in the city that provides . . . every kind . . . of support . . . to young carers and it doesn't have [to have] that city council social care badge over it. 'Cause that's a massive barrier. We are so successful compared to the city council projects because we don't have that stigma." A 2008 Labour government's report supported this view in its consultation with child carers; the SureStart scheme provided such a one-stop shop (Melhuish, Belsky, and Barnes 2009; Mason, Alexiou, Bennett 2021).

I have noted the impact of austerity policies on child support in the context of the 2008 crisis. In that context, the COVID-19 pandemic has also placed enormous strains on children's education and on their relations of care within the household,[11] intensifying their depletion: "Findings show that the level of care that young carers are required to provide had increased as external agency support for their families had been withdrawn while their own coping strategies had been challenged, in particular through school closures" (Blake-Holmes and McGowan 2022, 22). The cutbacks in public funding are, of course, further eroding the possibilities of local government support to child carers; their care labor is helping families fill in the gaps in care needed within households and provides a subsidy to the state (Ferguson 2017).

Nonstate actors such as the YCS can help replenish children and their families but need stable and adequate funding; their small team has been struggling with the number of families requiring support. YCS provides replenishment for families where children have caring responsibilities. However, they do this under conditions of austerity, unstable funding arrangements, and poor conditions of work, which depletes staff and undermines the stability of staffing over time.

Schools as Sites of Depletion

The importance of schools to support child carers was highlighted in the research, especially by Mark, who worked with schools to identify young carers. He explained that schools were often reluctant to start proactively identifying and supporting young carers, as this was seen as an extra workload for which they were not compensated. Schools are also underresourced and therefore cannot devote enough personnel to support children who care (see also Warhurst, Bayless, and Maynard 2022). Further, there is a lack of trust between the families and schools, which also affects practices of seeking and offering support (Warhurst, Bayless, and Maynard 2022). Out of 19 parents who participated in our survey, 8 said that the caring duties of their child were not recognized by the school. When asked what kind of support they would like to have from the school, parents called for general support and recognition of the fact that the child might be tired. The YCS staff explained that schools tended to interpret tardiness as a problem that had to be remedied through detention or other disciplinary methods, rather than asking why the young person was late. Making adjustments to schools' requirements was often considered out of the question, leaving it up to the young person to adjust their life according to school rules, which was very challenging with caring responsibilities. A lot could be done simply through a more flexible approach that recognizes that child carers sometimes cannot strictly follow the schedule and rules of a school day. Schools could help to reduce the amount of worrying that young carers do during the school day by allowing them to phone home between lessons. Schools could also be more patient with tardiness in the morning, considering that pupils might be a little late because of having to drop off their siblings at school. And yet the schools are also structurally placed in a neoliberal landscape of competition, attainment targets, and league tables; they are underfunded and underresourced, so ensuring that all children's needs are taken into account in a context where academic results matter becomes difficult.

Summary

Unrecognized and unsupported care work can deplete children's lives, and greater state support for organizations such as YCS is needed to mitigate the harm done to children. Children's unpaid labor is often central to the sustainability of their families as a unit and should form a core aspect of debates about poverty, austerity, education, welfare, and gendered biases in social policy. The research in Coventry shows that both boys and girls engage in this work, face different pressures, and need diverse support mechanisms to help them and their families. As Grugel, Macias, and Rai (2020, 13) argue in the context of children's care work in Mexico, "The idea that children should not participate in this work is misguided, especially where mitigation strategies are stymied because of poverty; rather . . . social policy needs to recognise the dilemmas and contradictions that social reproductive work poses and address it in ways that take into account the particular nature of this work, the support that children need—educationally and in terms of their well-being—and the lack of publicly funded good child care that is accessible to all" (see also Joseph et al. 2020).

We also know that the needs of the children and the parents, and the family as a whole, are interconnected and sometimes in tension with each other. In order to hold the household together—to ensure that one parent can go to work, to help with keeping the state (social services) at bay, to maintain the integrity of everyday rhythms of the family—children's care labor is needed and is mobilized. However, the attitudes of the state and social services to child labor more broadly frames this labor as problematic and something to be minimized or even eliminated. This in turn puts pressures on the parents, who on the one hand feel guilty for not seeking help and on the other hand feel unable to do so as this may bring to the family unwanted attention of social services, leading to the possibility of children being taken away. Discursive harm as stigma for poor families in need of care help can also result in bodily and emotional harm for both the child and the parent(s) and depletes households; replenishment is available but often compromised by the distrust of state bodies and social services.

There is a raft of challenges that children face as carers, and many of them resonate with adult carers that we focused on in the previous chapters. In the United Kingdom, children do this work within the parameters of household needs and national and local government social policy frameworks that they have little control over. Their households' social position—gender, race, and class in particular—affects their care work, their access to replenishment, and their personal choices. This dependence on and labor for the household presents some similar and some very different challenges for child and adult carers: how to manage time, negotiate spaces both public and private, and learn to avoid or cope with everyday violence—bullying at school, for example, or domestic or discursive violence. However, we need to think through these two sets of care agents in the same frame, with the same question: How can the depletion of carers be reversed through mitigation and replenishment strategies that are individual-, household-, and community-based but state supported?

Of course, state and nonstate provision differs a great deal in countries of the Global North compared to poorer countries of the Global South. If this chapter was written about child carers in Bangladesh, many of the provisions described and critiqued would be entirely absent or sparse. The reason I chose to write about children in the United Kingdom was because I wanted to show that nonrecognition of care work by children under conditions of austerity in one of the richest countries in the world continues to deplete their everyday lives.

Here is the conundrum: care work is not counted as work for adults, and it is seen as problematic for children, who are socially constructed and normatively framed as minors who need to play and study; they need protection. As a result, no longer seen as part of the capitalist labor force, "young people are now widely understood to be marginal, if relevant at all, to capitalist patterns of accumulation" (Ferguson 2017, 100). As we have seen in this chapter, this has led to separation of work and play and of care and work. Social policy builds on these separations, leaving little room for learning from the children who negotiate their care work through labor and play, even as they experience depletion. To address depletion of child carers, we need to shift our understanding of the Western model of childhood and the value of care work and how it is organized within families—especially those that are most economically vulnerable and unable to afford buying in labor of others. Recognizing this work of and by children is the first step toward reversing their depletion.

6

Postcards to the Future

Anticipatory Harms and Struggles against Extractivism

Introduction

Fazile Danca has a written a postcard to Mr. Gwede Mantashe, the minister of mineral resources in South Africa in 2016. She is worried about being moved from the land where her family is buried and laments, "Maybe others don't understand [the value of this sacred land] but it is very important [to her and her community]." The worry and the anticipation of the pain of loss is evident in these words, as she stands by a stone burial cross.

In this book, I have been examining depletion through social reproduction in everyday life as it unfolds in different contexts for individuals and their households. In this chapter, I study depletion and struggles to reverse it through examining the campaign of a community to protect its way of life. This is the story of the communities of the Xolobeni region—together called Amadiba—in the Wild Coast region of South Africa, whose world is now threatened by mining. By thinking through their struggles, I argue, first, that depletion accrues not just in *experiencing* harm but also in *anticipating* it; second, that depletion affects not only individuals and households (as in Chapters 3, 4, and 5) but also communities embedded in socioeconomic and environmental landscapes; and third, that legal strategies for reversing depletion are important but limited. To do this, I map the slow, structural violence against the environment of the Eastern Cape and the people inhabiting it, and their mobilization against it, in particular through the legal case brought by the Xolobeni community against the mining company.

Depletion. Shirin M. Rai, Oxford University Press. © Shirin M. Rai 2024.
DOI: 10.1093/oso/9780197535547.003.0007

Fazile Danca - Xolobeni, South Africa

Figure 6.1 Fazile Danca. "My family are buried on this land. My father, brother and grandchild are all here, as well as many others. In Pondo culture we cannot move them. If the mine comes we will have to leave and they will stay behind. This land is sacred to us. Maybe others don't understand but it is very important." Source: *Postcards from Xolobeni* © Thom Pierce.

Depletion, as we have seen in the previous chapters, is ongoing and affects individuals and their households unequally. Here, I examine *depletion in the future* and argue that anticipating harm to the environment in which people live their everyday lives can be deeply depleting. It is important to explore this temporality of future harm because anticipatory harm gets far less attention in public discourse and policy frameworks and therefore fewer resources to ward off that harm (DeLeo 2016). Recent prefigurative work on everyday utopias allows us to look to future alternatives to present-day problems (Levitas 2013; Cooper 2014; Swain 2019; Jeffrey and Dyson 2021); I suggest that we also need to pay attention to the ways in which people invoke everyday *dystopias* in response to real threats to themselves, their households, and their communities, which then spurs them to action to protect their lives and landscapes. As we see in the postcard written by Danca, under conditions of crisis the worry about the erosion of ways of life and struggles to protect them map onto already existing unequal distribution of social reproductive work, resulting in increased burdens of care and provisioning. This harms individuals, households, and communities as they struggle to find meaning of their everyday worlds in the present, which they see vanishing under the onslaught of other worlds being thrust upon them. As the story of the Xolobeni shows, "[t]he destruction of communal land regimes remains the backbone of the present phase of capitalist development and the cause of the surge of . . . violence" (Federici 2019, 3). The struggles to reverse depletion and destruction of alternative modes of living are inextricably linked.

The reason I find the story of the Amadiba of Xolobeni important is because it connects the depletion of individuals and households to the depletion of communities and their environment—the land/scape in which are emplaced their livelihoods, but also their "way of life": their ancestors, their places of rest and play. Also, because the struggle of the Xolobeni communities is for the "not-yet-real"—it is against anticipated harm, which will lead to depletion of the lives of Amadiba future generations, disconnected from their land and their way of life. The struggle of these communities is important to stop this depletion from undermining the communities now and in the future. Finally, in being a narrative about the importance of communities in protecting their environment, its struggles are social reproductive struggles— keeping alive not only the physical lives of its members but also the land on which they live and their traditions and indeed the future generations. It is a story of a struggle for replenishment—of holding the state accountable, of developing a politics of solidarity among the communities—and also a vision of transformation, of an insistence on a different way of life. In this chapter we will see, therefore, how the threat to the environment of a community produces anticipatory anx- iety that is individually and collectively depleting, and how the com- munity pushes back against this threat to generate a politics that aims to prevent, mitigate, replenish, and transform social relations on the ground through narratives and imaginaries that are grounded in their histories and the current politics of South Africa.

Collective action emerges as much from the experience of exploi- tation as it does from collective memory that is mobilized; I study this through the visual analysis of photographs of Thom Pierce, which are part of the story of affective mobilization of the Xolobeni.[1] There is a refusal here to accept modes of development that go against and at- tempt to delegitimize this collective memory. The struggles of the Amadiba discussed in this chapter take time, effort, and energy; they mobilize fear and anxiety and they can and do intensify depletion even as they provide routes out of it through alternative imaginaries of everyday lives.

As I outlined in Chapter 1, "depletion" is a borrowed term—we borrowed it from the work of environmental activists arguing for taking into account the depletion of the environment when calculating the GDP. We then extended it to the labors of caring to understand the costs of social reproduction. In this chapter I outline how it is not sufficient to think about depletion in either human or environmental terms but that both need to be brought into the same frame to gauge the intensity and extensity of depletion.[2] By focusing on extractive capitalism and its relations with the state, on the one hand, and the struggles of the affected communities, on the other, I show how depletion in/as capitalist social relations are imbricated as quotidian, exploitative, foundational, and violent. Depletion that is ongoing needs to be remedied; depletion that will occur needs to be prevented. Law is an important resource for the Xolobeni, but it is not a sufficient protection against future harms and the depletion that accrues through these. Building on feminist understandings of social reproduction as well as anticapitalist alternative imaginaries, we need transformative approaches to depletion of communities and of the environments in which they are embedded (Pardo 2023). The Xolobeni provide some of these as they push back against anticipatory harms that the mine represents.

The Xolobeni Struggle

"If the mine comes it will pollute our water and destroy our land. We will move away to live in township with out the space we need to farm. This land means everything to us," says Khanyisile Ndovela on a postcard in Thom Pierce's photographs. To study this story of depletion of the Xolobeni, I not only work through the political and legal literature but also visual and narrative cultures. Much of the work on "narrative imagination" focuses on possibilities—in making change happen through imagining a different world (Andrews 2014; Squire 2020). Specifically, Andrews (2014, 6) writes about narrative imagination as the mediation between the real, the not-real, and, following Sartre, the "not-yet-real": "We know that the not-real might also be the not-yet-real, and that that which is real is never a static category. Movement thus connects perception with vision, extending what one sees with what one imagines." I am interested in this liminal movement between the real, the not-real, and the not-yet-real and study it through a series of photographs by Pierce (2018a) titled *Postcards from Xolobeni*. The photographs of the postcards bring together the visual with the textual—the portraits of the Amadiba people in the landscape they are fighting to protect, as well as messages they have written to the mine owners and government officials outlining their fears.

The messages on the postcards are poignant, angry, reflective, and determined. The text reflects the worries of the individuals as well as their political resolution to protect their way of being. Mingled with the clear and defiant messages to the mine owners and the government that supports mining there is also fear about the future. Imagination, after all, can also be apocalyptic even as it helps us develop an understanding of positive, even utopian change; grounded in location/space it then brings to life imaginaries of harm in the context of eroding the everyday life of communities as well as visions of a sustainable, collective future. While terrifying, an apocalyptic imagination can help us think through the harm that overthrowing of the present in the future might entail and how to strategize to preserve what is valued. The postcards tell us about a community that values its history, even as it looks fearfully to the future and articulates alternative visions of development.

Environmental statisticians have argued that extractive and other forms of exploitation of the environment needs to be recognized by debiting the cost of environmental depletion from measures of economic growth, like the GDP (see Chapter 1). Building on this work, I argue that depletion of both humans and the environment subsidize economic growth through the unaccounted for harm that is inflicted and absorbed by human subjects and by the environment. To protect both communities and their environments takes organizational labor, opposition to and engagement with the state and the law, which, on top of unpaid work in the home and, for many, market labor, can increase the experience of depletion through temporal and spatial poverty and structural as well as physical violence. Transformative imagination in times of crisis can therefore also be a burden—to bring about transformation requires mobilizing to stop harm from happening, which requires courage, a democratic space for participation, time for taking action under conditions of threat as well as existing social inequalities. There is of course a considerable feminist literature on the "triple burden" that women carry: paid and unpaid work and organizational work in the public sphere (Lyon, Mutersbaugh, and Worthen 2017; Chant 2008; Moser 1993).

"Enough is enough, we are sick and tired of being dumping places, when children are sick they dump them on us, when men are sick from mining they dump on us. We need to speak up and say government put our lives first, profit is important, but not more important than life," said Nonhle Mbuthuma, one of the leaders of the leaders of the Amadiba Crisis Committee, campaigning against mining in their area (SABC News 2018).[3] This burden of care increases the depletion of women and causes harm. However, solidarity within the community and participation in the struggle can generate personal and political resources for reversing the depletion of individuals, households, and communities as well as the environments that they inhabit. So it is important to study how we might increase these resources to reduce levels of depletion through state and nonstate actions, as well as individual mitigatory strategies.

Mining as a Natural Resource Curse

Following the discovery of gold in South Africa in 1886, the mining industry played a central role in the country's economic, political, and social environment (Adler et al. 2007). The African continent is richly endowed with mineral reserves: it's estimated to hold 30% of the world's mineral resources. African nations with significant mining activity rely heavily on the sector for exports and tax revenue (Nalule 2020). The stakes are thus high for both the corporations that wish to make profit from mining and the states that need the revenue. The adoption of the new Constitution of 1996 and the Minerals and Petroleum Resources Development Act of 2002 in postapartheid South Africa meant that "natural resources became the people's collective property, with government acting as the central custodian. In addition, stakeholders were given the right to access information and to inform the policymaking process" (Adler et al. 2007, 34). Although this has given some protection to the people affected by mining, as we shall see, deficiencies in current legislation and policy and poor enforcement of protective laws remain challenges. The discourse and trajectory of development—what it means and how it is pursued—are also contested. Mining is not a win-win activity; on the contrary, for-profit, underregulated extractive industry leaves a heavy and often corrosive footprint on people's lives and land.

Mining is an important source of environmental depletion as it generates "large quantities of heavy metal laden wastes which are released in an uncontrolled manner, causing widespread contamination of the ecosystem" (Fashola, Ngole-Jeme, and Babalola 2016, 1). "Acid mine drainage is recognized as one of the more serious environmental problems in the mining industry" (Ochieng, Seanego, and Nkwonta 2010, 3351). Another source of environmental pollution from gold mines is the chemicals used in processing the gold; mercury and cyanidation method both result in the contamination of ground water, global warming, and dangerous waste (Fashola, Ngole-Jeme and Babalola 2016, Page 4 is from this source, not Ochieng, Seanego, and Nkwonta). As the evidence of this depletion and erosion of the environment marks the natural landscapes with ugly scars, people across the world are fearful but also determined to challenge this intrusion into and depletion of their lives. The Amadiba of Xolobeni are one such people, in whose life agriculture production supports community reproduction. This close and sustained link to the land means low levels of household food insecurity compared to other rural, Black African communities (Bennie 2019).

The website of the Mineral Resource Commodities (MRC), an Australian mining company, describes the Xolobeni titanium deposit "as being the 10th largest heavy mineral deposit in the world, with 346 million tonnes. Mining is proposed over 6 blocks over 25 years" (EJAtlas 2019). This attracted the MRC to explore the possibility of mining titanium in the Wild Coast area in 1996. As noted, mineral rights are vested in the state for the benefit of the country as a whole. This gives the state the right to be the final arbiter for mineral development in the country, which makes the Department of

Mineral Resources an active party in the story of the struggle of the Xolobeni community against the MRC—not as a source of replenishment but as contributor to depletion of the region and its people. The state-promoted development narrative focuses on jobs creation and taxation as reasons for promoting regulated mining. However, as research has shown, there are several reasons to push back against such a development model: "the degradation and pollution of local land, air and water and fossil fuel emissions . . . disease and migrant labour relations . . . damage to sacred sites and common spaces, and . . . community displacement and gendered violence . . . elite formation [and corruption] . . . [and] the depletion of natural capital wealth without sufficient returns" (Bond 2019, 74).

Mines pose a threat not only to the present but also to the future (Socker and Hublet 2022, n.p.)[4]—not only in their production of coal and minerals but also when they stop working after extraction is deemed unprofitable. "When a mining operation is shut down, both permanent and temporary installation is removed, and the mine is left to collapse," creating hazardous conditions for the local people (Bond 2019, 9; see also Limpitlaw et al. 2005). Campaigns against mining often result in human rights abuses, as we have seen across the African continent—the use of force against the Ogoni people in Nigeria, for example (Idowu 1999), and the violence perpetrated against the Kabwe community in Zambia through neglect of the effects of lead poisoning on the community (Chama 2010). Such violence, among other elements of extractivist investment, has been labeled the "resource curse"—attracting unaccountable corporations that deplete natural resources, send profits out of the country rather than reinvesting, and change the local landscape marked by maldevelopment (Bond 2019). The struggle of the Amadiba community, like so many others across the world, is against such maldevelopment.

The Amadiba Struggle and State Entanglements

The Xolobeni struggle is against extractivist politics of global capital and nation-states keen on economic rather than human development. It is a struggle to preserve a way of life for future generations; it is also a struggle to reshape our understanding of what is valuable in life: a healthy environment, clean air and water and land that is tended and embeds collective identities. Further, as Goldblatt and Hassim (2023, 247) underline, "At issue is not only protecting common resources, but also ensuring that they are governed sustainably and with full attention to gender inequalities." These are also elements of replenishment that have the potential to reverse depletion of individuals, households, and communities.

Worried about the proposed mining, the Xolobeni community established the Amadiba Crisis Committee (ACC) in 2007. The struggles of the Xolobeni have highlighted two particular issues that many communities face in their fight against mining: first, the nature of development in the region, and second, the issue of consent of the community to mining (Gqada 2011). In terms of the first issue, people were concerned about "their grazing land, the amounts of water that would be consumed, the impact on livestock and livelihoods, the destruction of medicinal plants, and the interference with ancestors' graves" (The Womin Collective 2017, 425). In terms of the second, the community stood firm on the issue, citing the ILO's Free, Prior and Informed Consent (FPIC) in its 1989 Convention on Indigenous and Tribal Peoples: "The necessary consent of indigenous peoples under the declaration is a recognition that the 'historic injustices' outlined in the preamble have allowed for the exploitation of their lands in violation of their right to choose forms of development that best meet their needs and interests" (McGee 2009, 571).

In Africa, provisions for public consultation (and not FPIC) are listed in the 2011 Action Plan of the Africa Mining Vision, adopted by heads of state at an African Union summit in 2009 (The Womin Collective 2017, 427). ACC were concerned that they had not been consulted adequately in the run-up to the Department of Mineral Resources (DMR) giving over mining rights to the MRC. Indeed, in July 2008, the DMR granted the mining rights to MRC's South African subsidiary, Transworld Energy and Minerals (TEM), which owns the Xolobeni Mineral Sands project (The Womin Collective 2017, 427). This mobilized the community, and they successfully campaigned against granting mining rights to TEM. In 2011 Susan Shabangu, the minister of mineral resources, withdrew the mining rights but gave the company 90 days to address the issues raised by the community. In her acceptance of the company's consultation process, she ignored the documented slipshod process, alarming the ACC (Gqada 2011, 5).

The company also tried to incite divisions within the community. Postapartheid, to increase Black ownership in the mining industry, the South African Mining Charter requires that transnational and white-dominated mining companies secure a Black economic empowerment partner; in 2003, together with MRC's first application to prospect, it also formed the cynically named Xolobeni Empowerment Company (XOLCO), which claimed to represent the local community but without any consultation with the community. In rural areas of South Africa, common property systems of landownership and management still prevail and have been used to open up indigenous areas for mining development: "The Communal Land Rights Act, which was struck down by the Constitutional Court in 2010, provided that traditional leaders would administer and control all land within their tribal boundaries [and] the Traditional Courts Bill, which was rejected by Parliament in 2014, would have empowered traditional leaders to strip anyone within their tribal boundaries of customary rights, including land rights, and would have made it a criminal offence to ignore a summons from a traditional leader" (Coleman 2016).

> This sits on top of a gendered history of colonial and apartheid collusion with designated chiefs as representatives of communities. The way that the traditional authority has been manipulated by both corporations and the state, means that the community is divided over mining and development and makes the role of traditional leaders and state actors contested and contentious. The Xolobeni struggle reflects these contestations. In 2015, MRC appointed Chief Lunga Baleni to the TEM board as a director and claimed that Amadiba Traditional Council with Chief Lunga Baleni at its helm is the only body that could challenge the mining rights application; Duduzile Baleni, the headwoman of the village and litigant against the state, was then superceded. (Huizenga 2019, 716)

There is, of course, a history of women having to fight for their positions as traditional leaders, including through the courts (Bentley

2005). In order to bypass such divisions of traditional authority, ACC has demanded that the process for seeking and attaining community consent be determined by the people themselves (Founding Affidavit 2016, cited in Huizenga 2019, 717).

However, racial discrimination and the development of mining in South Africa, which have gone hand in hand, has been "resistant to change and rural peoples continue to bear the violence of mineral extraction" (Huizenga 2019, 713). On February 22, 2016, planned drilling on the dunes was blocked by mass mobilization, and soon after this Bazooka Radebe, chairman of the ACC, was assassinated, leading the South African Human Rights Commission to issue a statement condemning the murder; the MRC has denied involvement but continues to refuse to meet with the community (Robertson 2016). There is also ongoing violence against the Xolobeni community: "The terror spree started on December 19 when armed men parked their car away from the village, turned off the lights, and came looking for the headwoman, Cynthia Baleni. Failing to find her, they fired volleys into the air and drove away. The next night they returned and repeated the performance. Eight days later three villagers were ambushed by men wielding knobkerries and bushknives. . . . Fear still reigns: a month later some villagers and their children are sleeping in the forest and nearby mealie fields" (Washinyira 2016). Campaigners against the mine and working with the community have been taken to court by the MRC in a Strategic Lawsuit Against Public Participation (SLAPP) suit[5]—the first of its kind in South Africa.

Women in Struggle against Extractivism

Women have been at the forefront of the antimining campaign by the Xolobeni to protect conditions for social reproduction; the gendered division of domestic labor and women's care roles ensure that "they deal most directly with the damaging effects of toxic pollution of the air and water on health and life" (Cock 2018, 216; see also Goldblatt and Hassim 2023). In Amadiba tradition unmarried women have the title to land (unmarried men do not have this title), which also means that they are directly connected to the care of the land and the way of life and to the community (The Womin Collective 2017, 431). Further, because of women's experience in the production and provision of food, they are better positioned to "promote a new narrative about our relationship with nature" (431). The Xolobeni women have therefore been acting in solidarity "to challenge corporate and patriarchal power as part of a larger struggle to end all forms of oppression" and to challenge extractivism (Cock 2018, 227). This has also resulted in women in Xolobeni playing a central role in community decision-making about the struggle and strategy and about future development in the area.

Consent—to the use of land and to personal and communal sovereignty—is an important issue for women (The Womin Collective 2017). As primary producers and processors of food, women are particularly affected by access to and preservation of land and sea for the subsistence and survival of their families and communities (ActionAid 2017, 3). The "opportunities for women in mines are either limited or more vulnerable, while women in mining communities bear the brunt of the negative impact of mining operations" (3). The health effects of mining are felt in the community as a whole; pollution of water and air has resulted in rising cases of leukemia, miscarriages, and deformity in children. Women take on the intimate, gendered work of caring for workers who became ill with lung diseases as a result of poor labor conditions in the mines in South Africa (Goldblatt and Rai 2018). Women have to walk long distances to collect clean drinking water, adding to their burdens of domestic work and increasing their depletion (ActionAid 2017, 14).

Based on a history of resistance to colonization in that part of the country, which is unusual in its success (South African History Online 2014),[6] the Xolobeni's campaign is also a response to the immediate threat to their lives and livelihoods and to extractivism as a settler colonial structure of harm (Yusoff 2023), which is both gendered and racialized. After the violence, murder and the strong pushback by the ACC, in September 2016 the DMR minister Mosebenzi Zwane declared an 18-month moratorium on mining in Xolobeni, until he was satisfied that the community conflict had been resolved; this was rejected by the ACC.

Legal Strategies: Opportunities and Limits

The ACC took the DMR to court, requesting that no license to mine the area be granted without the community's consent. In November 2018, the North Gauteng High Court ruled, "The applicants in this matter [have] the right to decide what happens with their land. As such they may not be deprived by their land without their consent. Where the land is held on a communal basis—as in this matter—the community must be placed in a position to consider the proposed deprivation and be allowed to take a communal decision in terms of their custom and community on whether they consent or not to a proposal to dispose of their rights to their land (International Commission of Jurists 2018).[7] The judgment shows the importance of legal strategies in the context of South Africa's postapartheid Constitution, which is widely regarded as equality focused. It also shows that the "plasticity of equality meant that it would always be open to different interpretations by the executive and parliament, as well as by courts tasked with enforcing the Constitution" (Albertyn 2018, 441). In response, the MRC has taken to court six South African activists, lawyers, and social workers it accuses of defaming it through public criticism (Davis 2020). Such intimidation through this SLAPP suit has raised important issues of freedom of speech and rights of corporations against citizens in South Africa (Davis 2020). Minister Mantashe also reacted against the judgment, complaining that within 10 years all mining and investment would stop in South Africa (Cele 2018) and that the government will appeal the judgment. Further, the case took advantage of the COVID-19 pandemic to push through "amendments to the Mineral Resources Development Act . . . which effectively strip mining-affected communities of key rights" (Rutledge 2020). This discourse of threat to the development of the country as a result of the struggle of the Xolobeni sought to shift the focus from the local to the national, while the Xolobeni sought to internationalize their struggle as part of the global struggle for insistence on Free, Prior and Informed Consent (FPIC) and for indigenous peoples' rights: "[T]his was now becoming the story of how a small group of rural agitators, branded 'anti-development' because of their commitment to the old ways, were standing in the path of state policy. It was becoming the story of the fight for water sovereignty, food sovereignty, and the sovereignty of their ancestors' graves . . . of non-violent resistance" (Tricontinental 2019, 7).

In September 2020, the North Gauteng High Court ruled that those affected by mining operations had a right to see applications for licenses and that "[m]eaningful consultation entails discussion of ideas on an equal footing, considering the advantages and disadvantages of each course and making concessions where necessary" (Ellis 2020). The struggle is ongoing, with judgment reserved on the case in April 2023 (Legalbrief 2023), but what effects is it having on the Xolobeni communities? One way of understanding this is by "reading" the photographic exhibition *Postcards from Xolobeni* by Thom Pierce (2018a), a photographer who has worked to bring their story to a global audience.

Visual Cultures of Depletion

Alpers et al. (1996, 28) argue that an image "is at least potentially a site of resistance and recalcitrance, of the irreducibly particular, and of the subversively strange and pleasurable." In other words, images have the potential to "do," in the Austinian sense, just by being seen. If a colonial, modernist aesthetic of destruction describes the landscape from afar, we need new modes of a resistance aesthetic to narrate alternative modes of living embedded in the land (Yusoff 2023). The photographs of the Xolobeni have this potential; Pierce's photographs allow us to connect the body, the landscape, and the text in an image. By making the images and texts available through this work, the struggle of the Xolobeni is connected with that of other communities across the world struggling against extractivist industries and depletion of the environment. These postcards are written by ordinary Xolobeni people to those who hold power to affect their lives; they are also a message to the past and the future—they imagine the "not-yet-real" but that which is present in the stories of other communities affected by mining; the imagined loss of their land and ways of life is therefore "real." The people are emplaced in their landscapes and their

Figure 6.2 Maxolo Mboyisa. "The best life I have is connected to this Pondo land. You can't have a good life if you are only concerned with money. I get herbs for my medicine from the land around my home. I respect the land and it provides for me. My ancestors are buried here and I need to protect them from the mining."
Source: *Postcards from Xolobeni* © Thom Pierce.

stories in the politics of mining that I have outlined above; the images recount both.

As Goldblatt and Rai (2018) have argued, a critical photographer is not simply a recorder of what is being done but, as the South African photographer David Goldblatt (2005, 94) put it, is a "witness": "I am a self-appointed observer and critic of the society into which I was born, with a tendency to doing honour or giving recognition to what is often overlooked or unseen." Pierce is clearly a critical photographer—his photographs do not make icons of the Xolobeni; they are self-consciously of the place, fighting for the place. Through his photo essay, Pierce clearly stands on the side of the subjects; his is not a "neutral" lens. As Squires (2006, 10) has pointed out, "[P]hotographs [can be] read through a spectrum of texts, including [the] photographer's interviews and writings, news reportage, political and social history. . . . [T]he images can be opened out into a broader field of understanding by texts that can help us comprehend the complexity of what the photographers confronted."

Through his photographs, Pierce is able to reveal the wild beauty of Wild Coast as well as expose the Xolobeni's anxieties about the imminent collapse of their worlds—their worry for their families and their way of life, their present and their future. There is a quiet intensity and quotidian practices of refusal (Campt 2017, 4) evident in these photographs and texts which is both powerful and vulnerable. The visuality of these images influence how I see and am able to see this struggle (Rose 2012, 2). In the words of Campt (2017, 3), photographs help us "recalibrate[e] vernacular photographs as quiet practices that give us access to affective registers through which images enunciate alternate accounts of their subjects." In Pierce's photographs, I see the body in the landscape—the sea and the land, the goat and the water—and sense the importance of these to the figure in the terrain: "we never look just at one thing; we are always looking at the relation between things and ourselves" (Berger 1972, 9). I cannot see but yet am constantly aware of other, invisible, nonseeable elements: the graves of Xolobeni ancestors to which they repeatedly gesture in their messages, their homes which they feel are under threat, as well as the titanium under their land that is so attractive as a commodity for both capital and the state. Through being in and writing the postcards, the people of the Xolobeni write and display their courage and determination in the face of a multinational corporation with clout and a state body with power.

Without claiming expertise as a visual researcher, my analysis of these photographs builds on a critical approach to visual culture, which means that we take "images seriously . . . think about the social conditions and effects of visual objects . . . [and consider our] own way of looking at images" (Rose 2012, 16–17). This entails, "among other things, thinking about how they offer very particular visions of social categories such as class, gender, race, sexuality, able-bodiedness" (12). Critical visual studies have also, with Berger (1972, 47), challenged images in which "men act and women appear." Pierce's postcards show both men and women standing firm and solidly on the ground that they call their home, which they are campaigning to keep safe, to hold on to.

The photographs are set in the landscape of the Wild Coast, whose beauty underlines the threat to it, to the Xolobeni community and its way of life and to the depletion of their environment posed by the MRC or XOLCO seeking to extract titanium. Their pain and anxiety are expressed in their bodies and in the texts they have written, both of which are integral to the photographs. These are postcards to their futures—to those who can destroy them and to those who could save them by changing course. (As we have seen, these messages have had little impact on either the state or the corporation.) They are poignant and brave responses to imminent threat—to their livelihoods, their landscapes, and their sense of themselves. These postcards are also intergenerational narratives—of their concern for their children and grandchildren but also for their community as a unit that needs to survive *for* their children and grandchildren. And these postcards are also indictments—the mining companies that would destroy the writers' habitat, their sense of well-being, and their traditions of the good life.

The individual figures in the photographs are rooted in the landscape, yet vulnerable to its loss. They stand there with their whole selves—carrying water on their heads, fishing tackle in their hands, standing by the graves of their ancestors, holding the fruits of their labor, or contemplating life. These seem to be lives that are difficult but also embedded in the Wild Coast—aware of their place in the fragile landscape of their ancestors and of the need for future generations to care for it if it is to be protected from exploitation. The portraits also underline "living otherwise"—a sense of well-being that is not the same as development that Minister Mantashe rues.

But the words on the postcards disturb the solidity of the photographs, aware that change is around the corner: change that they neither desire nor have control over, change that is being thrust upon them. The words bring into view what is out of sight in the photographs—their households and communities and the environment that supports these.

Fakazile Joyce Ndovela is worried. "I have cattle, sheep and goats," she writes. "I grow crops and plough my fields. I don't have a husband, I survive off the land. The water feeds everything, the crops, the animals and my family. I don't want to change the way I live" (Figure 6.3). Her photograph captures both the land and the water of the Xolobeni—the stream that gives Fakazile water to drink, and the sea that provides fish—the sources of life for the Xolobeni. Reading her words, we can see that Fakazile can imagine the land being gouged out by the machines,

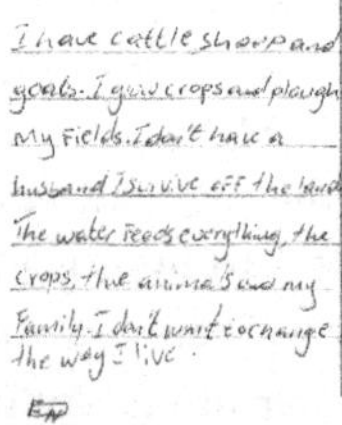

Figure 6.3 Fakazile Joyce Ndovela. "I have cattle, sheep and goats. I grow crops and plough my fields. I don't have a husband, I survive off the land. The water feeds everything, the crops, the animals and my family. I don't want to change the way I live."

Source: *Postcards from Xolobeni* © Thom Pierce.

Figure 6.4 Thabisa Mbuthuma. "If the mine comes we will have to leave this land. The noise and the sand will be too much. If we move away our lifestyle will change and we will have to leave our ancestors behind. We need to protect the land for future generations."

 Source: *Postcards from Xolobeni* © Thom Pierce.

the sweet water of the stream polluted by debris and metal run-offs, and the access to the sea blocked by fences to keep in the workers and keep out her community. Thabisa Mbuthuma is also anxious: "If the mine comes we will have to leave this land. The noise and the sand will be too much. If we move away our life style will change and we will have to leave our ancestors behind. We need to protect the land for future generations" (Figure 6.4). The not-yet-real is real in her words that tell of a ruined future if the mine is allowed to go ahead. Also evident in her words addressed to the company is the concern about leaving her ancestors behind, something that is of real concern to the Xolobeni communities and comes up again and again in their narratives—leaving behind those who were part of their lives, those who gave them life, and those who advised them is leaving behind part of themselves.

And Luleka Funwa is anxious that the land that "feeds our family and the sea is part of our lives. We come here to think and to collect water for our health. We need free access to the sea, it is our right as a community. Even if we are allowed access the mine will pollute the sea, it will never be the same" (Figure 6.5).

The Amadiba subjectivities and identities are tied to the land—to think, to feel, to appreciate what they have is to be on the land. There is a sense here of "knowing" the present and appreciating it; narratives of modernization and development recede in the face of what Funwa thinks is to *be* a/of the Xolobeni, the Amadiba community. She chooses to write to the MRC rather than the minister. I wonder why she thinks she may be able to explain to greedy strangers the importance of the sea to her and her community?

So, in anticipating harm, the Xolobeni communities experience depletion through fears of a futuristic dystopia. The fear that the mine will destroy their way of life, their access to life's resources, and their communities' histories is depleting: it raises levels of anxiety and stress as they imagine the threat to and the ruination of their present and a future full of loss.

Luleka Funwa - Xolobeni, South Africa

The land feeds our family and the sea is part of our lives. We come here to think and collect water for our health. We need free access to the sea. It is our rights as a community. Even if we are allowed access the mine will pollute the sea, It will never be the same.

—L.F.

MR GWEDE MANTASHE
DEPT. OF MINERAL RESOURCES
PRIVATE BAG X59
ARCADIA, PRETORIA
0007

Figure 6.5 Luleka Funwa. "The land feeds our family and the sea is part of our lives. We come here to think and to collect water for our health. We need free access to the sea, it is our right as a community. Even if we are allowed access the mine will pollute the sea, it will never be the same." Source: *Postcards from Xolobeni* © Thom Pierce.

It also adds to the burdens of campaigning against the MRC, XOLCO, and the government, and to the time poverty of the women engaged in work within the home and outside to provide for their families. The threat of violence—structural and physical, immediate and imagined—adds to the sense of precarity, so much at variance with the landscape on which they stand in the photographs. The anticipated harm, however, builds a determination to struggle against the mine; many voices shout out through these postcards: "My ancestors are buried here and I need to protect them from the mining" (Maxolo Mboyisa); "We are happy living off the land. We have everything we need; we don't need to be given hand outs. This is life we are used to and we don't want it [to] change. We say no to the mine" (Themba Yalo); "We cannot live without it, hands off our land" (Nokwakha Mboyisa). Despite the wins and the losses, the threats and the violence, the struggle is ongoing.

In anticipating harm to their land, the Xolobeni campaigners are not idealizing their way of life—they want improvement to their health and education, they want better schools and hospitals, they want "development"—but on their own terms and within their own frame:[8] " 'We are the holders of the land. . . . [W]e are not anti-development; we want development and the development that we want to see in Xolobeni is we want to see ecotourism, we want to see agriculture . . . not monoculture. . . . [W]e are talking about small scale, where people are practicing

Figure 6.6 Mashakumani Yalo. "We are happy living off the land. We have everything we need. We don't need to be given hand outs. This is the life we are used to and we don't want it to change. We say no to the mine."
Source: *Postcards from Xolobeni* © Thom Pierce.

agriculture for themselves,' says Mbuthuma" (SABC News 2018). It is neoliberal extractivism they are against, not an ecofriendly, communal, and participatory approach to development.

The Grant Thornton report on ecotourism found that "the benefits of tourism outweighed those of mining, in terms of the number of jobs created and its longevity—mining would last only 22 years, tourism as long as the sea, the environment and the people exist" (Bennie 2019). Indeed, in her judgment in *Baleni v. Minister of Mineral Resources and Others*, Judge Basson (2018, 12) noted, "A significant number of the community also rely on tourism and tourist-related activities. . . . The growth potential in tourism has, however, not [been] realised as a result of the repeated prospecting and mining right applications brought by TEM."

These alternative visions of development connect with the "what ifs" of future imaginaries—one path leads to displacement of life and traditions, the other to an integrated approach to development for all the community. As Claude Ake (1990, 8) noted, "Whatever people do not accept, whatever they do not assimilate as an integral part of their lives can never be properly construed as their development." The Xolobeni activists struggle against depletion that erodes life in multiple registers. They struggle for replenishment and even the possibility of transformation of both the community and the country, and indeed of new thinking about development as a concept and as a way of life. Social reproduction as care brings the care of the environment together with that of individuals and houscholds, of imaginaries of a good life with the distribution of resources to bring that about (Federici 2019; Rai 2018).

Social reproductive labor includes the labor of struggle and solidarity to maintain life and help it flourish. It is important to note that women's place among the Amadiba community places them as equal members of their community with rights to land and therefore a direct stake in its cultivation and preservation. This means that women not only worry at home but are part of the political struggle against mining and the destruction of their environment. While this participation is important, it also places added burdens on women as there is little redistribution of domestic labor in the home. The worry and anxiety about their future, the time spent in marching and meetings against the state-corporation axis, the labor in the home to keep life going, and the labor to support the family through paid work—all this is negotiated by Xolobeni women and men very differently and also together. The harm from violence against the land and against the communities that live on/off the land is significant—in anticipation and in struggle even though it is necessary and also empowering.

Harm and/as Depletion to the Xolobeni

Harm occurs when there is a measurable deterioration in the health and well-being of individuals and households and communities, and when the inflows required to maintain social reproduction fall below the sustainability threshold (Chapter 1). Through Pierce's photographs we have seen that in the context of mining, the harm to the Xolobeni creates "ripples of harm" that cross temporal boundaries—harm to here and now as well as harm to future generations (Goldblatt and Rai 2018; Ní Aoláin 2009). Goldstein (2017, 321) points out that harm can be invisible and that the "unseen nature of toxicity . . . enables the state to authorise its existence." We have seen that anticipatory harm works in the same way. As the mine has not started functioning, the Xolobeni cannot point to their experience of harm, which allows the mining company and the state to suggest that the anticipated harm might not occur, can be contained, or if it occurs can be mitigated. This of course obfuscates the fact that the anticipated harm may be invisible now but will be manifest tomorrow; such approaches "based in immediacy may speak to the potential for environmental damage and bodily harm" (321). The lack of recognition of these harms erodes the capabilities of those affected to cope emotionally; it challenges their place in society and their right to frame claims against the state and nonstate actors as entitlements rather than as the needs of subjects requiring support (Rai, Hoskyns, and Thomas 2014). The Xolobeni's ability to cope with harms is therefore not a given. The nonrecognition of harm can lead to disruption of households and communities as the individuals affected, both physically and mentally, lose capacity to cope (Ní Aoláin 2009).

Xolobeni women have been active in the struggle as they see their role in particular gendered terms—they are connected to the land not only in terms of tenure but also as farmers, as contributing to keeping alive the customs and rituals of the community for future generations. What the Xolobeni struggle reveals is that harm takes many forms; indeed, as we have seen, the harm experienced by the Xolobeni communities show different aspects of depletion as harm: that they are antidevelopment (discursive), stress and anxiety of anticipating the effects of mining (emotional), the threat of violence here and now and of ill health from anxiety and from the mine (bodily), and erosion of rights of the community to be listened to (citizenship-related) (Rai, Hoskyns, and Thomas 2014, 91–92). Of course, these are overlapping, as discursive harm is emotional, and emotional harm manifests in the body through stress-related illness, and the claim to citizenship rights in the struggle against mining can elicit physical violence against both the individuals involved as well as the households through attacks upon homes and cattle, as evidenced in the reports discussed above.

In South Africa, the law of delict (in other common law countries known as "tort") means that the courts allow for claims for damages for monetary loss caused by wrongful injuries to a person (such as loss of income and medical expenses), known as "special damages." The law also allows claims for wrongful injuries to a person's body leading to pain and suffering, loss of amenities of life, and disfigurement that are not readily calculable (non economic loss) but which can be given a monetary value by the courts as a form of compensation, known as "general damages" (Goldblatt and Rai 2018, 674). While the court ruled in favor of the Xolobeni communities on grounds of community rights to land and the importance of free, informed consent to prevent mining-based harms to the area and its people, the law cannot compensate for the depletion of individuals and communities, which is, the law believes, yet to happen. The mining has not started yet. In the meantime, women of the community continue to carry the triple burden of doing paid, unpaid, and community work of struggle. They are being depleted without a recognition of this depletion. The courts have, however, in some judgments, recognized the threat to the land

and the people that live on/off it, as in the *Beleni v. Minister of Mineral Resources and Others* (2018); arguably such a legal victory is recognition and is mitigating in some ways and maybe even replenishing in consolidating their rights. As Goldblatt and Hassim (2023, 248) point out, such legal victories need to be institutionalized if they are to be effective. The determination of the state to appeal against such judgments, the imposing of the SLAPP suit by the corporation, and the violence against the community, however, show that there is as yet a lack of recognition of present and continuing harm being experienced by the Xolobeni community and how they may be compensated.

In the South African context, the courts have a constitutional mandate to develop the common law consistent with the "spirit, purport and objects of the Bill of Rights" (Constitution of the Republic of South Africa, 1996, s. 8(3) and s. 39(2)). Could compensation for depletion in the context of anticipatory harm be one legal and replenishment strategy to explore? Could the courts develop the common law consistent with anticipatory harm not only to protect the environment but also to replenish the community that suffers from the threat to the environment? The awarding of legal costs, including punitive costs, is one form of recourse in litigation. If depletion in defending their land can be proven to be a measurable harm arising from the actions of the mining company and/or government through a demonstrable causal link, would depletion be compensable? These questions are posed in the context of the distress being experienced by the Xolobeni community, even as they fight the pressures from the state to open up their land for mining and from the corporations to profit from the minerals they can extract. Other remedial mechanisms that may be mobilized could be the United Nations' business and human rights framework, which is directed at specifically preventing and remedying the harms of corporate negligence and malpractice (Goldblatt and Rai 2020). This has yet to happen as this framework does not address the needs of those who care, and also does not challenge the growth agenda at the center of the South African state's development paradigm, which also remains at the heart of the Xolobeni struggle. Extractivism continues to function as an "ideological undercurrent to colonial dispossession, racial subjection and gendered violence" (Okoth 2023, 55), which depletes the individuals, households, and communities of the Amadiba.

The Commons as a Way of Life/Development

The story of the Xolobeni is a story of claims to replenishment and indeed of attempts at transformation. As we have seen, imagining the not-yet-real can be both dystopic and utopic, depleting and replenishing at the same time; the Xolobeni are having to cope with both as they push back against the state and MRC and also respond to accusations about being antidevelopment. When asked about whether the ACC is against development, Nonhle Mbthuma, a founding member of the ACC and resident of Xolobeni, responded with an alternative vision of development:

> We believe that we know who we are because of the land. We believe that once you have lost the land, you have lost your identity. We also believe that it is our right to live in a healthy environment, an environment which is not harmful to us, that has clean air with no air pollution, no pollution of the land and no contamination of the water . . . that women must be a part of decision making. There should be no discrimination in terms of gender. If we do that, we are going to build a healthy nation. (Cited in The Womin Collective 2017, 422)

Clearly, subjectivity has an important place in what development means to particular communities. Here we do not see what Ambreena Manji (2006) has quite correctly worried about: the use of law to strengthen property rights, which then leads to dispossession of thousands of farmers, including women. We need to be aware that customary laws do not always benefit women; whether state law or customary law, women often tend to lose out if land is privatized. But we also know that in the case of the Xolobeni (and in feminist imaginaries) this need not be so—women can have entitlement to land use, just as men do. We can see a powerful case being constructed by the Xolobeni based on the history of Pondoland, where women historically have rights on the land and the valorization of traditional land use patterns, the use of contemporary postapartheid South African law, and future-looking articulations of development "otherwise." As Goldblatt and Hassim (2023, 248) argue, "[I]nstitutional mechanisms

such as the law and Constitution can be allies as people mobilise. . . .
The Xolobeni example provides insights into strategies of resistance."
The Xolobeni seem to be aware of the politics "in and against the state"
(London Edinburgh Weekend Return Group 1979; Rai 1995)—using
the law but also working to change it. In so doing they can serve as
a (utopic) example of sustainable community and resistance against
colonization.

The Xolobeni are aware of the fact that erosion of community land
tenure, through the state's claim to it, will adversely affect their social
fabric, intensify land disputes, and block access not only to land but
also to the wider resources that the land held communally provides: the
river, the sea, the trees and herbs that they write about in the postcards.
As Federici (2019, 125) notes, "[T]he commons are shrinking and the
premise for a peaceful road to communal egalitarianism is more land."
A commoning of land and decisions about how to use it, for which the
Xolobeni are struggling, is also ultimately a struggle about how to reor-
ganize, reproduce, and maintain life: "One crucial reason for creating
collective forms of living is that the reproduction of human beings is
the most labour-intensive work on earth and, to a very large extent,
it is irreducible to mechanization. . . . For centuries, the reproduction
of human beings has been a collective process. It has been the work of
extended families and the communities upon which people could rely"
(110–111).

In the context of extractivism and its historic and multiple harms
(Barca 2014), the Xolobeni are struggling for an alternative politics—
of the commoning of land based not on historical exclusions of gender
and class, caste, and race but on equal access (Federici 2019) and care
of the environment. The story of the Xolobeni is inspiring because it
envisions a reversal of depletion—in the present and in the future—
and of a transformation of social reproduction.

Conclusion
Building Solidarities to Reverse Depletion

The woman in the painting on the cover of this book is ironing a huge pile of clothes, each one carefully made distinct by the painter's brush. There is an umbrella, I think shielding her from the fierce sun beating down in the saffron surrounding her. She is crouching, half-sitting as many Asian women do when they do cleaning or housework. She is laboring—perhaps paid, or perhaps ironing for the family, unpaid and unacknowledged. In the sky high above her there is an airplane, symbolic of modernity, showing the distance between this laboring figure and those who travel swiftly above her. The woman doesn't look up—she has work to do. I see the depletion in her tense face and wonder about her life under what Fraser (2023) calls cannibal capitalism that is hollowing out our life-worlds.[1]

Depletion as harm is a thread that runs throughout the book—past, present, and anticipated harm is experienced differently by individuals, households, and communities. Harm is also planetary—making our world increasingly fragile and affecting the health and wellbeing of people. Harm is manifested in the everyday—spatially, temporally, and through violence, both immediate and structural—as well as in times of crisis, when the pressures of life and work increase and resources to draw upon for mitigation decrease for the most economically vulnerable.

In this book I have argued that an intersectional analysis is imperative when assessing the costs of social reproduction as depletion (Chapter 1); that location—geographic and social—matters greatly in strategies of mitigation (Chapters 3, 4, 5, and 6); that intergenerational social reproductive work ensures depletion down the generational care chain, as much as it does along the migration care chain, not just for older people but also for children who care (Chapter 5); and that

Depletion. Shirin M. Rai, Oxford University Press. © Shirin M. Rai 2024.
DOI: 10.1093/oso/9780197535547.003.0008

depletion of humans is intimately entangled with the depletion of the planet, with those marginalized more at risk from being dispossessed of not only their present but their futures (Chapter 6).

Care, Crisis, and Depletion

Crises intensify depletion.

This book was largely written during a crisis—the COVID-19 pandemic. Daily death toll statistics, rounds of lockdowns that "locked in" people in shrinking spaces, stories of loneliness, of breakdown of intergenerational contact, of overflowing hospitals, and of growing public acknowledgment of the importance of care work by "clapping for carers," are the memories of that time. But, of course, this is not the only crisis that has been impinging on my work and the lives of so many. Other crises—environmental, financial, political, and social— have all seen the intensification of depletion as people struggle to re- source social reproduction, with racialized and gendered division of labor making life/work particularly difficult. Crises are historically layered; the pandemic struck when the regimes of austerity, of racism, and of precarity were already operative, intensifying the crisis of social reproduction and intensifying depletion (Bassel and Emejulu 2017).

The pandemic was a crisis of both health and social reproduction. Increasing commodification of care and state-enabling of corporatized care had made the care sector vulnerable to economic crisis. In turn, profit-oriented care regimes put those most in need into ever more precarious positions (Butler 2023, 12). The pandemic also revealed gendered, classed, and raced regimes of work; the overrepresentation of women and racialized minorities in the care sector made them more vulnerable to the virus, and death rates in these groups were, as a result, high (Aldridge et al. 2020). COVID-19-induced lockdowns resulted in sharp increases in care labor at home, which also became a work- site; children had to be home-schooled as schools closed down, family members stayed at home and had to be fed, more people at home generated more housework. Domestic violence and mental health is- sues increased too, as people coped with being locked in their homes and also locked out of sociality and hospitality of family and friends

(Akhter, Elias, and Rai 2019; Lingham, Rai, and Akhter forthcoming; Daly, Sutin, and Robinson 2020; UN 2020; Power 2020, 67).

We could say that instead of a caring society we were and are living in a careless society, one that depends on care but does not value the "doing" of care (Kaur and Rai 2021). As the pandemic underlined, the cost of this carelessness is heavy and is paid by society as a whole, but more so by those socially marginalized, intensifying their depletion through social reproductive and care labor. COVID-19 produced a "life-unfriendly regime," where even if the poorest survived they could not thrive; the systematic marketizing of social reproduction produced a chronic crisis of care (Mezzadri 2022, 383).

All crises have this potential of differentially intensifying depletion of those who have to cope every day with the constrained lives. We have seen that both the everyday and longer periods of crisis are historically embedded, complex and many layered. Social reproduction and depletion are grounded in this complexity. While difficult to do so, as we saw in Chapters 2 and 3, we can and must measure the scope, scale, and levels of depletion—measurement is a form of recognition that can aid in developing strategies of reversing depletion. The pandemic also showed that the state can (and many states did) contribute to the intensification of depletion by neglecting to invest in social infrastructure. However, individuals and communities are not without agency to negotiate (Chapters 3, 4, and 5) and to push back against depletion (Chapter 6). As Dengler and Lang (2022, 2) argue, "a multidimensional crisis requires multidimensional strategies." Reversing depletion that is unequally felt and intensified during crises also needs such multilayer and historically aware strategies.

Struggles to Reverse Depletion

I started this book by pointing out that depletion is not a cheery or optimistic concept. However, as I look back to the life stories of individuals, households, and communities covered in this book, I find much to be hopeful about. This is because despite the challenges of un/malrecognized social reproductive work, despite balancing care work with paid work, despite many being poor, marginalized and oppressed, we find individuals, households, and communities that struggle against the structures of everyday exploitation, imagine different lives, and come together in friendship and solidarity to try to reverse their own and their community's depletion—present and anticipated. Prefigurative approaches to change are already developing (Gibson-Graham 2008; Cooper 2014; Yates 2021; Cohen and Morgan 2023) and have the power of reimagining both care and caring such that those who care do not suffer continuing depletion for this work. These reimaginings are not new; there are long histories of communities bringing into being alternative modes of living, however precarious; as Mullings (2021,153) suggests, "Perhaps the most powerful form of resistance to the system of plantation capitalism took place when enslaved workers ran away either temporarily (petit marronage) or permanently (grand marronage) to form separate communities." Delinking, however, is not an option for most, especially for women enmeshed in family relations.

These prefigurative imaginaries therefore need to acknowledge the long histories of gendered, classed, and raced oppressions and locations, issues not only of recognition but of redistribution that are raised in the book. State and nonstate actors have a role to play in these reimaginings, but they do this within the constraints of the historical structures of empire and of capitalism (Mullings 2021). Also important are how these reimaginings translate into local struggles and why some are more successful than others (Törnberg 2021). So what form do these struggles to reverse depletion take? Building on the discussion in the book, I will briefly note some emerging strategies of reversing depletion that could be and are being mobilized to open up new avenues of reshaping social reproduction in the everyday at the three levels discussed in the book: mitigation, replenishment, and transformation.

Mitigation

There are attempts at shifting more and more unpaid care work to the monetized economy as a way of bridging the care gap for some. In the absence of states investing adequately in social infrastructures, corporations are investing in healthcare and care sectors in response to growing demand for care and the increasing care gaps. Deloitte's (2022) report on public health notes, "Reimagining the future of public health will require to forge new partnerships across public and private health care providers, new sources of investment for the wellness of communities, fresh market entrants bringing in diverse skills and expertise, and taking significant strides for digitizing public health." This allows for development of global practices of commercial caregiving in wealthy countries and for wealthy people, marginalizing the care and healthcare needs of others. This also makes the care sector vulnerable to the ups and downs of the global markets—of capital and of labor. Sudden closures of care homes as a result of market fluctuations, increases in the price of rents, electricity, food costs, and the racist migration policies of Western governments that play to populist politics in the context of need for care labor from global labor markets are becoming more visible. This undermines these mitigatory strategies and increases depletion in periods of economic crises.

Other innovative approaches to care imagine mitigation through the use of technology—film and television project AI robotic domestic workers, and experts in healthcare look to digital technology to save money and free up human clinical time (Darzi, Quilter-Pinner and Kibasi 2018; Butler 2023) and to build "hospitals without walls" (Deloitte 2022). Reducing social reproductive work through mobilizing technology is being explored in terms of labor-saving devices (lifting, carrying, reminding) versus emotional care devices (socially assistive robots for replacing human interaction) (Druckman and Mair 2019). This, of course, is not an entirely new approach; vacuum cleaners and washing machines were also hailed as mitigating domestic labor in the 1950s and 1960s; there was no redistribution of the domestic chores however. This also raises broader questions of ethics of care in this rapidly developing and commodifying care landscape—the transformation of care itself (Dowling 2021) as well as the re/shaping of social reproduction by deeply gendered and raced AI (Fortunati and Edwards 2022). Technology is also being mobilized to "nudge" gender equality in the home; for example, the Spanish government has developed a new app to register the work done in the home, in the hope that the visibility of gendered inequality in housework will encourage men to share more equally the burden of social reproductive work (Jones 2023).

However, as we saw in Chapters 3, 4, and 5, mitigation also emerges from friendship and familial networks. In Chapter 3 we saw women negotiate gendered familial norms or challenge these with the support of friends and family members; they reflected on where their sources of support and solidarity lay and tried to invest time in these and lamented its loss if they couldn't. They are aware of their depletion and the need for mitigating it. As care needs increase with aging populations, especially in the Global North, other than struggling with the issue of migration care chains and conditions of work of domestic workers, communities are developing new caring strategies (Cooper 2014). Advertisements for rent-free accommodation in return for care and domestic labor now abound in Europe[2] for example. There is also a revival of traditional woman-to-woman marriages in Kenya, where younger women "marry" older women, whom they care for, in anticipation of inheriting their property (Kereithi and Viljoen 2019; Stewart 2023).

Mitigation is the most prominent strategy of reversing depletion; however, it remains largely individualized and connects the worlds of unpaid and paid social reproduction. Fundamentally unequal, it also does not challenge the foundations of a capitalist socioeconomy of care and caring.

Replenishment

Replenishment, like mitigation, is an important but also a limited strategy to reverse depletion. As percentages of older people in the Global North increase, the issue of care has become an increasingly key political battleground for state intervention. Most feminist social policy debates on care focus on how to mobilize fiscal, discursive, and policy-oriented state resources, which address care gaps and gender asymmetries (Gornick and Meyers 2009; Chapter 1). The complexity of addressing this issue results in internal tensions in state policy—austerity, migration controls, regulation of care homes, funding of social care as opposed to health/medical care, taxation, insurance. All of these are connected and affect articulation of care policies in the Global North.

Changing family forms, urbanization, and precarious welfare regimes and increasingly issues of climate change and just transitions (Lake and Quaid 2023) affect policies and systems of care in the Global South.

At the international level, institutions such as the EU and the UN have accepted that "[t]he perceived narrative that the economic empowerment of women as a tool for economic growth is a winwin situation for all neglects the dangers of overwork among the poorest women, given that they struggle with intense and heavy paid and unpaid workloads, leading to time poverty and depletion" (UNWomen 2020, 17). Struggles for recognition of social reproductive work, especially unpaid care work, have resulted in shifts in international social policy. The UN has promoted a number of international conventions and treaties advancing the right of everyone to the "continuous improvement of living conditions" in Article 11 of the International Covenant on Economic, Social and Cultural Rights, the Convention on the Elimination of All Forms of Discrimination against Women, the Convention on the Rights of the Child, and the Convention on the Rights of Persons with Disabilities, ILO Convention 189, and SDG 5.4. All these agreements impose obligations on the state to address the issues of inequality and improvement in conditions of work. Of course, as I have argued, mitigation and replenishment are not unconnected. The continued mitigation of depletion for some throws light on the conditions of work for others, which requires both international and national regulation through legal instruments. ILO Convention 189 on Domestic Workers was enacted in 2011 as a global governance mechanism for making the conditions of work of domestic workers visible and ensuring decent conditions of work for domestic/care workers; this was a result of a long history of struggle by the workers and the NGOs working with them. The struggle continues as the many signatory nation-states fail to regulate the conditions of work they have signed up for (Marchetti 2018). However, as we have seen, there is practically no progress in revising the calculation parameters of GDP as a measure of growth, and indeed development, despite strong critiques of this measure, with ongoing consequences for reframing social reproductive work (Rai et al. 2019). These contradictory signals in international policy framing lead to a conceptual and policy logjam that is far from resolving the issues of depletion, and of recognizing, reducing, and redistributing unpaid care and domestic work (Triple Rs first articulated by Elson [2017]; see also Knobloch's [2019] 4 Vs).[3] This strategy of measuring social reproductive work, and in so doing recognizing its importance, can be politically mobilized to insist on the urgently needed investment in social infrastructure to support care work; this, however, in itself can only be replenishing and not transformative. State, nonstate, and market-based strategies do not shift the capitalist mode of production and social reproduction. However, as discussed below, such replenishing strategies can and do help in reducing depletion in the everyday; state investment in public services matters.

Focusing on nonstate and market actors, Butler and Hoskyns (2017) have outlined a novel replenishing strategy, an innovative community fair trade pricing model negotiated between The Body Shop International and the sesame-producing Nicaraguan Cooperativa Juan Francisco Paz Silva, that included recognition for the unpaid work of women. Butler and Hoskyns argue that "despite the uneven impact of fair trade on gender in the household, the recognition of the unpaid work of women in the price paid for sesame, coupled with other enabling factors explored in the chapter, can have a positive impact" (155). While this experiment and model is truly innovative and shows the power of collective bargaining between workers (who wanted this recognition in material terms) and business (Body Shop needing to work with the sesame producers on a sustained basis), I have not seen evidence of a scaling up of this model to all Body Shop suppliers. The importance and the limitations of this model are self-evident: "[T]he incorporation of gender equality into neoliberal rationalities and technologies of government, such as public-private partnerships," allows for "the production of new gendered subjectivities that flourish in liberal markets" (Prügl 2017, 46).

If international organizations, states, and capital can play a crucial part in mitigation and replenishment, so can struggles by communities and people affected by the precarity of care, care employment, and social reproduction practices in the context of economic and political crises. Here too we see different strategies deployed—both in and against the state, challenging corporatization and extraction of value from care of both human and nonhuman environments. New imaginings of the future of care and caring and of social reproduction also focus on the here and now, raising issues of gaps in care and investment in this sector, addressing the overlooking of women's labor or gender gaps in social investment and in paid work through gender budgeting, developing new small-scale "close to home" strategies of cooperative production of food (see Agarwal 2018), and mobilizing trade union campaigning for international institutions to gender-mainstream policies at the global and state levels.

Nonstate initiatives to care for the planet are taking off; some, bear witness to harms done to the land in the past, such as the Knitting Nannas of Australia working with indigenous women: "We want to leave this land no worse than we found it, for our children and grandchildren."[4] Others, like the Xolobeni, anticipate harm and take legal action (Chapter 6); An important legal initiative has been young people taking their governments to the courts to protect their futures: "[I]n a first, in the US's first constitutional climate trial in 2023, the judge ruled in favor of 'a group of young plaintiffs who had accused state officials in Montana of violating their right to a healthy environment'" (Noor 2023).[5]

But all this activism also requires labor, in addition to the everyday labors of social reproduction (Chapter 6). "Hope is a discipline," writes Mariame Kabe (2021). "It's work to be hopeful. . . . Like, you have to put in energy, time and . . . it is a hard thing to maintain. But it matters to have it, to believe that it's possible, to change the world." Depletion attaches itself to these labors for change, often leading to burnout; the sustainability of social movements requires the redistribution of social reproductive work. Constant vigilance against backsliding and backlash also generates depletion—the two steps forward, one step back, or the political stasis after campaigns can lead to disappointment, disengagement, and depletion of not only political communities of struggle but also imagining new futures of transformation.

Transformation

Struggles toward transformation need more radical approaches that challenge the current status quo. Debates about Universal Basic

Income, about degrowth, postdevelopment, about commoning—of land and labor—all seek to transform our current modes of social reproduction, of people's well-being, and of the environments that we are embedded in. There is also a returning interest in ideas of Marxism and of socialism, of "economic arrangements and social practices that supplant dominant capitalist forms" of social and ecological reproduction (Yates 2021, 1034; Moore 2015; Saito 2023). Earlier experiments by socialist states to communize reproductive work failed because they overlooked the need for an infrastructure of support for social reproduction and spaces of intimacy where human relations can flourish; without discursive shifts and redistribution of social reproduction, the double burden continued depleting those who did social reproductive work (Davin 1976). This is why we need a politics of a regenerative state that is redistributive and replenishing and supports social infrastructure that might replenish those who are depleted (Rai, True, and Tanyag 2019). Thinking about commoning social reproduction is now under way (Dengler and Lang 2022; Federici 2019). Attention to ecological crises is leading to new ways of thinking about planetary and societal care together; the ecological untenability of the Western "imperial mode of living" (Brand and Wissen 2018) is making scholars and activists imagine "incremental, emancipatory decommodification and a commonization of care" through developing strategies for "communitarian and transformative caring commons" (Dengler and Lang 2022, 1; Federici 2019), which go beyond the "common pool resourcing" of Elinor Ostrom (1990). While still in an embryonic stage, such thinking can help us imagine new horizons of social reproduction and ecology-centered societies.

Future-ing imaginaries also include methodological approaches—GDP including unpaid social reproduction, for example. Although one could argue that the HHSAs are already telling us the value of this labor, the fact that GDP does not include either the depletion of the environment or the value of social reproduction means that policies based on these calculations of economic growth continue to compound and exacerbate the consequences of depletion; thus, campaigns to include both environmental and social reproductive depletion in GDP calculations continue. Another methodological future-ing could be jumping scale—thinking of scale not spatially but discursively by linking local struggles to national or global movements of change. Jones (1998, 26) argues that "[j]umping scales is not synonymous with a leap up, rather one must consider all scales as mutually implicated in any conflict." The shifting geopolitics of a globalized world is making this approach to scale particularly useful in connecting local to global struggles to reverse depletion—with sometimes successful and sometimes unsuccessful results.

Further, bringing into view the gendered and racialized crisis of care under capitalism can also help us imagine a different approach to borders and bordering. A less racialized and more hospitable approach to migration can surely address some of the panic about declining birth rates and aging populations? Utopic though this may sound, reimagining migration with the lens of social reproduction and vice versa might help challenge the violent borders of today's nation-states and help reverse depletion.

If "practical," "concrete," and "everyday" utopias and reimaginings of the good life (Panitch and Gindin 2000; Ollman 2005; Gornick and Meyers 2009; Cooper 2014; Rai 2018) can help us reimagine our world, then how do we approach change? If recognizing the depletion caused by unrecognized social reproductive work is important, so is the redistribution of resources that underpin the current state of affairs. This redistribution of care responsibilities within the home and investment in social infrastructure to support social reproduction at the level of the state are both critical to reverse depletion. But neither can come about on its own. Redistribution can be generated only through struggle, for which cross-border alliances are essential—whether these borders are of identities, of class, or of nationalities. However, feminist mobilizations for change have also been marked by inequalities— of class, race, and sexuality. Without developing alliances across these border-differences, change cannot materialize; alliances without recognition of histories of oppression and of unequal social relations can only be tense, fragile, and, in the long run, unsustainable.

Solidaristic alliances that are equal and strong militate against what Giroux (1986, 247) calls "the sheer weight of apocalypse." Building sustainable and reflexive solidarities that link networks working to reverse depletion is therefore an urgent political task. Boundaries provoke struggles, as Fraser (2016) has argued, but through these struggles new solidarities may be forged to redistribute resources and reverse depletion. Struggles to generate viable and sustained change need to examine themselves; what can build sustained and equal solidarities?

Transforming Solidarities, Solidarities for Transformation

Adneia, a young indigenous Yanomami woman from the Amazon, looks straight at the camera and speaks:

> Help us! Bring health back to this place!
> We want to live in peace. Be firm!
> You white people, see our reality! Open your minds! Don't let us
>   talk so gallantly and do nothing.
> White people! Tell your fathers and mothers. Explain to them.
>   Support us!
> You people from far away, put up a barrier here against the invaders.
> They don't listen to FUNAI[6], they have tried to kill us.
> This is what I ask of you, my friends: don't film me for nothing. I
>   don't want that.
> I want you to really help me.
> My children are suffering. This is very sad for us. I had to run away
>   with my kids from our own house. This is harrowing.
> I am very angry about this! Very angry! We have had enough
>   suffering!
> I am very upset. (Yanomami 2022)

Adneia's speech shows that asking for help does not imply being a supplicant; on the contrary, she shares her rage, her disappointments, and her hopes with those she addresses and expects to be heard. She has grown tired of the hand-wringing and wants sympathy and empathy to be backed up by concrete action. Decolonization is not a metaphor (Tuck and Yang 2012; see also this book's introduction); solidarities need to be built on the solid ground of the recognition of historic cruelties and dispossessions and addressed through reparations and redistribution.

The history of mobilizations shows that while solidarity appears as a framework for working together—"sisterhood is global"—it can also be excluding. The history of suffragettes and second-wave feminism opened up questions of race and of class distinctions that were called out by working-class and Black and ethnic-minority feminists (Amos and Parmar 1984; Einwohner et al. 2021). Naming and challenging these exclusions, as well as "refusing the politics of origins" (Madhok 2021) is part of the story of solidarity movements and when this is not done, an explanation of the fragility of solidaristic politics.

Speaking and listening across boundaries of difference is difficult enough at a personal level; to scale it up politically takes a great deal of effort, energy, attention, and care. As Jabri (2007, 724) writes, the "challenge is to articulate a mode of international politics, indeed a cosmopolitan politics, that is at once both internationalist in orientation as well as being cognisant of the inequalities that constitute the terrain of the human." Solidarities are developed in time and need to be sustained over time; processes of communication are important not just for building solidarities but also for maintaining them. Like disinvestment in the economy or the fraying of political institutions, the fracturing of solidarity can leave deep scars on the social fabric of life and on the possibilities of future alliance making. Also important are strategies to prevent burnout—as we saw in Chapter 6, depletion can attach itself to mobilizations and struggles and undermine the sustainability of activism (Reagon 2015, 358; Madhok and Rai 2010). Solidarity "is, at its core, a symmetrical, mutual, and reciprocal relation. . . . [I]t seems somehow to transcend the very dichotomy between altruistic and egoistic motivations" (Jaeggi 2001, 52). Thinking through what constitutes a *reflexive solidarity* by standing with others in struggle defined by historical processes to develop concrete forms of sociality is therefore critically important for reversing depletion (Rai 2024).

In writing this book I had two objectives: first, mapping and revealing the intensity and extensity of the problem of depletion, and second, to suggest how it might be reversed over time, for both human and ecological worlds that are being depleted in tandem. A structural analysis of capitalism and the marginalized place that social reproduction continues to occupy within it suggests that depletion is intensifying in the context of nonrecognition of social reproductive ecologies; mitigation as an individualized and often marketized and always deeply gendered and racialized strategy continues to be the most visible strategy for addressing depletion under global capitalism. Replenishment through state and nonstate support for social reproduction continues to be vulnerable to conservative pushbacks and attacks as right-wing forces see their material interests, wealth, and power threatened. And yet, although transformation is not imminent, it is being struggled for every day; new imaginaries of progressive change are taking shape and being shared, provoking new ways of reflection and strategizing for a less depleted future.

Depletion is a plea to recognize the costs of social reproduction, and to stop the harm to the ecologies of life-making and its flourishing through mobilizations of new imaginaries and activism that is both reflexive and sustainable. Reversing depletion is urgent and demands a solidaristic and transformative approach to world-making.

Notes

Introduction

1. In this book, the research focused on households that are largely hetero-normative and male-headed. However, some of the households are multigenerational and extended. Of course, households come in many different forms across the world—female-headed households have risen sharply, migration has led to global households spanning different countries and continents, LGBTQI+ households are now commonplace in many parts of the world. Households also shape-shift over time—extended, nuclear, and global households organize social reproduction differently, with varied consequences for those constituting each. Depletion is experienced across these different households, and also mitigated through household support.
2. Well-being effects of volunteering, for example, which are coded as "forms of payment in kind calculated as income equivalents" (Dowling 2016, 453).
3. Of course, as Zelizer (1989, 344) has argued, money has a social meaning—within the domestic sphere, it is "obtained in special ways, used for designated purposes, and even [has] a special vocabulary: allowance, pin money." This also, I would argue, legitimizes gendered social relations.
4. Winders and Smith (2019) provide an excellent summary of the debates on and imaginaries of social reproduction, which helps in mapping as well as analyzing the different feminist approaches and arguments about the epistemologies and ontologies underpinning social reproduction.
5. Take, for example, the development of care homes for elder care—from a position of horror of these in many parts of the Global South, to offering these as cut-price luxury to the older people of the Global North, to now offering marketized care in care homes to the upper-classes of local populations, these spaces of caring are becoming increasingly commodified. Issues of such marketized care governance that arise from this expansion have also changed and are changing (Harbishettar et al. 2021; Stewart 2023).
6. According to the IMF (2021), "Globally, 58 per cent of employed women work in the informal sector, and are more likely to be in the most precarious and low-paid categories of informal employment."

7. Sophisticated work on not only the organization of social reproduction, important to this book, but also on the contribution of social reproduction to the financialization of life and "the creation of promissory financial value" (Adkins and Dever 2016, 129) is also underway to help us understand the complexity and timeliness of this concept.

8. Of course, as we saw during COVID-19, the home become a site of work in both the Global North and the Global South. However, here too differences of gender, class and location are important—stretching of the working day for white-collar workers as opposed to the gig economy workers, expulsions of small factory workers in countries in the Global South, and increasing the burden of social reproduction in the Global North and South.

9. Take, for example, the discussion about valuing social reproduction—is it integral to or outside of capitalist circuits of production? Post-Fordist production of value in the context of deindustrialization and increased (though not everywhere) participation of female labor force shifted gender roles in multiple-earner households, but also, I would argue, extended and intensified depletion through the double burden of household and waged work.

10. For Tuck and Yang (2012), decolonization means repatriation of land, which has a very different politics attached to it. However, the point I want to make here is that decentering requires structural change, without which it remains limited.

Chapter 1

1. Even as I make final edits to the book, the crisis in Gaza has erupted. While I cannot, at this late stage, assess the impact of this conflict on social reproduction, I note that this crisis is showing us evidence of not only the consequences of depletion through long-term erosion of social and political life because of conflict and the carceral politics of this region, but the utter collapse of social reproduction under this current round of settler-colonial state violence.

2. We used the term "depletion" rather than "depreciation," which is the commonly used economic term for loss of value in capital goods. Depreciation in that sense denotes an identifiable, measurable economic value and triggers a clearly defined process for replacement, which is not always possible when dealing with the loss of human well-being.

3. "Inflow" and "outflow" are words that indicate large volumes transferred inside and outside over time, without necessary intentionality—so they capture systemic flows better than the terms "input" and "output."

4. Similar discourses on race were seen during the COVID-19 pandemic when Muslim and racialized minority communities were framed as "spreaders" of the infection (see Lingham, Rai, and Akhter forthcoming).

5. Of course, both men and women benefit from engaging in paid work. The point here is not that women should not or need not enter the labor market but that their unpaid work and the outflow of resources need to be recognized and reversed.

6. For a sophisticated analysis of the complexities between disposability and empowerment, see Ruwanpura and Hughes (2016).

7. UK Trade Union Council (TUC) report shows that "Black and minority ethnic (BME) workers are disproportionately affected by the growth of insecure work. Since 2011, the proportion of the working population in insecure work grew from 10.7 per cent to 11.8 per cent. BME workers have borne the brunt of this increase. In the last 11 years the proportion of BME workers in insecure employment has risen from 12.2 per cent to 17.8 per cent" (Creagh 2023, 1).

Chapter 2

1. I hope that rehearsing these measures and methodologies will be of use to those readers less familiar with some of the political and economic concepts, measures, and indices that are referred to here.

2. Depletion Data Browser, https://pjbogdanski.shinyapps.io/depletion/?fbc lid=IwAR26165g5rzgaaKnMixwwTBc-QaUF-b7LN2phMqM1Iq482kw 0oeJOcVlmvE, accessed February 28, 2024.

3. I do not have the space here to go into the debates about objectivity and scientific research, but I suggest that my approach also moves away from setting up a binary between qualitative and quantitative methods which tend to "close down the possibilities for the building of a feminist objectivity, an objectivity which Haraway insisted was crucial if feminists were to be able to make any meaningful claims towards knowing the world" (Adkins 2009, 326; see also Nanda 1996 and 2016), which argues for some measure of objectivity as a political imperative for challenging relativism and religious and nationalist claims and for monopolizing claim-making.

4. The object of Marx's theory of value was of course not market price but "what the [workers] produce[d] and … how they produce[d]" it ("German Ideology," in Elson 1979, 123).

5. The debate about the current mobilization of women into paid labor (see Harris 2004; McRobbie 2007) also raises issues of class and of depletion (see Chapters 3 and 4). While women of middle-class families can earn high salaries that can offset their social reproductive labor, women of the racialized minorities and working class and lower middle class can only look to increased levels of labor—both paid and unpaid—that intensify levels of their depletion, even as their wages contribute to the increased well-being and resources of the household, which makes social reproduction increasingly commodified and increases inequalities among women.

6. This also "provided a new way of imagining geopolitical space," Mitchell (1998, 90–91) argues, as the national economies came to be measured and confirmed the continuing dependence of postcolonial states, on the one hand, and weaponized measurement of economic growth to assert the dominance of the United States in the context of the Cold War, on the other.

7. As Mitchell (1998) has pointed out, this articulation of the economy is very new, overtaking the older political economy approaches of Adam Smith, Ricardo, and Marx. "Fixing" the economy through discourse reflected three aspects, he argues: "a new way for the nation-state to represent itself, a new representation of the international order, and a novel conception of politics as growth" (89).

8. The disciplinary role of the SNA can be seen clearly in the case of Norway, where national accounts for the period 1935–1943 and 1946–1949 included estimates of the value of unpaid household work. However, the introduction of the first UN international standard for national accounts caused Norway to omit the value of unpaid labor from 1950 in the interest of producing internationally comparable national account figures (Aslaksen and Koren 1996; Hoskyns and Rai 2007).

9. While I do not have the space to discuss this fully, environmental accountants have also developed the System of Integrated Environmental-Economic Accounting (SEEA) to "measure more accurately the structure, level and trends of socioeconomic performance for purposes of environmentally sound and sustainable development planning and policies" (Bartelmus Stahmer, and Tongeren 1991, 113; see also Bain 2007). The starting point for SEEA is that the negative effects of environmental pollution, the environmental externalities, lead to two different forms of

depletion: reduced output (when environmental depletion affects production such as the quality of water on agriculture), which is counted in the SNA, and reduced human welfare (health being affected by poor air quality), which is not counted. Further, while estimates of depreciation of manmade capital stocks are included in the national accounts, natural stocks, such as forests, which are "used up" in production increase net national product—but their loss is not recorded. Another measure of environmental depletion is the Index of Sustainable Economic Welfare introduced by Cobb and Daly (1989), which took into account long-term climate change costs and showed that U.S. sustainable economic welfare has risen much more slowly than GNP; the same has been revealed in the context of Indonesia and in China (Zhu, Liu, and Fang 2022, 12). Rai, Hoskyns, and Thomas (2014) built on these arguments about environmental depletion in their conceptualization of depletion through social reproduction.

10. For a discussion of the South African TUS, see Budlender (1999).

11. See Folbre (2006a, 193) for a discussion on this important issue: "The Australian Time Use Surveys of 1992 and 1997 registered large amounts of secondary care for two reasons. First, they included an explicitly coded activity that called attention to supervisory responsibilities. . . . Second, written instructions to respondents regarding secondary activities listed childminding as an example."

12. Bauman, Bittman, and Gershuny (2019) outline how time-use diaries can help measure health; however, they do not focus on issues of gendered inequality in time-use affecting stress levels and health outcomes.

13. While this is a rather old study, I think it is still valuable for two reasons: first, for its focus on stress as a depleting outcome of social reproductive labor, and second, as a reminder that very few such studies have been done, but more need to be done if we are to fully understand the important of measuring depletion.

14. See, for example, Topping and Butler (2023) on the U.K. Conservative government's policy of pushing people on benefits to take full-time work.

15. See, for example, the Multinational Time Use Study, https://timeuse.org/mtus.

16. Interestingly, she is not in favor of a monetary valuation of unpaid work, seeing this as an abstraction from the real situation.

17. I trialed this method first in New Delhi (see Chapters 3 and 4), then Jacqui True trialed it in Ukraine; we then applied this method in a major study of social reproduction and depletion under conditions of conflict in Myanmar and Sri Lanka (Rai and True 2020; Johnson and Lingham 2020).

Chapter 3

1. The names of the women we interviewed have been changed to ensure anonymity.
2. We hoped to write a paper together on the methodology, but Pujya's master's work made this impossible, and I too didn't write this until much later (Rai and True 2020).
3. While this group of women live in and are representative of the dominance of heteronormative male-headed families in India—in 2019 82.5% of households were headed by men (Statista 2024)—it is important to note the globally growing number of women-headed households. Households headed by women are most common in Northern America, at 47%; figures for Europe are 37%, Latin America and the Caribbean, 34%, and Oceania, 33%. The median prevalence of female-headed households is much lower in Africa, 27%, and lowest in Asia, 19% (UN 2017). Similarly, social reproductive work in LGBTQ+-headed families would raise similar but different issues for social reproduction and depletion.
4. It is important to note that households and homemaking vary according to household formations across class, religion, and caste; they would vary even more across urban/rural and national borders (Ruwanpura 2007).
5. A "regular social meeting of a group of women, held at either a member's house or a restaurant, where each person gives an amount of money and one is chosen to receive the whole sum," Oxford Learner's Thesaurus, https://www.oxfordlearnersdictionaries.com/definition/english/kitty-party#:~:text=(especially%20Indian%20English),to%20receive%20the%20whole%20sum.

Chapter 4

1. As before, it was Pujya Ghosh who mapped their journeys on the day.
2. In some countries, including India, public transport is gender segregated, with few separate carriages and some assigned seating in metro and buses, which are not enough during peak-time travel for work.
3. https://pjbogdanski.shinyapps.io/depletion/?fbclid=IwAR26165g5rzga aKnMixwwTBc-QaUF-b7LN2phMqM1Iq482kw0oeJOcVlmvE, accessed August 2, 2024.

4. Korzhenevych and Jain (2018, 733) also note that in higher income groups "women often choose to commute by car rather than using green modes of transportation."

5. The number of domestic workers in India ranges from official estimates of 4.2 million to unofficial estimates of more than 50 million. Girls and women make up the significant majority of domestic workers. Between 2000 and 2010, women accounted for 75% of the increase in the total number of domestic workers in India (http://ndwm.org/domestic-workers/).

6. In India, generally referred to as "auto."

7. In my study of this issue, I found that we still need much more work here; most of the studies I was able to access focused on women with disability and employment barriers or inequalities but with little to say about their care duties.

8. Chittaranjan Park is a Bengali-dominant area; Sabina is Bengali. So in deciding to live in Vasant Vihar she is not only paying more in monetary terms but also letting go of a community where she would feel socially comfortable.

9. In the United Kingdom claim to universal credit is linked to finding a job within a 90-minute travel limitation. According to the Department of Work and Pensions, "If any claimant does not take up a job within the 90 minute travelling limitation, Jobcentre advisers must explore the reason behind the claimant not taking up the job to establish whether they had 'good reason' to do so. The guidance on good reason sets out a nonexhaustive list of circumstances which should be considered when deciding this. This includes whether the claimant had caring responsibilities, and whether there are unavoidable expenses, such as travel or child care costs, which would be incurred if they amount to an unreasonably high proportion of the income they would have received from the job in question." Many women are falling foul of this regulation. https://www.whatdotheyknow.com/request/151018/response/368266/attach/2/reply.FoI.888.pdf?cookie_passthrough=1

10. As we found when researching care and caring during COVID-19, public transportation stoppages during lockdowns in the United Kingdom wreaked havoc with schedules of both paid and unpaid careers, leading to mental stress and physical exhaustion and therefore intensified depletion (Lingham, Rai, and Akhter forthcoming).

11. Return to workplaces is rapidly rising and hybrid working is being curtailed as companies try to make employees return to offices ('Never again': is Britain finally ready to return to the office? https://www.theguard

ian.com/business/2023/aug/12/never-again-is-britain-finally-ready-to-return-to-the-office). But for many gig economy workers this was never a choice.

12. There are new initiatives that are focused on walking in the city—the 15-minute city for instance, which suggests that all the amenities for everyday life should be within 15 minutes' walking or cycling distance of households. However, where introduced without consultation, and in absence of alternative systems of transport, this also leads to opposition, especially by libertarians and those invested in car-based economies (Partington 2023).

Chapter 5

1. The construction of the figure of "womenandchildren" (Enloe 2014) in the context of care has produced tensions between feminists who have challenged this elision and "those concerned with challenging the oppression of children [who] have often ended up in antagonistic oppositions" (Rosen and Twamley 2018, 2; Lim and Roche 2000).

2. The literature on children's care work largely uses the word "care" rather than "social reproduction" to describe this work; this chapter reflects this.

3. Twum-Danso et al. (2022) argue that childhood studies is framed by Global North scholars, journals, and epistemic hierarchies in the construction of a transnational childhood scientific discourse which does not reflect the complexities of childhoods in the Global South; assumptions about both Global North and Global South childhoods need to be challenged to develop more complex and sophisticated approaches to childhood studies.

4. Article 4 of the UNCRC: "Governments have a responsibility to take all available measures to make sure children's rights are respected, protected and fulfilled. This includes assessing domestic legislation and practice to ensure that the minimum standards set by the Convention are being met." Article 41 of the Convention points out that when a country already has higher legal standards than those seen in the Convention, the higher standards always prevail.

5. Olivier de Schutte, the current special rapporteur on poverty, underlined the Alston report and said that the levels of child poverty in the United Kingdom are "simply not acceptable" and the government is violating

international law (https://www.theguardian.com/society/2023/nov/05/ United Kingdom-poverty-levels-simply-not-acceptable-says-un-envoy-olivier-de-schutter).

6. The current Labour Party leadership has decided not to lift this cap if the party comes into power in 2024.

7. The Children and Family Act of 2014 further outlines, "A local authority that carry out a young carer's needs assessment must consider the assessment and decide—(a) whether the young carer has needs for support in relation to the care which he or she provides or intends to provide; (b) if so, whether those needs could be satisfied (wholly or partly) by services which the authority may provide under section 17; and (c) if they could be so satisfied, whether or not to provide any such services in relation to the young carer."

8. YCS is a charitable NGO that focuses on providing support for child carers in families where at least one person required care. YCS is also dependent upon soft money—the Big Lottery, Children in Need—and therefore is not able to extend its services, increase its reach, or sustain a strong staff over the long term. They are underfunded and overworked, unable to strategically plan ahead because of lack of resources. YCS has a target of 80 assessments done in a year. A referral leads to an assessment and an Action Plan. Sometimes referrals are prompted by what the social care sector calls "inappropriate care," such as bathing and changing clothes of disabled adults. This is work that most distinguishes child carers from their peers (Warren 2007) and can sometimes lead to triggering the interest of social care officials.

9. After consultation with the children, we decided that FEOT was not appropriate for this research; the children felt uncomfortable being recorded, and we felt that we would mark them out in school if we did shadow them.

10. Luttrell (2020) has also noted how the children in their study value their relationship with their mothers and appreciate the support that their mothers give them http://www.childrenframingchildhoods.com/digita linterludes/feeding-the-family/.

11. See Figure 2, "Percentage of unpaid carers and non-carers by age, Great Britain, 31 March to 25 April 2021: Coronavirus and the social impacts on unpaid carers in Great Britain" (UK Office for National Statistics). Child carers younger than 16 years are not included in this report, which makes analysis of the impact of COVID-19 on the younger cohort difficult.

Chapter 6

1. You can access this exhibition at *Postcards from Xolobeni* (2018), https:// thompierce.com/postcards-from-xolobeni. I am most grateful to Thom Pierce for allowing me to use his beautiful pictures. He says, "Being a photographer is not about being interested in photography, it's about being interested in the world" (https://www.itsnicethat.com/articles/thom-pierce-postcards-from-xolobeni-photography-290518). His generosity in sharing his work is part of his commitment to change.

2. See, for example, Chapter 4 and the effects of pollution on the health of those commuting to work.

3. For a discussion of mining, harm, care, and recognition of social reproduction, see Goldblatt and Rai (2018).

4. *Sharma v. Minister for the Environment in Australia* was a case focused on the duty of care of the environment minister to future generations; after an initial judgment in favor of the litigants, the Federal Court ruled that the minister had "no duty of care to Australian children to exercise her powers to approve the expansion of a coalmine so as to avoid the harmful effects of climate change." Sharma v Minister for the Environment: A setback for climate change claimants as landmark decision is overturned on appeal | White & Case LLP (whitecase.com).

5. SLAPP refers to a lawsuit filed strategically by a corporation against a group or activist opposing certain action taken by the corporation, usually in the realm of an environmental protest. Typical claims underlying a SLAPP suit are libel, slander, or restraint of business." Legal Information Institute, Cornell Law School, https://www.law.cornell.edu/wex/slapp_suit.

6. The Pondoland revolt of 1950–1961 is valorized in the Xolobeni area, and its history of struggle inspires those who struggle today. It was a popular struggle against the Bantu Authorities Act of 1951, which increased the power of the chiefs and increased taxes, a shift away from elected authority and reduction in popular participation; the Act was imposed without consultation. See https://www.sahistory.org.za/article/pondoland-revolt-1950-1961.

7. See the full judgment: http://www.saflii.org/za/cases/ZAGPPHC/2018/829.html.

8. Within international human rights law, this ambition for improvement is encapsulated in the right of everyone to the "continuous improvement of living conditions" in Article 11 of the International Covenant on Economic, Social and Cultural Rights. See Hohmann and Goldblatt (2021).

Conclusion

1. The painting by Soma Das is titled *Stupa*—in Sanskrit it means "heap" and in Buddhism it is a shrine used for meditation. Does the woman meditate on reversing depletion as she irons the heap of clothes before her?

2. See for example SpareRoom "Free accommodation in exchange for 15 hrs work p/w" Room to Rent from SpareRoom, https://www.spareroom.co.uk/flatshare/london/bayswater/2381695.

3. The continued separation of social reproductive and paid care work is evident in the ILO's formulation of the "5R framework for decent care work": "Recognize, reduce, **and redistribute unpaid** care work, and reward and represent paid care work by promoting decent work for care workers and guaranteeing their representation, social dialogue, and collective bargaining." This overlooks conditions of decent work for unpaid carers—absence of violence, adequate rest and sleep—as well as representation, which are needed for societal and state recognition of unpaid work. Ulrike Knobloch's (2013) 4 Vs are (1) avoiding (*vermeiden*), (2) modifying (*verändern*), (3) shifting (*verlagern*), and (4) redistributing (*verteilen*) unpaid care work.

4. https://knitting-nannas.com/about-us/the-nannafesto/.

5. Other such legal challenges to state policies, in Australia and India, for example, have failed. This strategy has, however, opened up a fertile terrain of political action to protect the environment.

6. FUNAI (National Indian Foundation) is the Brazilian government body that establishes and carries out policies relating to Indigenous peoples.

References

Abt, K. 1987. "Descriptive Data Analysis: A Concept between Confirmatory and Exploratory Data Analysis." *Methods of Information in Medicine* 26 (2): 77–88.

ActionAid. 2017. "Living Next to the Mine: Women's Struggles in Mining Affected Communities." https://www.actionaid.org.za/living-next-to-the-mine-womens-struggles-in-mining-affected-communities/.

Addati, L., U. Cattaneo, V. Esquivel, and I. Valarino. 2018. *Care Work and Care Jobs for the Future of Decent Work*. Geneva: International Labor Organization.

Abebe, T., and A. T. Kjørholt. 2009. "Social Actors and Victims of Exploitation: Working Children in the Cash Economy of Ethiopia's South." *Childhood* 16 (2): 175–194. https://doi.org/10.1177/0907568209104400.

Adkins, Lisa. 2009. "Feminism after Measure." *Feminist Theory* 10 (3): 323–339.

Adkins, Lisa, and Maryanne Dever. 2016. "The Financialisation of Social Reproduction: Domestic Labour and Promissory Value." In *The Post-Fordist Sexual Contract: Working and Living in Contingency*, edited by Lisa Adkins and Maryanne Dever, 129–145. Basingstoke: Palgrave Macmillan.

Adler, Rebecca A., Marius Claassen, Linda Godfrey, and Anthony R. Turton. 2007. "Water, Mining, and Waste: An Historical and Economic Perspective on Conflict Management in South Africa." *The Economics of Peace and Security Journal* 2 (2): 33–41. https://doi.org/10.15355/epsj.2.2.33.

Agarwal, Bina. 1994. *A Field of One's Own: Gender and Land Rights in South Asia*. Cambridge: Cambridge University Press.

Agarwal, Bina. 2018. "Can Group Farms Outperform Individual Family Farms? Empirical Insights from India." *World Development* 108: 57–73.

Ahmad, Sara. 2021. *Complaint!* Durham, NC: Duke University Press.

Ajunwa, Ifeoma, Kate Crawford, and Jason Schultz. 2017. "Limitless Worker Surveillance." *California Law Review* 105 (3): 735–776.

Ake, Claude. 1990. "Sustaining Development on the Indigenous." In *The Long-Term Perspective Study of Sub-Saharan Africa*, 7–21. Institutional and Sociopolitical Issues 3. Washington, DC: World Bank.

Akhter, Shahnaz, Juanita Elias, and Shirin M. Rai. 2022. "Being Cared for in the Context of Crisis: Austerity, COVID-19, and Racialized Politics." *Social Politics: International Studies in Gender, State & Society* 29 (4): 1121–1143.

Albertyn, Catherine. 2018. "African Constitution: Beyond Social Inclusion towards Systemic Justice." *South African Journal on Human Rights* 34 (3): 441–468.

Aldridge, Jo, and Saul Becker. 1993a. "Inside the World of Young Carers." *Care Link* (Kings Fund Journal) 19: 3.

Aldridge, Jo, and Saul Becker. 1993b. "Punishing Children for Caring: The Hidden Cost of Young Carers." *Children & Society* 74 (4): 376–387.

Aldridge, Jo, and Saul Becker. 2003. *Children Caring for Parents with Mental Illness: Perspectives of Young Carers, Parents and Professionals.* Bristol: Policy Press.

Aldridge J, and D. Sharpe. 2007. "Supporting Mum." *Mental Health Today* (Jul–Aug):16–17. PMID: 17712887.

Aldridge, J., and Wates, M. 2005. "Young Carers and Their Disabled Parents: Moving the Debate On." In *Disabled Parents and Their Children: Building a Better Future*, edited by T. Newman and M. Wates, 80–99. Ilford, UK: Barnardos.

Aldridge, Robert W., Dan Lewer, Srinivasa Vittal Katikireddi, Rohini Mathur, Neha Pathak, Rachel Burns, Ellen B. Fragaszy, et al. 2020. "Black, Asian and Minority Ethnic Groups in England Are at Increased Risk of Death from COVID-19: Indirect Standardisation of NHS Mortality Data." Wellcome Open Research 5. https://www.ncbi.nlm.nih.gov/pmc/articles/PMC7317462/#:~:text=Conclusion%3A%20Our%20analysis%20adds%20to,based%20on%20the%202011%20census, (Accessed 01.03.2024).

Alpers, Svetlana, Emily Apter, Carol Armstrong, Susan Buck-Morss, Tom Conley, Jonathan Crary, Thomas Crow, et al. 1996. "Visual Culture Questionnaire". *October* (77): 25–70. https://disparata.files.wordpress.com/2010/03/visualcultureoctober1996.pdf, (Accessed February 28, 2024).

Alston, Philip. 2018. Statement on Visit to the United Kingdom, by Professor Philip Alston, United Nations Special Rapporteur on Extreme Poverty and Human Rights. London, November 16. https://www.ohchr.org/documents/issues/poverty/eom_gb_16nov2018.pdf.

Amos, Valerie, and Pratibha Parmar. 1984. "Challenging Imperial feminism." Feminist Review 17.1: 3–19.

Andrews, Molly. 2014. *Narrative Imagination and Everyday Life.* Oxford: Oxford University Press.

Angelou, Maya. 1986. *Poems.* London: Bantam Books.

Angelou, Maya. 2013. *And Still I Rise.* New York: Random House.

Aoláin, Fionnuala Ní. 2009. "Exploring a Feminist Theory of Harm in the Context of Conflicted and Post-conflict Societies." *Queen's Law Journal* 35: 219.

Aradau, Claudia, and Jef Huysmans. 2014. "Critical Methods in International Relations: The Politics of Techniques, Devices and Acts." *European Journal of International Relations* 20 (3): 596–619.

Arif, Yasmeen. 2015. "The Audacity of Method." *Economic and Political Weekly* (Special Article) L (1) : 53–61.

As, Dagfinn. 1978. "Studies of Time-Use: Problems and Prospects." *Acta Sociologica* 21 (2): 125–141.

Ashwini, Deshpande, and Jitendra Singh. "Dropping Out, Being Pushed Out or Can't Get In? Decoding Declining Labour Force Participation of Indian Women." Discussion Paper series, IZA Institute of Labour Economics. IZA DP No. 14639. https://docs.iza.org/dp14639.pdf.

Aslaksen, Julie, and Charlotte Koren. 1996. "Unpaid Household Work and the Distribution of Extended Income: The Norwegian Experience." *Feminist Economics* 2 (3): 65–80.

Aslanbeigui, Nahid, Guy Oakes, and Nancy Uddin. 2010. "Assessing Microcredit in Bangladesh: A Critique of the Concept of Empowerment." *Review of Political Economy* 22 (2): 181–204.

Baek, Chung-Ah. 2022. "Lived Experiences of Cyclone Nargis: An Analysis of the Gendered Displacement of Burmese Women and Men." PhD diss., University of Warwick.

Bain, David. 2007. "Depletion of Renewable Environmental Resources." Issue paper for the London Group Meeting, Rome, December 17–19. https://mdgs.un.org/unsd/envaccounting/seearev/docs/LG12_14a.pdf.

Bakker, I. 2007. "Social Reproduction and the Constitution of a Gendered Political Economy." *New Political Economy* 12 (4): 541–556.

Bakker, I., and S. Gill. 2019. "Rethinking Power, Production, and Social Reproduction: Toward Variegated Social Reproduction." *Capital & Class* 43 (4): 503–523. https://doi.org/10.1177/0309816819880783.

Baleni and Others v Minister of Mineral Resources and others. 2018. High Court of the Republic of South Africa, Gauteng Division, Pretoria. Case No. 73768/2016. November 22, 2018. https://cer.org.za/wp-content/uploads/2018/11/Baleni-and-others-v-Minister-of-Mineral-Resources-and-others.pdf, (Accessed February 28, 2024),

Banerjee, Sneha, and Prabha Kotiswaran. 2021. "Divine Labours, Devalued Work: The Continuing Saga of India's Surrogacy Regulation." *Indian Law Review* 5 (1): 85–105.

Banks, Nina. 2020. "Black Women in the United States and Unpaid Collective Work: Theorizing the Reorganisation of Life, Work and Death." *Organization* 29 (3): 379–400.

Bannerji, Himani. 1995. *Thinking Through: Essays in Feminism, Marxism, and AntiRacism*. Toronto: Women's Press.

Barca, Stefania. 2014. "Telling the Right Story: Environmental Violence and Liberation Narratives." *Environment and History* 20 (4): 535–546.

Barker, K. 2004. *Review of Housing Supply: Delivering Stability—Securing Our Future Housing Needs. Final Report—Recommendations*. London: H.M. Treasury.

Barry, Monica. 2011. "'I Realised That I Wasn't Alone': The Views and Experiences of Young Carers from a Social Capital Perspective." *Journal of Youth Studies* 14 (5): 523–539.

Bartelmus, Peter, Carsten Stahmer, and Jan Van Tongeren. 1991. "Integrated Environmental and Economic Accounting: Framework for a SNA Satellite System." *Review of Income and Wealth* 37 (2): 111–148. https://doi.org/10.1111/j.1475-4991.1991.tb00350.x.

Basham, Victoria M., and Sergio Catignani. 2018. "War Is Where the Hearth Is: Gendered Labor and the Everyday Reproduction of the Geopolitical in the Army Reserves." *International Feminist Journal of Politics* 20 (2): 153–171. doi:10.1080/14616742.2018.1442736.

Bassel, Leah, and Akwugo Emejulu. 2017. *Minority Women and Austerity: Survival and Resistance in France and Britain*. Bristol: Policy Press.

Bauhardt, Christine. 2014. "Solutions to the Crisis? The Green New Deal, Degrowth, and the Solidarity Economy: Alternatives to the Capitalist Growth Economy from an Ecofeminist Economics Perspective." *Ecological Economics* 102: 60–68.

Bauhardt, Christine. 2018. "Nature, Care and Gender: Feminist Dilemmas." In *Feminist Political Ecology and the Economics of Care: In Search of Economic Alternatives*, edited by Christine Bauhardt and Wendy Harcourt, 16–35. London: Routledge.

Bauhardt, Christine, and Wendy Harcourt, eds. 2018. *Feminist Political Ecology and the Economics of Care: In Search of Economic Alternatives*. Routledge.

Bauman, Adrian, Michael Bittman, and Jonathan Gershuny. 2019. "A Short History of Time Use Research: Implications for Public Health." *BMC Public Health* 19 (Suppl 2): 607. https://doi.org/10.1186/s12889-019-6760-y.

Baxter, Richard, and Katherine Brickell. "For Home Unmaking." *Home Cultures* 11:133–144.

Beaujot, Roderic, and Robert Anderson. 2004. "Stress and Adult Health: Impact of Time Spent in Paid and Unpaid Work, and Its Division in Families." PSC Discussion Papers Series 18 (8): 1.

Becker, S. 2007. "Global Perspectives on Children's Unpaid Caregiving in the Family." *Global Social Policy* 7: 23–50.

Becker, Saul, Chris Dearden, and Jo Aldridge. 2001. "Children's Labour of Love? Young Carers and Care Work." In *Hidden Hands: International Perspectives on Children's Work and Labour*, edited by Phil Mizen, Chris Pole, and Angela Bolton, 70–88. London: Routledge Falmer Press.

Becker, Saul, Chris Dearden, and Jo Aldridge. 2000. "Young Carers in the UK: Research, Policy and Practice." *Research Policy and Planning* 18 (2): 13–22.

Bellis, Mark A., Karen Hughes, Kat Ford, Katie A. Hardcastle, Catherine A. Sharp, Sara Wood, Lucia Homolova, and Alisha Davies. 2018. "Adverse Childhood Experiences and Sources of Childhood Resilience: A Retrospective Study of Their Combined Relationships with Child Health and Educational Attendance." *BMC Public Health* 18: 792. https://doi.org/10.1186/s12889-018-5699-8.

Benaton, Tonimarie, Tamsin Bowers-Brown, Thomas Dodsley, Alix Manning-Jones, Jade Murden, Alexander Nunn, and The Plus One Community.

2020. "Reconciling Care and Justice in Contesting Social Harm through Performance and Arts Practice with Looked After Children and Care Leavers. *Children and Society* 34 (5): 337–459. doi:10.1111/chso.12370.

Bennie, Andrew. 2019. "Mining Will Not Bring Jobs to Xolobeni." *Daily Maverick*, January 15. https://www.dailymaverick.co.za/article/2019-01-15-mining-will-not-bring-jobs-to-xolobeni/?tl_inbound=1&tl_gro ups%5b0%5d=80895&tl_period_type=3&utm_medium=email&utm_c ampaign=First%20Thing%20Tuesday%2015%20January%202019%20C ell%20C%20Fibre&utm_content=First%20Thing%20Tuesday%2015%20 January%202019%20Cell%20C%20Fibre+CID_89a3f76ba9ca03f4b0d4e 725c8766a5b&utm_source=TouchBasePro&utm_term=Mining%20w ill%20not%20bring%20jobs%20to%20Xolobeni.

Bentley, Kristina A. 2005. "Are the Powers of Traditional Leaders in South Africa Compatible with Women's Equal Rights? Three Conceptual Arguments." *Human Rights Review* 6: 48–68.

Berger, John. 1972. *Ways of Seeing: Based on the BBC Television Series with John Berger*. London: British Broadcasting Corporation.

Berik, Günseli. 2018. "To Measure and to Narrate: Paths toward a Sustainable Future." Feminist Economics 24 (3): 136–159.

Bertolani, Barbara, and Paolo Boccagni. 2021. "Two Houses, One Family, and the Battlefield of Home: A Housing Story of Home Unmaking in Rural Punjab." *Geoforum* 127: 57–66.

Bhambra, Gurminder K. 2021. "Colonial Global Economy: Towards a Theoretical Reorientation of Political Economy." *Review of International Political Economy* 28 (2): 307–322.

Bhattacharya, Sumanta, and Bhavneet Kaur Sachdev. 2021. "Women Health in India: A Crucial Area Which Requires Attention and Change in the Outlook of Society." *International Journal of Recent Advances in Multidisciplinary Topics* 2 (11): 113–116. https://www.ijramt.com.

Bhattacharya, Tithi. 2017. *Social Reproduction Theory: Remapping Class, Recentering Oppression*. London: Pluto Press.

Bhattacharyya, Gargi. 2018. *Rethinking Racial Capitalism: Questions of Reproduction and Survival*. London: Rowman & Littlefield.

Bhowmick, Nilanjana. 2022. *Lies Our Mothers Told Us*. New Delhi: Aleph.

Biesecker, Adelheid, and Sabine Hofmeister. 2010. "(Re)productivity: Sustainable Relations Both between Society and Nature and between the Genders." *Ecological Economics* 69: 1703–1711.

Bird, Cassieleigh. 2018. "To What Extent Does Being a Young Carer Impact on an Individual's Educational Opportunities and Peer Group Relations?" Undergraduate diss., University of Derby.

Bird, Chloe E., and Allen M. Fremont. 1991. "Gender, Time Use, and Health." *Journal of Health and Social Behavior* 32 (June): 114–129.

Bissell, David. 2018. "How Your Commute is Changing You." World Economic Forum, in Collaboration with The Conversation. August 6. https://www.

weforum.org/agenda/2018/08/how-the-everyday-commute-is-changing-who-we-are/.

Biswas, Samata. 2021. "Bringing the Border Home: India Partition 2020." In *India's Migrant Workers and the Pandemic*, edited by Ritajyoti Bandyopadhyay, Paula Banerjee, Ranabir Samaddar, 250–262. London and New York: Routledge.

Bittle, Jake. 2023. *The Great Displacement: Climate Change and the Next American Migration*. New York: Simon & Schuster.

Blake-Holmes, Kate, and Andy McGowan. 2022. "'It's Making His Bad Days into My Bad Days': The Impact of Coronavirus Social Distancing Measures on Young Carers and Young Adult Carers in the United Kingdom." *Child & Family Social Work* 27 (1): 22–29.

Blanton, R., S. Blanton, and D. Peksen. 2019. "The Gendered Consequences of Financial Crises: A Cross-National Analysis." *Politics & Gender* 15 (4): 941–970. doi:10.1017/S1743923X18000545

Bloom, Kevin. 2019. "Mantashe in Xolobeni: A Master-Class in Coercive Dissembling." *Daily Maverick*, January 17. https://www.dailymaverick.co.za/article/2019-01-17-mantashe-in-xolobeni-a-master-class-in-coercive-diss embling/?tl_inbound=1&tl_groups[0]=80895&tl_period_type=3&utm_medium=email&utm_campaign=First%20Thing%20Thursday%2017%20 January%202019%20Mi-Plan&utm_content=First%20Thing%20Thurs day%2017%20January%202019%20Mi-Plan+CID_9a942eca1e6d87a57 1450c7371b9dde2&utm_source=TouchBasePro&utm_term=Mantashe%20 in%20Xolobeni%20A%20master-class%20in%20coercive%20dissembling.

BMA. 2018. "Feeling the Squeeze: The Local Impact of Cuts to Public Health Budgets in England." https://www. bma. org. uk/ collective- voice/ policy- and- research/ public- andpopulation-health/ public- health-budgets.

Boeri, Natascia. 2018. "Challenging the Gendered Entrepreneurial Subject: Gender, Development, and the Informal Economy in India." *Gender & Society* 32 (2): 157–179. https://doi.org/10.1177/0891243217750119.

Bolas, Helen, Anna Van Wersch, and Darren Flynn. 2007. "The Well-being of Young People Who Care for a Dependent Relative: An Interpretative Phenomenological Analysis." *Psychology and Health* 22 (7): 829–850.

Bond, Patrick. 2019. "Ecological-Economic Narratives for Resisting Extractive Industries in Africa." In *Environmental Impacts of Transnational Corporations in the Global South*, edited by Paul Cooney and William Sacher, 73–110. Bingley: Emerald. https://books.google.co.uk/books?id= XqB5DwAAQBAJ&pg=PA106&dq=multinational+corporations+and+ mining+south+africa&hl=en&sa=X&ved=2ahUKEwi_wcezjsjrAhWxolw KHd1kAbYQ6AEwBnoECAgQAg#v=onepage&q=multinational%20c orporations%20and%20mining%20south%20africa&f=false.

Boyden, J., C. Porter, I. Zharkevich, and K. Heissler. 2016. "Balancing School and Work with New Opportunities: Changes in Children's Gendered Time Use in Ethiopia (2006–2013)." *Young Lives Working Paper* 16.

Bray, Rachel. 2009. "A Literature Review on Child Carers in Angola, Nigeria, Uganda and Zimbabwe." Save the Children UK. https://resourcecentre.save thechildren.net/node/3738/pdf/3738.pdf.

Brenner, Johanna. 2000. *Women and the Politics of Class*. New York: Monthly Review Press.

Brensell and Habermann. 2001. "Community as a Site of Production." *Review of Black Political Economy* 47 (4): 343–362.

Brickell, Katherine, Fiorella Picchioni, Nithya Natarajan, Vincent Guermonda, Laurie Parsons, Giacomo Zanello, and Milford Batemane. 2020. "Compounding Crises of Social Reproduction: Microfinance, Over-indebtedness and the COVID-19 Pandemic." *World Development* 136: 1–4. https://doi.org/10.1016/j.worlddev.2020.105087.

Broom, Alex, Michelle Peterie, Katherine Kenny, Gaby Ramia, and Nadine Ehlers. 2023. "The Administration of Harm: From Unintended Consequences to Harm by Design." *Critical Social Policy* 43 (1): 51–75.

Broome, André. 2022. "Gaming Country Rankings: Consultancies as Knowledge Brokers for Global Benchmarks." *Public Administration* 100 (3): 554–570. doi:10.1111/padm.12809

Bryson, Valerie. 2007. *Gender and the Politics of Time: Feminist Theory and Contemporary Debates*. Policy Press.

Bubeck, Diemut Elisabet. 1995. *Care, Gender and Justice*. Oxford: Oxford University Press.

Buckingham, Susan. 2020. *Gender and Environment*. Routledge.

Buck-Morss, Susan. 1986. "The Flaneur, the Sandwichman and the Whore: The Politics of Loitering." *New German Critique* 39: 99–140.

Buckley, Doris, and Deirdre Budzyna. 2023. *The Whole Child: Development in the Early Years*. Creative Commons.

Budlender, Debbie, ed. 2010a. *Time Use Studies and Unpaid Care Work*. London: Routledge.

Budlender, Debbie. 2010b. "What Do Time Use Studies Tell Us about Unpaid Care Work? Evidence from Seven Countries." In *Time Use Studies and Unpaid Care Work*, edited by Debbie Budlender, 23–67. London: Routledge.

Burden-Stelly, Charisse. 2020. "Modern U.S. Racial Capitalism: Some Theoretical Insights." *Monthly Review*, July 1. monthlyreview.org/2020/07/01/modern-u-s-racial-capitalism/.

Buss, Doris. 2015. "Measurement Imperatives and Gender Politics: An Introduction." *Social Politics: International Studies in Gender, State & Society* 22 (3): 381–389.

Butler, Felicity, and Catherine Hoskyns. 2017. "Valuing Unpaid Labour in Community Fair Trade Products: A Case Study of the Contract between The Body Shop International and a Nicaraguan Sesame Cooperative." In *Gender Equality and Responsible Business*, edited by Kate Grosser, Lauren McCarthy, Maureen A. Kilgour, 154–169. New York: Routledge.

Butler, James. 2023. "This Concerns Everyone." *London Review of Books*, March 2.

Bywaters, Paul, Geraldine Brady, Lisa Bunting, Brigid Daniel, Brid Featherstone, Chantel Jones, Kate Morris, Jonathan Scourfield, Tim Sparks, and Calum Webb. 2017. "Inequalities in English Child Protection Practice under Austerity: A Universal Challenge?" *Child and Family Social Work* 23 (1): 53–61. https://doi.org/10.1111/cfs.12383.

Camey Castañeda, Itzá, Laura Sabater, Cate Owren, and A. Emmett Boyer. 2020. *Gender-Based Violence and Environment Linkages: The Violence of Inequality*. International Union for Conservation of Nature and Natural Resources, USAID.

Camilletti, Elena, Prerna Banati, and Sarah Cook. 2018. "Children's Roles in Social Reproduction: Re-examining the Discourse on Care through a Child Lens." *Journal of Law, Social Justice and Global Development* (21). http://www.lgdjournal.org/wp-content/uploads/2018/06/3_CAMILLETTI_BANATI_COOK_LDG_GDSI_I21_2018.pdf.

Campt, Tina M. 2017. *Listening to Images*. Durham, NC: Duke University Press.

Cantillon, Sara, Odile Mackett, and Sara Stevano. 2023. *Feminist Political Economy: A Global Perspective*. Newcastle upon Tyne, UK: Agenda.

Carers' Trust UK. n.d. "Know Your Rights." https://carers.org/downloads/help-and-advice-section/knowyourrights.pdf, (Accessed on 29 February 2024).

Cass, Bettina, Ciara Smyth, Trish Hill, Megan Blaxland, and Myra Hamilton. 2009. "Young Carers in Australia: Understanding the Advantages and Disadvantages of Their Care Giving." Social Policy Research Paper No. 38. Australian Government Department of Families, Housing, Community Services and Indigenous Affairs, Canberra. https://www.arts.unsw.edu.au/sites/default/files/documents/26_Social_Policy_Research_Paper_38.pdf.

Cavallero, Lucí, and Verónica Gago. 2021. *A Feminist Reading of Debt*. London: Pluto Press.

Cele, S'thembile. 2018. "Mantashe: Xolobeni Ruling Means We Could Have No Mining in SA." *City Press*, November 22. https://www.news24.com/citypress/Business/mantashe-xolobeni-ruling-means-we-could-have-no-mining-in-sa-20181122.

Centre for Cities. 2024. City Factsheet: Coventry. https://www.centreforcities.org/city/coventry/, (Accessed February 27, 2024).

Chakraborty, Shiney. 2019. Why Are So Few Delhi Women Participating in the Workforce?" *The Wire*. https://thewire.in/labour/why-are-so-few-delhi-women-participating-in-the-workforce.

Chama, Brian. 2010. "Economic Development at the Cost of Human Rights: China Nonferrous Metal Industry in Zambia." *Human Rights Brief* 17 (2): 2–7.

Chant, Sylvia. 2008. "The 'Feminisation of Poverty' and the 'Feminisation' of Anti-Poverty Programmes: Room for Revision?" *Journal of Development Studies* 44 (2): 165–197. doi:10.1080/00220380701789810.

Chattopadhyay, Raghabendra, and Esther Duflo. 2004. "Impact of Reservation in Panchayati Raj: Evidence from a Nationwide Randomised Experiment." *Economic and Political Weekly* 39 (9): 979–986.

Chattopadhyay, S., and S. Chowdhury. 2022. "Female Labour Force Participation in India: An Empirical Study." *The Indian Journal of Labour Economics*. 65: 59–83. https://doi.org/10.1007/s41027-022-00362-0.

Chatzidakis, Andreas, Jamie Hakim, Jo Littler, Catherine Rottenberg and Lynne Segal. 2020. *The Care Manifesto: The Politics of Interdependence*. London: Verso Books.

Chaudhary, Ruchika, and Sher Verick. 2014. "Female Labour Force Participation in India and Beyond. ILO Asia-Pacific Working Paper Series. http://www.oit.org/wcmsp5/groups/public/---asia/---ro-bangkok/---sro-new_delhi/documents/publication/wcms_324621.pdf.

Chelli, Francesco Maria, Mariateresa Ciommi, and Chiara Gigliarano. 2013. "The Index of Sustainable Economic Welfare: A Comparison of Two Italian Regions. *Procedia: Social and Behavioral Sciences* 81: 443–448.

Chhachhi, Amrita. 2022. "Crisis, Care and Transformation: A Conversation with Diane Elson." *Development and Change* 53 (6).

Chikhradze, Nino, Christiane Knecht, and Sabine Metzing. 2017. "Young Carers: Growing Up with Chronic Illness in the Family—A Systematic Review 2007–2017." *Journal of Compassionate Health Care* 4: 12. doi:10.1186/s40639-017-0041-3.

Children's Commissioner. 2019. "Vulnerable Groups and Latest Data." https://www.childrenscommissioner.gov.uk/wp-content/uploads/2019/07/cco-vulnerability-2019-summary-table.pdf.

Children's Commissioner. 2022. The Big Ask Voices: Shining a Light on Young Carers. https://www.childrenscommissioner.gov.uk/blog/the-big-ask-voices-shining-a-light-on-young-carers/#:~:text=The%20Children's%20Society%20says%20there,aware%20of%20their%20caring%20responsibilities. (Accessed 01.03.2024).

Children's Society a. n.d. "Can I Claim a Carers Allowance?" https://www.childrenssociety.org.uk/advice-hub/can-i-claim-young-carers-allowance.

Children's Society b. n.d. "Child Refugee Statistics." https://www.childrenssociety.org.uk/what-we-do/our-work/refugee-and-migrant-children/child-refugee-statistics#:~:text=Currently%20the%20UK%20is%20home,result%20of%20their%20asylum%20cases.&text=Wherever%20they're%20from%2C%20refugees,in%20their%20new%20home%20countries.

Children's Society n.d.c. "10 Facts about Child Refugees." https://www.childrenssociety.org.uk/what-we-do/our-work/refugee-and-migrant-children/facts-about-child-refugees.

Children's Society d. n.d. "Facts about Young Carers." childrenssociety.org.uk.

Children's Society. 2013. "Hidden from View: The Experiences of Young Carers in England." https://www.childrenssociety.org.uk/sites/default/files/2020-10/hidden_from_view_final.pdf, (Accessed February 27, 2024).

Chilmeran, Yasmin, and Nicola Pratt. 2019. "The Geopolitics of Social Reproduction and Depletion: The Case of Iraq and Palestine." *Social Politics: International Studies in Gender, State & Society* 26 (4, Winter): 586–607. https://doi.org/10.1093/sp/jxz035.

choi, shine, Natália Maria Félix de Souza, Amy Lind, Swati Parashar, Elisabeth Prügl, and Marysia Zalewski. 2022. "Nurturing a Robust Dialogic and Collaborative Space of Accountability and Transformation." *International Feminist Journal of Politics* 24:1–4.

Chopra, D., and E. Zambelli. 2017. "No Time to Rest: Women's Lived Experiences of Balancing Paid Work and Unpaid Care Work." Report, IDS, November. https://www.ids.ac.uk/publications/no-time-to-rest-womens-lived-experiences-of-balancing-paid-work-and-unpaid-care-work/.

Christensen, Hilda Rømer. 2019. "Gendering Mobilities and (In)Equalities in Post-Socialist China." In *Integrating Gender into Transport Planning: From One to Many Tracks*, edited by Christina Lindkvist Scholten and Tanja Joelsson, 249–269. Cham: Palgrave Macmillan.

Clark, Ben, Kiron Chatterjee, Adam Martin, and Adrian Davis. 2020. "How Commuting Affects Subjective Wellbeing." *Transportation* 47: 2777–2805.

Clay, Dan, Caitlin Connors, Naomi Day, Marina Gkiza, with Jo Aldridge. 2016. "The Lives of Young Carers in England." Qualitative Report to DfE. https://assets.publishing.service.gov.uk/government/uploads/system/uploads/attachment_data/file/498115/DFE-RR499_The_lives_of_young_carers_in_England.pdf.

Clement, Viviane, Kanta Kumari Rigaud, Alex de Sherbinin, Jones Bryan, Susana Adamo, Jacob Schewe, Nian Sadiq, and Elham Shabahat. 2021. *Groundswell Part 2: Acting on Internal Climate Migration Groundswell*. Washington, DC: World Bank.

Cobb, John, and Herman Daly. 1989. *For the Common Good: Redirecting the Economy toward Community, the Environment and a Sustainable Future*. Boston, MA: Beacon Press.

Cock, Jacklyn. 2018. "The Climate Crisis and a 'Just Transition' in South Africa: An Eco-Feminist-Socialist Perspective." In *Climate Crisis: South African and Global Democratic Eco-Socialist Alternatives*, edited by Vishwas Satgar, 210–230. Wits University Press

Cohen, A., and B. Morgan. 2023. "Prefigurative Legality." *Law & Social Inquiry* 48 (3): 1053–1082. https://doi.org/10.1017/lsi.2023.4.

Cohen, Philip. 2013. "'Women Own 1% of World Property': A Feminist Myth That Won't Die." *The Atlantic*, March. https://www.theatlantic.com/sexes/archive/2013/03/women-own-1-of-world-property-a-feminist-myth-that-wont-die/273840/.

Coleman, Mike. 2016. "A Triumph for Rural Land Rights Holders." Wild Coast. December 14. https://www.wildcoast.co.za/xolobeni.

Collins, Jane L. 2016. "Expanding the Labor Theory of Value. *Dialect Anthropology* 40:103–123. doi:10.1007/s10624-016-9418-5.

Conaghan, Joanna. 2002. "Law, Harm and Redress: A Feminist Perspective." *Legal Studies* 22 (3): 319–339. https://doi.org/10.1111/j.1748-121X.2002.tb00196.x.

Conde, Marta. 2017. "Resistance to Mining: A Review." *Ecological Economics* 132: 80–90.

Connell, Raewyn. 2014. "The Sociology of Gender in Southern Perspective." *Current Sociology* 62 (4): 550–567.

Conradi, Elisabeth. 2020. "Theorising Care: Attentive Interaction or Distributive Justice?" *International Journal of Care and Caring* 4 (1): 25–42 https://doi.org/10.1332/239788219X15633663863542.

Conway, Zoe. 2016. "Care Workers Sue Council Contractor in Minimum Wage Battle. BBC, September 14. https://www.bbc.co.uk/news/uk-37350750.

Cooney, Paul, and William Sacher Freslon, eds. 2018. "Environmental Impacts of Transnational Corporations in the Global South. Special issue of *Research in Political Economy* 33. https://doi.org/10.1108/S0161-723020180000033010.

Cooper, Davina. 2014. *Everyday Utopias*. London: Duke University Press.

Cornwell, Benjamin, Jonathan Gershuny, and Oriel Sullivan. 2019. "The Social Structure of Time: Emerging Trends and New Directions." *Annual Review of Sociology* 45: 301–320.

Costa, Pedro, and Luísa Ribas. 2019. "AI Becomes Her: Discussing Gender and Artificial Intelligence." *Technoetic Arts: A Journal of Speculative Research* 17 (1–2): 171–193. https://doi.org/10.1386/tear_00014_1.

Coventry City Council. 2019. "Coventry Carers' Strategy 2016–2019: Improving Lives for Coventry Carers." https://www.coventry.gov.uk/carers-support/coventry-carers-strategy#:~:text=Coventry%20Carers'%20Strategy%202016%20%2D%202019&text=The%20strategy%20is%20based%20on,areas%20to%20support%20these%20priorities.

Coventry City Council. n.d. "Young Carers and Young Adult Carers." https://www.coventry.gov.uk/info/76/carers_support/923/young_carers_and_young_adult_carers.

Cox, Tom, Jonathan Houdmont, and Amanda Griffiths. 2006. "Rail Passenger Crowding, Stress, Health and Safety in Britain." *Transportation Research Part A: Policy and Practice* 40 (3): 244–258.

Creagh, Matt. 2023. "Insecure Work in 2023: The Impact on Workers and an Action Plan to Deliver Decent Work for Everyone." TUC. https://www.coventry.gov.uk/carers-support/coventry-carers-strategy#:~:text=Coventry%20Carers'%20Strategy%202016%20%2D%202019&text=The%20strategy%20is%20based%20on,areas%20to%20support%20these%20priorities.

Crenshaw, Kimberlé. 1989. "Demarginalizing the Intersection of Race and Sex: A Black Feminist Critique of Antidiscrimination Doctrine, Feminist Theory and Antiracist Politics." *University of Chicago Legal Forum* 1989 (1): 139–167.

Criado Perez, Caroline. 2019. *Invisible Women: Exposing Data Bias in a World Designed for Men*. New York: Abrams Press.

Cusicanqui, Silvia Rivera. 2012. "Ch'ixinakax utxiwa: A Reflection on the Practices and Discourses of Decolonization." *South Atlantic Quarterly* 111 (1): 95–109.

Dalla Costa, Mariarosa, and Selma James. 1972. *The Power of Women and the Subversion of the Community*. Bristol: Falling Wall Press.

Daly, M., A. R. Sutin, and E. Robinson. 2020. "Longitudinal Changes in Mental Health and the COVID-19 Pandemic: Evidence from the UK Household Longitudinal Study." *Psychological Medicine* 52 (13): 2549–2558. https://doi.org/10.1017/S0033291720004432. https://www.ncbi.nlm.nih.gov/pmc/articles/PMC7737138/.

Daly, Mary. 2021. "The Concept of Care: Insights, Challenges and Research Avenues in COVID-19 Times." *Journal of European Social Policy* 31 (1): 108–118.

Dannemann, Teodoro, Boris Sotomayor-Gómez, and Horacio Samaniego. 2018. "The Time Geography of Segregation during Working Hours." *Royal Society Open Science* 5 (10): 180749.

Dannreuther, Charles. 2019. "Silencing the Social: Debt and Depletion in UK Social Policy." *Capital & Class* 43 (4): 599–615.

Dasgupta, Partha. 2021. *The Economics of Biodiversity: The Dasgupta Review*. London: HM Treasury.

Dasgupta, Jashodhara, and Sona Mitra. 2020. "A Gender-Responsive Policy and Fiscal Response to the Pandemic." *Economic and Political Weekly* 55 (22) May 30.

Darzi, Ara, Harry Quilter-Pinner, and Tom Kibasi. 2018. *Better Health and Care For All: A 10-Point Plan For the 2020s*. The Lord Darzi Review of Health and Care Final Report. Institute For Public Policy Research.

Datta, Ayona. 2020. "The 'Smart Safe City': Gendered Time, Speed, and Violence in the Margins of India's Urban Age." *Annals of the American Association of Geographers* 110 (5): 1318–1334. doi:10.1080/24694452.2019.1687279.

Davies, Christine. 2020. "A Quick Guide to Quantitative Research in the Social Sciences."

Davies, Karen. 2001. "Responsibility and Daily Life: Reflections over Timespace." In *Timespace*, edited by Jon May and Nigel Thrift, 133–148. London: Routledge.

Davin, Delia. 1976. *Women-Work: Women and the Party in Revolutionary China*. Oxford: Clarendon Press.

Davis, Angela. 1983. *Women, Race and Class*. New York: Vintage Books.

Davis, Rebecca. 2020. "Mining Case Poses Big Questions about the Right of Business to Silence Dissent. *Daily Maverick*, June 9. https://www.dailymaverick.co.za/article/2020-06-09-mining-case-poses-big-questions-about-the-right-of-business-to-silence-dissent/.

Dearden, Chris, and Jo Aldrich. 2010. "Young Carers: Needs, Rights and Assessment." In *The Child's World: The Comprehensive Guide to Assessing Children in Need*, edited by Jan Horwath, 214–228. London: Jessica Kingsley.

de Certeau, Michel. 1988. *The Practice of Everyday Life*. Translated by Steven Rendall. University of California Press.

DfE (Department of Education). 2018. "The Annual Report of Her Majesty's Chief Inspector of Education, Children's Services and Skills 2017/18." Ofsted. December 4. https://assets.publishing.service.gov.uk/media/5c0692f6ed915 d7460c9dba9/29523_Ofsted_Annual_Report_2017-18_041218.pdf.

DeLeo, Rob. 2016. *Anticipatory Policymaking: When Government Acts to Prevent Problems and Why It Is So Difficult*. New York: Routledge.

Deloitte. 2022. Global Health Care Outlook. https://www.deloitte.com/global/en/Industries/life-sciences-health-care/perspectives/global-health-care-sector-outlook.html, (Accessed February 29, 2024).

Dengler, Corinna, and Miriam Lang. 2022. "Commoning Care: Feminist Degrowth Visions for a Socio-Ecological Transformation." *Feminist Economics* 8 (1): 1–28. doi:10.1080/13545701.2021.1942511.

Dengler, Corinna, and Birte Strunk. 2017. "The Monetized Economy versus Care and the Environment: Degrowth Perspectives on Reconciling an Antagonism." *Feminist Economics* 24 (3): 160–183 doi:10.1080/13545701.2017.1383620.

Deshpande, Ashwini, and Naila Kabeer. 2019. "(In)visibility, Care and Cultural Barriers: The Size and Shape of Women's Work in India." Discussion Papers Series in Economics, DP No.04/19. London School of Economics. http://eprints.lse.ac.uk/100992/.

Deshpande, Ashwini, and Jitendra Singh. 2021. "Dropping Out, Being Pushed Out or Can't Get In? Decoding Declining Labour Force Participation of Indian Women." IZA Discussion Papers, No. 14639. Institute of Labor Economics, Bonn.

Dewan, Ritu, Jashodhara Dasgupta, Sona Mitra, and Sruthi Kutty. 2023. "Towards a Feminist Fiscal Policy in a Post-pandemic Economy." *Economic and Political Weekly* 58 (27). https://www.epw.in/journal/2023/27/special-articles/towards-feminist-fiscal-policy-%C2%A0-post-pandemic.html, (Accessed February 29, 2024).

Di Chiro, Giovanna. 2008. "Living Environmentalisms: Coalition Politics, Social Reproduction, and Environmental Justice." *Environmental Politics* 17 (2): 276–298. doi:10.1080/09644010801936230.

DNA India. 2013. "Only 15% Women Feel Safe in Public Transport." https://www.dnaindia.com/mumbai/report-only-15-women-feel-safe-in-public-transport-1884478. doi:10.1177/02537176211021785.

Doron, Assa, and Ira Raja. 2015. "The Cultural Politics of Shit: Class, Gender and Public Space in India." *Postcolonial Studies* 18 (2): 189–207.

Dowling, Emma. 2016. "Valorised but Not Valued? Affective Remuneration, Social Reproduction and Feminist Politics beyond the Crisis." *British Politics* 11: 452–468. https://doi.org/10.1057/s41293-016-0036-2.

Dowling, Emma. 2021. *The Care Crisis: What Caused It and How Can We End It?* London: Verso.

Druckman, Angela, and Simon Mair. 2019. "Wellbeing, Care and Robots: Prospects for Good Work in the Health and Social Care Sector." CUSP Working Paper 21. University of Surrey, Guildford.

Dugarova, Esuna. 2020. "Unpaid Care Work in Times of the COVID-19 Crisis: Gendered Impacts, Emerging Evidence and Promising Policy Responses." Paper prepared for the UN Expert Group Meeting Families in Development: Assessing Progress, Challenges and Emerging Issues. https://www.un.org/development/desa/family/wp-content/uploads/sites/23/2020/09/Duragova.Paper_.pdf.

Duijs, Saskia Elise, Anouk Haremaker, Zohra Bourik, Tineke A. Abma, and Petra Verdonk. 2021. "Pushed to the Margins and Stretched to the Limit: Experiences of Freelance Eldercare Workers during the Covid-19 Pandemic in the Netherlands." *Feminist Economics* 27 (1–2): 217–235. https://doi.org/10.1080/13545701.2020.1845389.

Durante, Federica, and Susan T Fiske. 2017. "How Social-Class Stereotypes Maintain Inequality." *Current Opinion in Psychology* 18: 43–48. https://doi.org/10.1016/j.copsyc.2017.07.033.

Duryea, Suzanne, and Mary Arends-Kuenning. 2003. "School Attendance, Child Labor and Local Labor Market Fluctuations in Urban Brazil." *World Development* 31 (7): 1165–1178.

Ebrahim, Zofeen T. 2023. "How Many More Poor Child Workers Must Die in Pakistan before Change Happens?" *Guardian*, August 28. https://www.theguardian.com/global-development/2023/aug/28/fatima-furiro-how-many-more-poor-child-workers-must-die-in-pakistan-before-change-happens.

Economic Times. 2019. "Indians Spend 7% of Their Day Getting to Their Office." September 3. https://economictimes.indiatimes.com/jobs/indians-spend-7-of-their-day-getting-to-their-office/articleshow/70954228.cms?utm_source=contentofinterest&utm_medium=text&utm_campaign=cppst.

Edholm, F., O. Harris, and K. Young. 1978. "Conceptualising Women." *Critique of Anthropology* 3 (9–10): 101–131.

Edmonds, Eric V., and Nina Pavcnik. 2005. "Child Labor in the Global Economy." *Journal of Economic Perspectives* 19 (1, Winter): 199–220.

Einwohner, Rachel L., Kaitlin Kelly-Thompson, Valeria Sinclair-Chapman, Fernando Tormos-Aponte, S. Laurel Weldon, Jared M. Wright, and Charles Wu. 2021. "Solidarity in Action." *Social Politics: International Studies in Gender, State & Society* 28 (3): 704–729.

EJAtlas. 2019. "Pondoland Wild Coast Xolobeni Mining Threat, South Africa." Environmental Justice Atlas. https://ejatlas.org/conflict/pondoland-wild-coast-xolobeni-mining-threat-south-africa, (Accessed February 29, 2024).

Elias, Juanita. 2009. "Gendering Liberalisation and Labour Reform in Malaysia: Fostering 'Competitiveness' in the Productive and Reproductive Economies." *Third World Quarterly* 30 (3): 469–483.

Elias, Juanita, Ruth Pearson, Belinda Phipps, Shirin M. Rai, Samantha Smethers, and Daniela Tepe-Belfrage. 2016. "Towards a New Deal for Care and Carers." Report of the PSA Commission on Care. https://wrap.warwick.ac.uk/92935/7/WRAP-web-care-comission-towards-a-new-deal-for-care-and-carers-2017.pdf.

Elias, Juanita, and Shirin M. Rai. 2015. "The Everyday Gendered Political Economy." *Politics & Gender* 11 (2): 424–429.

Elias, Juanita, and Shirin M. Rai. 2019. "Feminist Everyday Political Economy: Space, Time, and Violence." *Review of International Studies* 45 (2): 201–220.

Elias, Juanita, and Adrienne Roberts. 2016. "Feminist Global Political Economies of the Everyday: From Bananas to Bingo." *Globalizations* 13 (6): 787–800.

Ellis, Estelle. 2020. "Game-Changing Xolobeni Judgment Orders Applications for Mining Licences to Be Made Public." *Daily Maverick*, September 14. https://www.dailymaverick.co.za/article/2020-09-14-game-changing-xolobeni-judgment-orders-applications-for-mining-licences-to-be-made-public/.

Elson, Diane. 1979. *Value: The Representation of Labour in Capitalism*. London: CSE Books.

Elson, Diane. 1998. "The Economic, the Political and the Domestic: Businesses, States and Households in the Organisation of Production." *New Political Economy* 3 (2): 189–208.

Elson, Diane. 2000. "The Progress of Women: Empowerment and Economics." In *The Progress of the World's Women*, edited by Karen Judd, 16–36. New York: UNIFEM.

Elson, Diane. 2012. "Social Reproduction in the Global Crisis: Rapid Recovery or Long-Lasting Depletion?" In *The Global Crisis and Transformative Social Change*, edited by Peter Utting, Shahra Razavi, and Rebecca Varghese Buchholz, 63–80. UK: Palgrave Macmillan.

Elson, Diane. 2017. "Recognize, Reduce, and Redistribute Unpaid Care Work: How to Close the Gender Gap March." *New Labor Forum* 26 (2): 109579601770013. doi:10.1177/1095796017700135.

Elson, Diane, and Ruth Pearson. 1981. "'Nimble Fingers Make Cheap Workers': An Analysis of Women's Employment in Third World Export Manufacturing." *Feminist Review* (7, Spring): 87–107.

Enloe, Cynthia. 2014. *Bananas, Beaches and Bases: Making Feminist Sense of International Politics*. 2nd Edition. Berkeley: University of California Press.

Ernaux, Annie. 2018. *The Years*. Translated by Alison L. Strayer. London: Fitzcarraldo Editions.

Esquivel, Valeria, Debbie Budlender, Nancy Folbre, and Indira Hiraway. 2008. "Explorations: Time-Use Surveys in the South." *Feminist Economics* 14 (3): 107–152.

Eurostat. 2019. "Time-Use Survey (TUS)." https://ec.europa.eu/eurostat/cache/metadata/en/tus_esms.htm#cost_burden1644268709276.

Evans, R. 2010. "Children's Caring Roles and Responsibilities within the Family in Africa." *Geography Compass* 4 (10): 1477–1496.

FAO. 2018. "The Gender Gap in Land Rights. http://www.fao.org/3/I8796EN/i8796en.pdf.

FAO. n.d. "Women Feed the World." http://www.fao.org/3/x0262e/x0262e16.htm.

Farber, Steven, Morton O'Kelly, Harvey J. Miller, and Tijs Neutens, l. 2015. "Measuring Segregation Using Patterns of Daily Travel Behavior: A Social Interaction Based Model of Exposure." *Journal of Transport Geography* 49: 26–38.

Farris, Sara R. 2019. "Social Reproduction and Racialized Surplus Populations." In *Capitalism: Concept, Idea, Image. Aspects of Marx's Capital Today*, edited by Peter Osborne, Éric Alliez, and Eric-John Russell, 121–134. London: CRMEP Books.

Fashola, Muibat Omotola, Veronica Mpode Ngole-Jeme, and Olubukola Oluranti Babalola. 2016. "Heavy Metal Pollution from Gold Mines: Environmental Effects and Bacterial Strategies for Resistance." *International Journal of Environmental Research and Public Health Review* 26 (13): 1047. doi:10.3390/ijerph13111047.

Fawcett, Robyn, Emily Gray, and Alexander Nunn. 2023. "Depletion through Social Reproduction and Contingent Coping in the Lived Experience of Parents on Universal Credit in England." *Social Politics: International Studies in Gender, State & Society* 30 (Winter, 4): 1040–1063. https://doi.org/10.1093/sp/jxad018.

Federici, Silvia. 1975. "Wages against Housework." https://caringlabor.wordpress.com/2010/09/15/silvia-federici-wages-against-housework/.

Federici, Silvia. 2004. *Caliban and the Witch: Women, the Body and Primitive Accumulation*. New York: Autonomedia.

Federici, Silvia. 2019. *Re-Enchanting the World: Feminism and the Politics of the Commons*. Oakland: PM Press.

Federici, Silvia, Selma James, and Mariarosa Dalla Costa. 1975. *Wages against Housework*. Bristol: Power of Women Collective and Falling Wall Press.

Fellows, Mary Louise, and Sherene Razack. 1998. "The Race to Innocence: Confronting Hierarchical Relations among Women." *Journal of Gender Race & Justice* 1: 335–352. https://scholarship.law.umn.edu/ faculty_articles/274.

Felski, Rita. 2000. *Doing Time: Feminist Theory and Postmodern Culture*. New York: NYU Press.

Ferguson, Sue. 2008. "Canadian Contributions to Social Reproduction: Feminism, Race and Embodied Labor." Journalism 4. https://scholars.wlu.ca/brantford_jn/4.

Ferguson, Susan. 2016. "Intersectionality and Social-Reproduction Feminisms: Toward an Integrative Ontology." *Historical Materialism* 24 (2): 38–60.

Ferguson, Susan. 2017. "Children, Childhood and Capitalism." In *Social Reproduction Theory*, edited by Tithi Bhattacharya, 112–130. London: Pluto Press.

Fernandes, M., L. Lupo, A. Benya, S. Dedeoğlu, A. Mezzadri, and E. Prügl. 2023. "Social Reproduction, Women's Labour and Systems of Life: A Conversation." *Dialogues in Human Geography* 13 (3): 473–483. https://doi.org/10.1177/20438206231177072.

Fernandez, Bina. 2017. "Dispossession and the Depletion of Social Reproduction." *Antipode* 50 (1): 142–163. https://doi.org/10.1111/anti.12350.

Ferrant, Gaëlle, Luca Maria Pesando, and Keiko Nowacka. 2014. "Unpaid Care Work: The Missing Link in the Analysis of Gender Gaps in Labour Outcomes." OECD. https://www.oecd.org/dev/development-gender/Unpaid_care_work.pdf.

Fisher, Berenice, and Joan C. Tronto. 1991. "Toward a Feminist Theory of Care." In *Circles of Care: Work and Identity in Women's Lives*, edited by Emily Abel and Margaret Nelson. Albany: State University of New York Press.

Flor, Luisa S., Joseph Friedman, Cory N. Spencer, John Cagney, Alejandra Arrieta, Molly E. Herbert, Caroline Stein, et al. 2022. "Quantifying the Effects of the COVID-19 Pandemic on Gender Equality on Health, Social, and Economic Indicators: A Comprehensive Review of Data from March, 2020, to September, 2021." *The Lancet* 399 (10344): 2381–2397.

Floro, Maria S. 2021. "Time Allocation and Time-Use Surveys." In *The Routledge Handbook of Feminist Economics*, 148–156. London: Routledge.

Floro, Maria S., and Anant Pichetpongsa. 2010. "Gender, Work Intensity, and Well-being of Thai Home-Based Workers." *Feminist Economics* 16 (3): 5–44.

Folbre, Nancy. 2006a. "Measuring Care: Gender, Empowerment, and the Care Economy." *Journal of Human Development* 7 (2): 183–199. doi:10.1080/14649880600768512.

Folbre, Nancy. 2006b. "Rethinking the Child Care Sector." *Community Development* 37 (2): 38–52.

Foreman, Ann. 1977. *Femininity as Alienation: Women and the Family in Marxism and Psycholanalysis*. London: Pluto Press.

Fortier, Nikki. 2020. "COVID-19, Gender Inequality, and the Responsibility of the State." *International Journal of Wellbeing* 10 (3): 77–93.

Fortunati, Leopoldina, and Autumn Edwards. 2022. "Gender and Human-Machine Communication: Where Are We?" *Human-Machine Communication* 5: 7–47. https://doi.org/10.30658/hmc.5.1.

Francesco, Maria Chelli, Mariateresa Ciommi, and Chiara Gigliarano. 2013. "The Index of Sustainable Economic Welfare: A Comparison of Two Italian Regions." *Procedia: Social and Behavioral Sciences* 81: 443–448. doi:10.1016/j.sbspro.2013.06.457

Fraser, Nancy. 2014a. "Behind Marx's Hidden Abode." *New Left Review*, 86 (March–April).

Fraser, Nancy. 2014b. "Can Society Be Commodities All the Way Down? Post-Polanyian Reflections on Capitalist Crisis." *Economy and Society* 43 (4): 541–558.

Fraser, Nancy. 2016. "Contradictions of Capital and Care." *New Left Review* 100 (July–August): 99–118. https://newleftreview.org/issues/ii100/articles/nancy-fraser-contradictions-of-capital-and-care.

Fraser, Nancy. 2017. "Crisis of Care? On the Social-Reproductive Contradictions of Contemporary Capitalism." In *Social Reproduction Theory: Remapping Class, Recentering Oppression*, edited by Tithi Bhattacharya, 21–36. London: Pluto Press.

Fraser, Nancy. 2023. *Cannibal Capitalism*. London: Verso.

Fraser, Nancy, and Rahel Jaeggi. 2018. *Capitalism: A Conversation in Critical Theory*. London. Verso.

Fuentes, Lorena, and Tara Patricia Cookson. 2020. "Counting Gender (In)Equality? A Feminist Geographical Critique of the 'Gender Data Revolution.'" *Gender, Place & Culture* 27 (6): 881–902.

Fukuda-Parr, Sakiko, Alicia Ely Yamin, and Joshua Greenstein. 2014. "The Power of Numbers: A Critical Review of Millennium Development Goal Targets for Human Development and Human Rights." Journal of Human Development and Capabilities 15 (2–3): 105–117.

Geronimus, Arline T. 1992. "The Weathering Hypothesis and the Health of African-American Women and Infants: Evidence and Speculations." *Ethnicity & Disease* 2 (3): 207–221.

Geronimus, Arline T., Cynthia G. Colen, Tara Shochet, Lori Barer Ingber, and Sherman A. James. 2006. "Urban-Rural Differences in Excess Mortality among High-Poverty Populations: Evidence from the Harlem Household Survey and the Pitt County, North Carolina Study of African American Health." *Journal of Health Care for the Poor and Underserved* 17 (3): 532–558.

Geronimus, Arline T., Margaret Hicken, Danya Keene, and John Bound. 2006. "'Weathering' and Age Patterns of Allostatic Load Scores among Blacks and Whites in the United States." *American Journal of Public Health* 96 (5, May): 826–833.

Gersbuny, Jonathan, and Oriel Sullivan. 1998. "The Sociological Uses of Time-Use Diary Analysis." *European Sociological Review* 14 (1): 69–85.

Gibson-Graham, J. K. 2008. "Diverse Economies: Performative Practices for 'Other Worlds.'" *Progress in Human Geography* 32 (5): 613–632. doi:10.1177/0309132508090821.

Gill, Rebecca. 2011. "The Shadow in Organizational Ethnography: Moving beyond Shadowing to Spect-acting." *Qualitative Research in Organizations and Management: An International Journal* 6 (2): 115–133.

Gilligan, Carol. 1982. *In a Different Voice: Psychological Theory and Women's Development*. Cambridge, MA: Harvard University Press.

Giroux, Henry A. 1986. "Solidarity, Struggle, and the Discourse of Hope: Theory, Practice, and Experience in Radical Education, Part II." *Review of Education* 12 (4): 247–255.

Giuntoli, G., S. Hughes, K. Karban, and J. South. 2015. "Towards a Middle-Range Theory of Mental Health and Well-being Effects of Employment

Transitions: Findings from a Qualitative Study on Unemployment during the 2009–2010 Economic Recession." *Health* 19 (4): 389–412.

Goldblatt, Beth. 2022. "The Work of Living-Social Reproduction and the Right to the Continuous Improvement of Living Conditions." SSRN 4050686.

Goldblatt, Beth, and Shireen Hassim. 2023. "'Grass in the Cracks': Gender, Social Reproduction and Climate Justice in the Xolobeni Struggle." In *Feminist Frontiers in Climate Justice: Gender Equality, Climate Change and Rights*, edited by Cathi Albertyn, Meghan Campbell, Helena Alviar García, Sandra Fredman, and Marta Rodriguez de Assis Machado, 246–267. Edward Elgar Publishing, Open Access. https://www.elgaronline.com/disp lay/book/9781803923796/9781803923796.xml.

Goldblatt, Beth, and Shirin M. Rai. 2018. "Recognizing the Full Costs of Care? Compensation for Families in South Africa's Silicosis Class Action." *Social & Legal Studies* 27 (6): 671–694.

Goldblatt, Beth, and Shirin M. Rai. 2020. "Remedying Depletion through Social Reproduction: A Critical Engagement with the United Nations' Business and Human Rights Framework." *European Journal of Politics and Gender* 3 (2): 185–202.

Goldblatt, David, Mark Haworth-Booth, and Christoph Danelzik-Brüggemann. 2005. *David Goldblatt: South African Intersections.* Germany: Prestel.

Goldstein, Donna M. 2017. "Invisible Harm: Science, Subjectivity and the Things We Cannot See." *Culture, Theory and Critique* 58 (4): 321–329.

González de la Rocha, Mercedes. 2001. "From the Resources of Poverty to the Poverty of Resources? The Erosion of a Survival Model, Mexico in the 1990s: Economic Crisis, Social Polarization, and Class Struggle, Part 2." *Latin American Perspectives* 28 (4, July): 72–100.

Gornick, Janet C., and Marcia K. Meyers. 2009. "An Institutional Proposal." In *Gender Equality: Transforming Family Divisions of Labour*, edited by Janet C. Gornick and Marcia K. Meyers, 3–66. London: Verso Books.

Government of NCT of Delhi, Planning Department. 2019. "Demographic Profile." In *Economic Survey of Delhi 2019–20*. https://delhiplanning.delhi. gov.in/sites/default/files/Planning/chapt1.pdf.

Gqada, Ichumile. 2011. "Setting the Boundaries of a Social Licence for Mining in South Africa: The Xolobeni Mineral Sands Project." Occasional Paper No. 99. SAIIA. file:///C:/Users/Shirin/Downloads/Occasional-Paper-99.pdf.

Griffin, Penny. 2015. "Crisis, Austerity and Gendered Governance: A Feminist Perspective." *Feminist Review* 109: 49–72.

Grimm, Pamela. 2010. "Social Desirability Bias." In *Wiley International Encyclopedia of Marketing*, edited by J. Sheth and N. Malhotra, Part 2 *Marketing Research*, 258. https://oj8k.gitee.io/knowledge_managem ent/files/readings/sdb_intro.pdf.

Grimshaw, Damian, and Jill Rubery. 2015. "The Motherhood Pay Gap: A Review of the Issues, Theory and International Evidence." Conditions of Work and

Employment Series No. 57. Inclusive Labour Markets, Labour Relations and Working Conditions Branch, International Labour Office, Geneva. https://www.ilo.org/wcmsp5/groups/public/@dgreports/@dcomm/@publ/documents/publication/wcms_348041.pdf.

Grove, Kevin, Savannah Cox, and Allain Barnett. 2020. "Racializing Resilience: Assemblage, Critique, and Contested Futures in Greater Miami Resilience Planning." *Annals of the American Association of Geographers* 110 (5): 1613–1630. doi:10.1080/24694452.2020.1715778

Grugel, J., and L. Fontana. 2015. "'To Eradicate or to Legalize': Child Labor Debates and ILO Convention 182 in Bolivia." *Global Governance* 21 (1): 61–78.

Grugel, J., S. Macias, and S. Rai. 2020. "Depletion, Intersectionality and the Limits of Social Policy: Child Carers in Mexico City." *European Journal of Politics and Gender* 3 (2): 1–16. doi:10.1332/251510820X15858427067832.

Grugel, Jean, and Frederico Poley Martins Ferreira. 2012. "Street Working Children, Children's Agency and the Challenge of Children's Rights: Evidence from Minas Gerais, Brazil." *Journal of International Development* 24 (7, October): 828–840.

Guardian. 2023. "Japan's Ageing Population Poses Urgent Risk to Society, Says PM." January 23. https://www.theguardian.com/world/2023/jan/23/japans-ageing-population-poses-urgent-risk-to-society-says-pm.

Guermond, Vincent, Dalia Iskander, Sebastien Michiels, Katherine Brickell, Grainne Fay, Long Ly Vouch, Nithya Natarajan, Laurie Parsons, Fiorella Picchioni, and W. Nathan Green. 2023. "Depleted by Debt: 'Green' Microfinance, Over-indebtedness, and Social Reproduction in Climate-Vulnerable Cambodia." *Antipode* 0 (0): 1–23. doi:10.1111/anti.12969.

Gunawardana, S. J. 2016. "'To Finish, We Must Finish': Everyday Practices of Depletion in Sri Lankan Export-Processing Zones." *Globalizations* 13 (6): 861–875.

Gupta, Poorvi. 2018. "Limited Choices, Expensive Transport: How Do Indian Women Commute?" SheThePeople TV. https://www.shethepeople.tv/news/choices-indian-women-commute/, (Accessed February 29, 2024).

HABITABLE. 2021. "Climate Migration: Why Focusing on Women and Girls Matters." https://habitableproject.org/news/climate-migration-why-focusing-on-women-and-girls-matters/, (Accessed February 29, 2024).

Hacking, Ian. 1990. *The Taming of Chance.* No. 17. Cambridge: Cambridge University Press.

Hamed, Sarah, Suruchi Thapar-Björkert, Hannah Bradby, and Beth M. Ahlberg. 2020. "Racism in European Health Care: Structural Violence and Beyond." *Qualitative Health Research* 30 (11): 1662–1673. doi:10.1177/1049732320931430.

Hamilton, K. 2016. "Measuring Sustainability in the UN System of Environmental-Economic Accounting." *Environmental and Resource Economics* 64: 25–36. https://doi.org/10.1007/s10640-015-9924-y.

Hamington, Maurice. 2004. *Embodied Care: Jane Addams, Maurice Merleau-Ponty, and Feminist Ethics*. Champaign: University of Illinois Press.

Hamunen, Eeva, Johanna Varjonen, and Katri Soinne. 2012. "Satellite Accounts on Household Production: Eurostat Methodology and Experiences to Apply It." Paper prepared for the 32nd General Conference of the International Association for Research in Income and Wealth. http://old.iariw.org/papers/2012/HamunenPaper.pdf.

Harbishettar, Vijaykumar, Mahesh Gowda, Saraswati Tenagi, and Mina Chandra. 2021. "Regulation of Long-Term Care Homes for Older Adults in India." *Indian Journal of Psychological Medicine* 43 (5 Suppl): S88–S96. doi:10.1177/02537176211021785.

Harding, Sandra, ed. 1987. *Feminism and Methodology: Social Science Issues*. Bloomington: Indiana University Press.

Hargreaves, C., P. Hodgson, J. N. Mohamed, and A. Nunn. 2019. "Contingent Coping? Renegotiating 'Fast' Disciplinary Social Policy at Street Level: Implementing the UK Troubled Families Programme." *Critical Social Policy* 39 (2): 289–308. https://doi.org/10.1177/0261018318780094.

Harlan, Sharon L., David N. Pellow, J. Timmons Roberts, Shannon Elizabeth Bell, William G. Holt, and Joane Nagel. 2015. "Climate Justice and Inequality." In *Climate Change and Society: Sociological Perspectives*, edited by Riley E. Dunlap, and Robert J. Brulle, 127–163. New York: Oxford Academic.

Harp, Kathi L. H., and Amanda M. Bunting. 2020. "The Racialized Nature of Child Welfare Policies and the Social Control of Black Bodies." *Social Politics: International Studies in Gender, State & Society* 27 (2, Summer): 258–281. https://doi.org/10.1093/sp/jxz039.

Harvey, Andrew S., and Arun K. Mukhopadhyay. 2007. "When Twenty-Four Hours Is Not Enough: Time Poverty of Working Parents." *Social Indicators Research* 82 (1): 57–77.

Harvey, David. 1990. "Between Space and Time: Reflections on the Geographical Imagination." *Annals of the Association of American Geographers* 80 (3): 418–434. https://www.jstor.org/stable/2563621.

Hassim, Shireen. 2009. "Whose Utopia." In *Gender Equality: Transforming Family Divisions of Labour*, edited by Janet C. Gornick and Marcia K. Meyers. London: Verso Books.

Hassim, Shireen, and Shahra Razavi. 2006. "Gender and Social Policy in a Global Context: Uncovering the Gendered Structure of 'the Social.'" In *Gender and Social Policy in a Global Context: Uncovering the Gendered Structure of 'the Social*, edited by Shahra Razavi and Shireen Hassim, 1–39. London: Palgrave Macmillan.

Hearn, Jeff, Sofia Strid, Anne Laure Humbert, Dag Balkmar, and Marine Delaunay. 2022. "From Gender Regimes to Violence Regimes: Re-thinking the Position of Violence." *Social Politics: International Studies in Gender, State & Society* 29 (2, Summer): 682–705. https://doi.org/10.1093/sp/jxaa022.

Held, Virginia. 2006. *The Ethics of Care: Personal, Political, and Global.* Reprint Edition. Oxford: Oxford University Press.

Heller, A. 1984. "Marx and Modernity." *Thesis Eleven* 8 (1): 44–58. https://doi.org/10.1177/072551368400800104.

Herrera, Gioconda. 2012. "Starting Over Again? Crisis, Gender, and Social Reproduction among Ecuadorian Migrants in Spain." *Feminist Economics* 18 (2): 125–148. doi:10.1080/13545701.2012.688997

Hirway, Indira. 2005. "Measurements Based on Time Use Statistics: Some Issues." Seminar on Unpaid Work and Economy: Gender, Poverty and Millennium Development Goals, Levy Economics Institute, New York, October. https://www.researchgate.net/publication/242175843_Measurements_Based_on_Time_Use_Statistics_Some_Issues1, (Accessed February 29, 2024).

Hirway, Indira, and U. Sunny Jose. 2011. "Understanding Women's Work Using Time-Use Statistics: The Case of India." *Feminist Economics* 17 (4, October): 67–92.

Hiswåls, Anne-Sofie, A. Marttila, E. Mälstam, and G. Macassa. 2017. "Experiences of Unemployment and Well-being after Job Loss during Economic Recession: Results of a Qualitative Study in East Central Sweden." *Journal of Public Health Research* 6 (3): 995. https://doi.org/10.4081/jphr.2017.995.

Hobson, J. M. 2020. *Multicultural Origins of the Global Economy beyond the Western-Centric Frontier.* Cambridge: Cambridge University Press.

Hochshild, Arlie. 2012. *The Managed Heart: Commercialization of Human Feeling.* Berkeley: University of California Press.

Hofmeister, Heather. 2005. "Geographic Mobility of Couples in the United States: Relocation and Commuting Trends." *Zeitschrift für Familienforschung* 17 (2): 115–128. https://doi.org/10.1007/s11116-019-09983-9.

Hohmann, Jessie, and Beth Goldblatt, eds. 2021. *The Right to the Continuous Improvement of Living Conditions: Responding to Complex Global Challenges.* Oñati International Series in Law and Society. London: Hart.

Holloway, Sue, Sandra Short, and Sarah Tamplin. 2002. *Household Satellite Account (Experimental) Methodology.* London: Office for National Statistics.

hooks, bell. 2000. *Where We Stand: Class Matters.* 1st Edition. New York: Routledge.

Hoskyns, Catherine. 2016. "Social Reproduction." In *Handbook on Gender in World Politics*, edited by Jill Steans and Daniela Tepe-Belfrage, 394–404. London: Edward Elgar.

Hoskyns, Catherine, and Shirin M. Rai. 2007. "Recasting the International Political Economy: Counting Women's Unpaid Work." *New Political Economy* 12 (3): 297–317.

House of Lords and House of Commons Joint Committee on Human Rights. 2015. *The UK's Compliance with the UN Convention on the Rights of the Child: Eighth Report of Session 2014–15.* London: HM Stationery Office.

https://publications.parliament.uk/pa/jt201415/jtselect/jtrights/144/144.pdf.

Hozic, Aida A., and Jacqui True, eds. 2016. *Scandalous Economics: Gender and the Politics of Financial Crises*. Oxford: Oxford University Press.

Hughes, Karen, Mark A. Bellis, Katherine A. Hardcastle, Dinesh Sethi, Alexander Butchart, Christopher Mikton, Lisa Jones, and Michael P. Dunne. 2017. "The Effect of Multiple Adverse Childhood Experiences on Health: A Systematic Review and Meta-analysis." *Lancet Public Health* 2 (8):356–366. https://www.sciencedirect.com/science/article/pii/S2468266717301184, (Accessed February 29, 2024).

Huizenga, Daniel. 2019. "Governing Territory in Conditions of Legal Pluralism: Living Law and Free, Prior, and Informed Consent (FPIC) in Xolobeni, South Africa." *The Extractive Industries and Society* 6 (3): 711–721.

Human Rights Watch. 2019 "Nothing Left in the Cupboards: Austerity, Welfare Cuts, and the Right to Food in the UK." May 20. https://www.hrw.org/report/2019/05/20/nothing-left-cupboards/austerity-welfare-cuts-and-right-food-uk.

Idowu, Amos Adeoye. 1999. "Human Rights, Environmental Degradation and Oil: Multinational Companies in Nigeria: The Ogoniland Episode Netherlands." *Quarterly Journal of Human Rights* 17 (2): 161–184.

ILO. 2008. "Measurement of Working Time." 18th International Conference of Labour Statisticians. Report II, Geneva, November 24–December 5. https://www.ilo.org/wcmsp5/groups/public/---dgreports/---stat/documents/publication/wcms_099576.pdf.

IMF. 2021. "Five Things to Know about the Informal Economy." https://www.imf.org/en/News/Articles/2021/07/28/na-072821-five-things-to-know-about-the-informal-economy#:~:text=Globally%2C%2058%20per%20cent%20of,paid%20categories%20of%20informal%20employment.

Indian Ministry of Statistics and Programme Implementation, Central Statistical Organisation. 2000. "Report of the Time Use Survey." New Delhi. https://mospi.gov.in/sites/default/files/publication_reports/Report%20of%20the%20Time%20Use%20Survey-Final.pdf, (Accessed February 29, 2024).

International Commission of Jurists. 2018. "South Africa: ICJ Welcomes Landmark Judgment on Free and Informed Consent of Communities Prior to the Award of Mining Rights." November 22. https://www.icj.org/south-africa-icj-welcomes-landmark-judgment-on-free-and-informed-consent-of-communities-prior-to-the-award-of-mining-rights/.

IPCC. 2023. "The Sixth Assessment Report." https://www.ipcc.ch/assessment-report/ar6/.

Irani, Laili, and Vidya Vemireddy. 2020. "Getting the Measurement Right! Quantifying Time Poverty and Multitasking from Childcare among Mothers With Children across Different Age Groups in Rural

North India." *Asian Population Studies.* https://www.researchgate.net/deref/https%3A%2F%2Fdoi.org%2F10.1080%2F17441730.2020.1778854?_tp=eyJjb250ZXh0Ijp7ImZpcnN0UGFnZSI6InB1YmxpY2F0aW9uIiwicGFnZSI6InB1YmxpY2F0aW9uIiwicG9zaXRpb24iOiJwYWdlQ29udGVudCJ9fQ.

Ironmonger, Duncan, and Faye Soupourmas. 2009. "Estimating Household Production Outputs with Time Use Episode Data." *Electronic International Journal of Time Use Research* 6 (2): 240–268.

Ishizuka, Patrick. 2021. "The Motherhood Penalty in Context: Assessing Discrimination in a Polarized Labor Market." *Demography* 58 (4): 1275–1300. doi: 10.1215/00703370-9373587. PMID: 34236402.

Jabri, Vivienne. 2007. "Solidarity and Spheres of Culture: The Cosmopolitan and the Postcolonial." *Review of International Studies* 33 (4): 715–728.

Jaeggi, Rahel. 2001. "Solidarity and Indifference." In *Solidarity in Health and Social Care in Europe*, 287–308. Dordrecht: Springer Netherlands.

Jagori. 2010. *A Report on Domestic Workers: Conditions, Rights and Responsibilities: A Study of Part-Time Domestic Workers in Delhi.* https://www.jagori.org/wp-content/uploads/2006/01/Final_DW_English_report_10-8-2011.pdf, (Accessed February 29, 2024).

James Allison, and Adrian L. James. 2004. *Constructing Childhood: Theory, Policy and Social Practice.* London: Red Globe Press.

Jeffrey, Craig, and Jane Dyson. 2021. "Geographies of the Future: Prefigurative Politics." *Progress in Human Geography* 45 (4): 641–658.

Jerven, Morten. 2013. *Poor Numbers, How We Are Misled by African Development Statistics and What to Do about It.* Ithaca, NY: Cornell University Press.

Jochimsen, Maren, and Ulrike Knobloch. 1997. "Making the Hidden Visible: The Importance of Caring Activities and Their Principles for Any Economy." *Ecological Economics* 20 (2): 107–112.

Johari, Aarefa. 2022. "The Historic Injustice Served to Care Workers by India's Highest Court." *Scroll*, April 20. https://scroll.in/article/1022099/the-historic-injustice-served-to-care-workers-by-indias-highest-court.

John, Mary E. 2013. "The Problem of Women's Labour: Some Autobiographical Perspectives." *Indian Journal of Gender Studies* 20 (2):177–212. https://doi.org/10.1177/0971521513482213.

Johnson, Holly. 2015. "Degendering Violence." *Social Politics* 22: 390–410.

Johnson, Melissa, and Jayanthi Lingham. 2020. "Inclusive Economies, Enduring Peace in Myanmar and Sri Lanka: Field Report." https://bridges.monash.edu/articles/report/Inclusive_Economies_Enduring_Peace_in_Myanmar_and_Sri_Lanka_Field_Report/12826130.

Johnston-Anumonwo, Ibipo. 1995. "Racial Differences in the Commuting Behavior of Women in Buffalo, 1980–1990." *Urban Geography* 16 (1): 23–45. doi:10.2747/0272-3638.16.1.23.

Jones, Katherine T. 1998. "Scale as Epistemology." *Political Geography* 17 (1): 25–28.

Jones, Ray. 2015. "The End Game: The Marketisation and Privatisation of Children's Social Work and Child Protection." *Critical Social Policy* 35 (4): 447–469.

Jones, Sam. 2023. "Spain Hopes Domestic Tasks App Will Ensure Men Pull Their Weight." *Guardian*, May 19. https://www.theguardian.com/world/2023/may/19/spain-domestic-tasks-app-chores-family-members.

Joseph, Stephen, Joe Sempik, Agnes Leu, and Saul Becker. 2020. "The Impact of a Parent's/Carer's Physical and Mental Health or Domestic Violence on Child Wellbeing: Young Carers Research, Practice and Policy: An Overview and Critical Perspective on Possible Future Directions." *Adolescent Research Review* 5: 77–89.

Kabe, Mariame. 2021. "Hope Is a Discipline: Mariame Kaba on Dismantling the Carceral State." *The Intercept*, March 17. https://theintercept.com/2021/03/17/intercepted-mariame-kaba-abolitionist-organizing/.

Kabeer, Naila, Shahra Razavi, and Yana van der Meulen Rodgers. 2021. "Feminist Economic Perspectives on the COVID-19 Pandemic." *Feminist Economics* 27 (1–2): 1–29. doi:10.1080/13545701.2021.1876906.

Kahneman, Daniel, A. B. Krueger, D. Schkade, N. Schwarz, and A. A. Stone. 2006. "Would You Be Happier If You Were Richer? A Focusing Illusion." *Science* 312 (5782): 1908–1910.

Kaiser, Steffen, and Gisela C. Schulze. 2015. "Between Inclusion and Participation: Young Carers Who Are Absent from School." *Journal of Cognitive Education and Psychology* 14 (3): 314–328.

Kannabiran, Kalpana. 2009. "Judicial Meanderings in Patriarchal Thickets: Litigating Sex Discrimination in India." *Economic and Political Weekly* 44 (44): 88–98.

Kareithi, M., and F. Viljoen. 2019. "An Argument for the Continued Validity of Woman-to-Woman Marriages in Post-2010 Kenya." *Journal of African Law* 63 (3): 303–328. doi:10.1017/S0021855319000263.

Kaur, Raminder, and Shirin M Rai. 2021. "COVID-19, Care and Carelessness." Countercurrents. https://countercurrents.org/2021/06/covid-19-care-and-carelessness/.

Kearns, Matthew. 2017. "Gender, Visuality and Violence: Visual Securitization and the 2001 War in Afghanistan." *International Feminist Journal of Politics* 19 (4): 491–505.

Kelly, Elaine, Tom Lee, Luke Sibieta, and Tom Waters. 2018. "Public Spending on Children in England: 2000 to 2020." Institute for Fiscal Studies. https://www.childrenscommissioner.gov.uk/wp-content/uploads/2018/06/Public-Spending-on-Children-in-England-CCO-JUNE-2018.pdf.

Kennedy, Ann. 2018–2019. "Chronic Harm," in "Power and Identity Politics: The Intersections of Marginalization and Social, Economic, and Political

Ascension," special issue. *William & Mary Journal of Race, Gender, and Social Justice* 25 (1): 131–162.

Kettell, Lynn. 2020. "Young Adult Carers in Higher Education: The Motivations, Barriers and Challenges Involved–a UK Study." *Journal of Further and Higher Education* 44 (1): 100–112.

Khaliq, Muhammed. 2020. "Child Poverty and Education Outcomes by Ethnicity." UK Office for National Statistics. https://www.ons.gov.uk/econ omy/nationalaccounts/uksectoraccounts/compendium/economicreview/ february2020/childpovertyandeducationoutcomesbyethnicity.

Kingdom, Elizabeth. 1991. *What's Wrong with Rights? Problems for Feminist Politics of Law*. Edinburgh: Edinburgh University Press.

Kittay, Eva Feder. 1999. *Love's Labor: Essays on Women, Equality and Dependency*. London: Routledge.

Kley, Stefanie. 2015. "The Impact of Job-Related Mobility and Migration Intentions on Union Dissolution." In *Spatial Mobility, Migration, and Living Arrangements*, edited by Can M. Aybek, Johannes Huinink, and Raya Muttarak, 139–158. Cham Heidelberg, New York, Dordrecht, London: Springer.

Knobloch, Ulrike. 2019. "Feminist Economics and Ethics." In *The Oxford Handbook of Ethics and Economics*, edited by Mark White, 248–269. Oxford: Oxford University Press.

Korzhenevych, Artem, and Manisha Jain. 2018. "Area- and Gender-Based Commuting Differentials in India's Largest Urban-Rural Region." *Transportation Research Part D: Transport and Environment* 63: 733–746.

Kotef, Hagar. 2015. *Movement and the Ordering of Freedom: On Liberal Governances of Mobility*. Durham, NC: Duke University Press.

Kotiswaran, Prabha. 2021a. "An Ode to Altruism: How Indian Courts Value Unpaid Domestic Work." *Economic & Political Weekly* 56 (36, September 4): 45–52.

Kotiswaran, Prabha. 2021b. "Toward a Model of Universal Care, One Manifesto at a Time." *Social Politics* 28 (4): 854–864. https://doi.org/ 10.1093/sp/jxab040.

Kundani, Arun. 2023. *What Is Antiracism? And Why It Means Anticapitalism: Racial Capitalism and the Limits of Liberalism*. London: Verso.

Künn-Nelen, Annemarie. 2015. "Does Commuting Affect Health?" IZA Discussion Papers No. 9031. Institute for the Study of Labor (IZA), Bonn.

Kunz, Rahel. 2010. "The Crisis of Social Reproduction in Rural Mexico: Challenging the 'Re-privatization of Social Reproduction' Thesis." *Review of International Political Economy* 17 (5): 913–945. http://www.jstor.org/sta ble/41061580.

Kuznets, Simon. 1934. *National Income, 1929–1930*. National Bureau of Economic Research. https://www.nber.org/system/files/chapters/c2258/ c2258.pdf.

Lake, Osprey Orielle, and Katherine Quaid. 2023. *Prioritizing Care Work Can Unlock a Just Transition for All.* https://www.wecaninternational.org/_files/ugd/d99d2e_371549ec6a0f48449e9a4b306e8fc72e.pdf.

Laslett, B., and J. Brenner. 1989. "Gender and Social Reproduction: Historical Perspectives." *Annual Review of Sociology* 15: 381–404. http://www.jstor.org/stable/2083231.

Laugier, Sandra. 2020. *Politics of the Ordinary: Care, Ethics, and Forms of Life.* Lueven: Peeters.

Lefebvre, Henri. 1984. *Everyday Life in the Modern World.* Vol. 2. New Brunswick, NJ: Transaction.

Lefebvre, Henri. 2002 [1961]. *Critique of Everyday Life.* Vol. 2. London: Verso.

Lefebvre, Henri. 2004. *Rhythmanalysis: Space, Time and Everyday Life.* London: Continuum.

Legalbrief. 2023. "Judgment Reserved in Xolobeni Mining Case." April. https://legalbrief.co.za/diary/legalbrief-environmental/story/mining-and-communities-the-consent-issue/pdf/, (Accessed February 29, 2024).

Leu, A., and S. Becker. 2019. "Young Carers." In *Oxford Bibliographies in Childhood Studies*, edited by H. Montgomery. New York: Oxford University Press.

Levitas, Ruth. 2023. *Utopia as Method: The Imaginary Reconstitution of Society.* London: Palgrave Macmillan.

Liebowitz, Debra J., and Susanne Zwingel. 2014. "Gender Equality Oversimplified: Using CEDAW to Counter the Measurement Obsession." International Studies Review 16 (3): 362–389.

Liedberg, Gunilla M., and Chris M. Henriksson. 2002. "Factors of Importance for Work Disability in Women with Fibromyalgia: An Interview." *Stud Arthritis & Rheumatism (Arthritis Care & Research)* 47 (3, June 15): 266–274. doi:10.1002/art.10454.

Lim, Hilary, and Jeremy Roche. 2000. "Feminism and Children's Rights." In *Feminist Perspectives on Child Law*, edited by Jo Bridgeman and Daniel Monk, 227–249. London: Routledge-Cavendish.

Limpitlaw, D., M. Aken, H. Lodewijks, and J. Viljoen. 2005. "Post-Mining Rehabilitation, Land Use and Pollution at Collieries in South Africa." Paper presented at the Colloquium: Sustainable Development in the Life of Coal Mining, South African Institute of Mining and Metallurgy, Boksburg, July 13. https://www.researchgate.net/profile/Daniel_Limpitlaw/publication/237436743_POST-MINING_REHABILITATION_LAND_USE_AND_POLLUTION_AT_COLLIERIES_IN_SOUTH_AFRICA/links/0f31753bfe3ef79d2c000000.pdf.

Lingham, Jayanthi Thiyaga, and Melissa Johnston. 2024. "Running on Empty: Depletion and Social Reproduction in Myanmar and Sri Lanka." *Antipode.* https://doi.org/10.1111/anti.13016.

248 REFERENCES

Lingham, Jayanthi, Shirin M. Rai, and Shahnaz Akhter. Forthcoming. *Race, Gender and Class under COVID-19-19: Narratives of Care, Caring and Carers.*

Lloyd, Katrina. 2013. "Happiness and Well-Being of Young Carers: Extent, Nature and Correlates of Caring among 10 and 11 Year Old School Children." *Journal of Happiness Studies* 14: 67–80. doi:10.1007/s10902-011-9316-0.

Lombardozzi, Lorena. 2020. "Gender Inequality, Social Reproduction and the Universal Basic Income." *Political Quarterly* 91 (2): 317–323.

London-Edinburgh Weekend Return Group. 1979. *In and Against the State: Discussion Notes for Socialists.* London: Pluto Press.

Lugones, Maria. 2008. "Toward a Decolonial Feminism." *Hypatia* 25 (4): 742–759.

Luttrell, Wendy. 2013. "Children's Counter-Narratives of Care: Towards Educational Justice." *Children & Society* 27 (4): 295–308.

Luttrell, Wendy. 2020. *Children Framing Childhoods: Working-Class Kids' Visions of Care.* Bristol: Policy Press.

Lutz, Helma. 2011. *The New Maids: Transnational Women and the Care Economy.* London: Bloomsbury.

Lutz, Helma. 2018. "Care Migration: The Connectivity between Care Chains, Care Circulation and Transnational Social Inequality." *Current Sociology* 66 (4): 577–589.

Lux, J., and S. Wöhl. 2015. "Gender Inequalities in the Crisis of Capitalism: Spain and France Compared." In *New Directions in Comparative Capitalisms Research*, edited by M. Ebenau, I. Bruff, and C. May, 101–117. International Political Economy Series. London: Palgrave Macmillan. https://doi.org/10.1057/9781137444615_7.

Lyon, Sarah, Tad Mutersbaugh, and Holly Worthen. 2017. "The Triple Burden: The Impact of Time Poverty on Women's Participation in Coffee Producer Organizational Governance in Mexico." *Agriculture and Human Values* 34: 317–331. https://doi.org/10.1007/s10460-016-9716-1.

Lyon, Scott, Marco Ranzani, and Furio C. Rosati. 2013. "Unpaid Household Services and Child Labour." UNICEF Understanding Children's Work Programme. http://ucw-project.org/attachment/unpaid_household_services_child_labour20130503_173956.pdf.

Lyons, Glenn, and Kiron Chatterjee. 2008. "A Human Perspective on the Daily Commute: Costs, Benefits and Trade-offs." *Transport Reviews* 28 (2): 181–198.

Macfarlane, Robert. 2013. *The Old Ways: A Journey on Foot.* Penguin.

Mackintosh, Maureen. 1981. "Gender and Economics: The Sexual Division of Labour and the Subordination of Women." In *Of Marriage and the Market*, edited by Kate Young, Carol Wolkowitz, and Roslyn McCullagh, 3–17 London: CSE Books.

Macpherson, Iain, Mami Taniguchi, and Fabian Jintae Froese. 2021. "Numbers and Needed Nuances: A Critical Analysis of the Gender Equity Index

(GEI)." In *Handbook on Diversity and Inclusion Indices*, edited by Eddy S. Ng, Christina L. Stamper, Alain Klarsfeld, and Yu J. Han, 101–116. London: Elgaronline.

Madgavkar, Anu, Olivia White, Mekala Krishnan, Deepa Mahajan, and Xavier Azcue. 2020. "COVID-19 and Gender Equality: Countering the Regressive Effects." McKinsey Global Institute. https://www.mckinsey.com/~/media/McKinsey/Featured%20Insights/Future%20of%20Organizations/COVID%2019%20and%20gender%20equality%20Countering%20the%20regressive%20effects/COVID-19-and-gender-equality-Countering-the-regressive-effects-vF.pdf, (Accessed 29 February).

Madhok, Sumi. 2020. "A Critical Reflexive Politics of Location, 'Feminist Debt' and Thinking from the Global South." *European Journal of Women's Studies* 27 (4): 394–412.

Madhok, Sumi, and Shirin M. Rai. 2012. "Agency, Injury, and Transgressive Politics in Neoliberal Times." *Signs: Journal of Women in Culture and Society* 37 (3): 645–669.

Madhok, Sumi. 2021. *Vernacular Rights Cultures*. Cambridge: Cambridge University Press.

Mahon, Rianne. 2020. "Redressing Harms to Migrant Domestic Workers: Global and Regional Spaces." *European Journal of Politics and Gender* 3 (2): 203–219.

Mander, H., I. Roy, P. Jain, R. Raman, R. G. Ray, A. Bhattacharya, and U. J. Siddiqi. 2019. "Stolen Citizenship, Stolen Freedoms: Locating the Rights of India's Circular Labour Migrants." *Esclavages & Post-esclavages: Slaveries & Post-Slaveries* 1: 1–17. Doi: 10.4000/slaveries/602.

Manji, Ambreena S. 2006. *The Politics of Land Reform in Africa: From Communal Tenure to Free Markets*. Zed Books.

Manning, Alan. 2003. "The Real Thin Theory: Monopsony in Modern Labour Markets." *Labour Economics* 10 (2): 105–131.

Marazzi, Christian. 2007. "Rules for the Incommensurable." *SubStance* 36 (1): 11–36.

Marchetti, Sabrina. 2018. "The Global Governance of Paid Domestic Work: Comparing the Impact of ILO Convention No. 189 in Ecuador and India." *Critical Sociology* 44 (7–8): 1191–1205.

Martin, Jarred H. 2022. "Exploring the Affective Atmospheres of the Threat of Sexual Violence in Minibus Taxis: The Experiences of Women Commuters in South Africa." *Mobilities* 17 (3): 301–316. doi:10.1080/17450101.2021.1942171.

Mason, Kate E., Alexandros Alexiou, Davara Lee Bennett, Carolyn Summerbell, Ben Barr, and David Taylor-Robinson. 2021. "Impact of Cuts to Local Government Spending on Sure Start Children's Centres on Childhood Obesity in England: A Longitudinal Ecological Study." *Journal of Epidemiology and Public Health* 75 (9): 860–866. https://jech.bmj.com/content/75/9/860.

Mau, Søren. 2021. "'The Mute Compulsion of Economic Relations': Towards a Marxist Theory of the Abstract and Impersonal Power of Capital." *Historical Materialism* 29 (3): 3–32.

Marx, Karl, and Friedrich Engels, 1965. *The German Ideology*. Lawrence & Wishart, London.

Mbembé, J-A. 2003. "Necropolitics." Translated by Libby Meintjes. *Public Culture* 15 (1): 11–40.

McDonald, S. 2018. "Going with the Flow: Shadowing in Organisations." In *The Sage Handbook of Qualitative Business and Management Research Methods*, edited by C. Cassell, A. L. Cunliffe, and G. Grandy, 205–218. London: Sage. doi:10.4135/9781526430236

McDowall, Duncan. 2008. *The Sum of the Satisfactions: Canada in the Age of National Accounting*. Montreal: McGill-Queen's University Press.

McGee, Brant. 2009. "The Community Referendum: Participatory Democracy and the Right to Free, Prior and Informed Consent to Development." *Berkeley Journal of International Law* 27: 570–635.

McGoey, Linsey. 2019. *The Unknowers: How Strategic Ignorance Rules the World*. London: Zed Books.

McLafferty, Sara. 1997. "Gender, Race, and the Determinants of Commuting: New York in 1990." *Urban Geography* 18 (3): 192–212.

McLaughlin, Kenneth. 2016. *Empowerment: A Critique*. London: Routledge.

McRobbie, Angela. 2007. "Top Girls? Young Women and the Post-feminist Sexual Contract." Cultural *Studies* 21 (4–5): 718–737.

Melamed, Jodi. 2015. "Racial Capitalism." *Critical Ethnic Studies* 1 (1): 76–85. doi:10.5749/jcritethnstud.1.1.0076.

Melhuish, E., J. Belsky, and J. Barnes. 2009. "Evaluation and Value of Sure Start." *Arch Dis Child* 95: 159–161.

Metzing-Blau, Sabine, and Wilfried Schnepp. 2008. "Young Carers in Germany: To Live On as Normal as Possible—A Grounded Theory Study." *BMC Nursing* 7 (15): 1–9. doi:10.1186/1472-6955-7-15.

Mezzadri, Alessandra. 2020. "A Value Theory of Inclusion: Informal Labour, the Homeworker, and the Social Reproduction of Value." *Antipode* 53 (4): 1186–1205. doi:10.1111/anti.12701.

Mezzadri, Alessandra. 2022. "Social Reproduction and Pandemic Neoliberalism: Planetary Crises and the Reorganisation of Life, Work and Death. *Organization* 29 (3): 379–400.

Mezzadri, Alessandra, Susan Newman, and Sara Stevano. 2022. "Feminist Global Political Economies of Work and Social Reproduction." *Review of International Political Economy* 29 (6): 1783–1803. doi:10.1080/09692290.2021.1957977

Mezzadri, Alessandra, Shirin M. Rai, Sara Stevano, Donatella Alessandrini, Hannah Bargawi, Juanita Elias, Shireen Hassim, et al. Forthcoming. *Pluralising Social Reproduction Approaches*.

Middleton, J. 2009. "'Stepping in Time': Walking, Time, and Space in the City." *Environment and Planning A: Economy and Space* 41 (8): 1943–1961. https://doi.org/10.1068/a41170.

Mies, Maria, and Federici, Silvia 2014. *Patriarchy and Accumulation on a World Scale: Women in the International Division of Labour.* London: Zed Books.

Mies, Martha, and Shiva, Vandana. 1993. *Ecofeminsim.* London: Zed Books.

Mitchell, Timothy. 1998. "Fixing the Economy." *Cultural Studies* 12 (1): 82–101. doi:10.1080/095023898335627.

Mohanty, Chandra Talpade. 1995. "European Women and the Second British Empire." *Signs* 20 (4, Summer): 1058–1061.

Montgomerie, Johnna, and Daniela Tepe-Belfrage. 2016. "A Feminist Moral-Political Economy of Uneven Reform in Austerity Britain: Fostering Financial and Parental Literacy." *Globalizations* 13 (6): 890–905.

Moore, Jason. 2015. *Capitalism in the Web of Life: Ecology and the Accumulation of Capital.* London: Verso.

Moore, Phoebe, and Andrew Robinson. 2016. "The Quantified Self: What Counts in the Neoliberal Workplace." *New Media & Society* 18 (11): 2774–2792.

Morgan, Robin. 1984. *Sisterhood Is Global: The International Women's Movement Anthology.* New York: The Feminist Press at CUNY.

Morris, L. 2010. "Welfare, Asylum and the Politics of Judgment." *Journal of Social Policy* 39: 119–138.

Moser, Caroline. 1993. *Gender Planning and Development: Theory, Practice and Training.* London: Routledge.

Mosse, Richard. Broken Spectre, 30, September 2022–23 April 2023, 180 The Strand, London, https://www.theguardian.com/artanddesign/2022/oct/01/you-cant-unsee-this-richard-mosses-all-consuming-plea-to-save-the-amazon, Accessed 01.03.2024.

Muegge, Daniel. 2022. "Economic Statistics as Political Artefacts." *Review of International Political Economy* 29 (1): 1–22. doi:10.1080/09692290.2020.1828141.

Muller, Beatrice. 2019. "The Careless Society—Dependency and Care Work in Capitalist Societies." *Frontiers in Sociology* 3 (44): 1–10. doi:10.3389/fsoc.2018.00044.

Mullings, Beverley Caliban. 2021. "Social Reproduction and Our Future Yet to Come." *Geoforum* 118: 150–158.

Naidu, Sirisha C. 2023. "Circuits of Social Reproduction: Nature, Labor, and Capitalism." *Review of Radical Political Economics* 55 (1): 93–111.

Nalule, V. R. 2020. *Introduction to Mining in Africa: Mining and the Law in Africa.* Cham, Switzerland: Palgrave Pivot. https://doi.org/10.1007/978-3-030-33008-8_1.

Nanda, Meera. 1996. "The Science Question in Post-colonial Feminism." *Economic and Political Weekly* 31(16/17): WS2–WS8, Apr. 20-27.

Nanda, Meera. 2016. *Science in Saffron: Skeptical Essays on History of Science.* New Delhi: Three Essays Collective.

Nedelsky, J. 2011. *Law's Relations.* New York: Oxford University Press.

Neetha, N. 2010. "Estimating Unpaid Care Work: Methodological Issues in Time Use Surveys." *Economic and Political Weekly* 45 (44–45): 73–80.

Neetha, N., and Rajni Palriwala. 2010. "Unpaid Care Work." In *Time Use Studies and Unpaid Care Work*, edited by Debbie Budlender, 92–117. London: Routledge.

Nelson, Julie. 2013. "'Would Women Leaders Have Prevented the Global Financial Crisis?' Teaching Critical Thinking by Questioning a Question." *International Journal of Pluralism and Economics Education* 4 (2): 192–209. doi:10.1504/IJPEE.2013.055444

Neumayer, Eric. 1999. "The ISEW: Not an Index of Sustainable Economic Welfare." *Social Indicators Research*, 48 (1): 77–101. doi:10.1023/A:1006914023227

Newell, Sarah. 2019. "In the Drivers' Seat: Why the ILO Should Care about the Commute." OpenDemocracy, June 13. https://www.opendemocracy.net/en/beyond-trafficking-and-slavery/in-the-drivers-seat-why-the-ilo-should-care-about-the-commute/.

Ní Aoláin, Fionnuala. 2009. "Exploring a Feminist Theory of Harm in the Context of Conflicted and Postconflict Societies." *Queen's Law Journal* 35 (1): 219–224.

Ní Aoláin, Fionnuala, and Michael Hamilton. 2009. "Gender and the Rule of Law in Transitional Societies." *Minnesota Journal of International Law* 18: 380. https://scholarship.law.umn.edu/faculty_articles/101.

Nodding, Nel. 1992. *Caring: A Feminine Approach to Ethics and Moral Education.* Berkeley: University of California Press.

Nolas, Sevasti-Melissa, Christos Varvantakis, and Vinnarasan Aruldoss. 2017. "Children of the Financial Crisis." Discover Society 44 (May 2). https://archive.discoversociety.org/2017/05/02/children-of-the-financial-crisis/.

Noor, Dharna. 2023. "'Gamechanger': Judge Rules in Favor of Young Activists in US Climate Trial." *Guardian*, August 14. https://www.theguardian.com/us-news/2023/aug/14/montana-climate-trial-young-activists-judge-order?CMP=Share_iOSApp_Other.

Nunn, A., and D. Tepe-Belfrage. 2019. "Social Reproduction Strategies: Understanding Compound Inequality in the Intergenerational Transfer of Capital, Assets and Resources." *Capital & Class* 43 (4): 617–635. https://doi.org/10.1177/0309816819880795.

Oakley, Ann. 1998. "Gender, Methodology and People's Ways of Knowing: Some Problems with Feminism and the Paradigm Debate in Social Science." *Sociology* 32 (4): 707–731.

Ochieng, George M., Ephrahim S. Seanego, and Onyeka I. Nkwonta. 2010. "Impacts of Mining on Water Resources in South Africa: A Review."

Scientific Research and Essays 5 (22): 3351–3357. http://www.academicj ournals.org/SRE.

Ofsted. 2021. "Main Findings: Children's Social Care in England 2021. https://www.gov.uk/government/statistics/childrens-social-care-data-in-england-2021/main-findings-childrens-social-care-in-england-2021, (Accessed February 29, 2024).

O'Hara, Sabine U. 1997. "Toward a Sustaining Production Theory." *Ecological Economics* 20 (2): 141–154.

Okoth, Christine. 2023. "Extraction Then and Now." In *Re/Sisters: A Lens on Gender and Ecology*, edited by Alona Pardo. London: Barbican Prestel.

Ollman, Bertell. 2005. "The Utopian Vision of the Future (Then and Now): A Marxist Critique." *Monthly Review*, July 1. https://monthlyreview.org/2005/ 07/01/the-utopian-vision-of-the-future-then-and-now-a-marxist-criti que/#:~:text=More%20specifically%2C%20the%20main%20critici sms,it%20really%20is%20the%20%E2%80%9Cgood%E2%80%9D.

Ortiz, Isabel, and Matthew Cummins. 2022. "End Austerity: A Global Report on Budget Cuts and Harmful Social Reforms in 2022–25." https:// www.eurodad.org/end_austerity_a_global_report, (Accessed February 29, 2024).

Ortiz-Ospina, Esteban, Sandra Tzvetkova, and Max Roser. 2018. "Women's Employment." Our World in Data. https://ourworldindata.org/female-labor-supply.

Osman-Elasha, Belgis. 2009. "In the Shadow of Climate Change." *UN Chronicle* 46 (3–4). https://www.un.org/en/chronicle/article/womenin-shadow-clim ate-change.

Ostrom, Elinor. 1990. *Governing the Commons: The Evolution of Institutions for Collective Action*. Cambridge: Cambridge University Press.

Oxfam. 2020. "On Women's Backs: India Inequality Report 2020." https://d1n s4ht6ytuzzo.cloudfront.net/oxfamdata/oxfamdatapublic/2020-01/Oxfam Inequality%20Report%202020%20single%20lo-res%20%281%29.pdf.

Oyěwùmí, O. 1997. *The Invention of Women: Making an African Sense of Western Gender Discourses*. Minneapolis: University of Minnesota Press.

Ozawa, Harumi. 2012. "Woman Is Japan's Secret Economic Weapon." Agence France-Presse, November 23.

Palriwala, R., and N. Neetha. 2011. "Stratified Familialism: The Care Regime in India through the Lens of Childcare." *Development and Change* 42 (4): 1049–1078.

Panitch, Leo, and Sam Gindin. 2000. "Transcending Pessimism: Rekindling Socialist Imagination." Socialist Register 36. file:///C:/Users/sr86/ Downloads/titusland,+SR_2000_Panitch_Gindin%20(1).pdf.

Pardo, Alona. 2023. "Reweaving the Web of Womainst Ecopolitics." In Re/ Sisters: A Lens on Gender and Ecology, edited by Alona Pardo. London: Barbican Prestel.

Parpart, Jane L, Shirin M. Rai, and Kathleen A. Staudt, eds. 2002. *Rethinking Empowerment Gender and Development in a Global/Local World*. Routledge.

Partington, Richard. 2023. "Tackling the 15-Minute Cities Conspiracy Means Fixing Inequality." *Guardian*, February 26.

Pemberton, S. 2007. "Social Harm Future(s): Exploring the Potential of the Social Harm Approach." *Crime, Law and Social Change* 48 (1–2): 27–41.

Pemberton, Simon A. 2015. *Harmful Societies: Understanding Social Harm*. Bristol: Bristol University Press.

Peng, I. 2019. "The Care Economy: A New Research Framework." Sciences Po LIEPP Working Paper No. 89. Paris: Sciences Po.

Pereira, R. H., T. Schwanen, and D. Banister. 2017. "Distributive Justice and Equity in Transportation." *Transport Reviews* 37 (2): 170–191.

Pereyra-Iraola, Victoria, and Samanthi J. Gunawardana. 2019. "Carceral Spaces and Social Reproduction: Exploring Export Processing Zones in Sri Lanka and Prisons in Argentina." *Social Politics: International Studies in Gender, State and Society* 26 (4): 538–560.

Peterson, V. Spike. 2020. "Family Matters in Racial Logics: Tracing Intimacies, Inequalities, and Ideologies." *Review of International Studies* 46 (2): 177–196.

Phadke, Shilpa, Shilpa Ranade, and Sameera Khan. 2009. "Why Loiter? Radical Possibilities for Gendered Dissent." In *Dissent and Cultural Resistance in Asia's Cities*, edited by Melissa Butcher and Selvaraj Velayutham, 199–217. New York: Routledge.

Picchio, A. 1992. *Social Reproduction: The Political Economy of the Labour Market*. Cambridge: Cambridge University Press.

Pierce, Thom. 2018a. "Postcards from Xolobeni." *Daily Maverick*, April 20. https://www.dailymaverick.co.za/article/2018-04-20-postcards-from-xolobeni/.

Pierce, Thom. 2018b. "South Africa's Wild Coast Under Threat of Mining: Photo Essay." *The Guardian*, August 20. https://www.theguardian.com/environment/2018/aug/20/the-australian-mining-threat-to-south-africas-wild-coast-photo-essay.

Pitkin, Hanna F. 1967. *The Concept of Representation*. Berkeley: University of California Press.

Porter, Theodore M. 1995. *Trust in Numbers: The Pursuit of Objectivity in Science and Public Life*. Princeton, NJ: Princeton University Press.

Power, Kate. 2020. "The COVID-19 Pandemic Has Increased the Care Burden of Women and Families." *Sustainability: Science, Practice and Policy* 16 (1): 67–73.

Power, Michael. 1997. *The Audit Society: Rituals of Verification*. Oxford: Oxford University Press.

Press Information Bureau. 2022. "Sex Ratio at Birth." Press Release by Ministry of Women and Child Development. March 16. https://pib.gov.in/PressReleasePage.aspx?PRID=1806605.

Preston, Valerie, Sara McLafferty, and Xiaofeng F. Liu. 1998. "Geographical Barriers to Employment for American-Born and Immigrant Workers." *Urban Studies* 35 (3): 529–545.

Price, Sophia. 2019. "The Risks and Incentives of Disciplinary Neoliberal Feminism: The Case of Microfinance." *International Feminist Journal of Politics* 21 (1): 67–88. doi:10.1080/14616742.2018.1454843

Proctor, Robert N., and Londa Schiebinger. 2008. *Agnotology: The Making and Unmaking of Ignorance*. Stanford, CA: Stanford University Press.

Proto, Eugenio, and Climent Quintana-Domeque. 2021. "COVID-19 and Mental Health Deterioration by Ethnicity and Gender in the UK." *PLoS ONE* 16 (1): e0244419. https://doi.org/10.1371/journal.pone.0244419.

Prügl, Elisabeth. 2017. "Corporate Social Responsibility and the Neoliberalization of Feminism." In *Gender Equality and Responsible Business*, edited by Kate Grosser, Lauren McCarthy, Maureen A. Kilgour, 46–55. New York: Routledge.

Prügl, Elisabeth, and J. Ann Tickner. 2018. "Feminist International Relations: Some Research Agendas for a World in Transition." *European Journal of Politics and Gender* 1 (1–2): 75–91. https://doi.org/10.1332/251510818X152 72520831193.

Public Health England. 2020. "No Child Left Behind: Understanding and Quantifying Vulnerability." https://assets.publishing.service.gov.uk/media/ 5f4f72c68fa8f523f4c3c0ed/Understanding_and_quantifying_vulnerabili ty_in_childhood.pdf, (Accessed February 27, 2024).

Puig de la Bellacasa, María. 2017. *Matters of Care: Speculative Ethics in More Than Human Worlds*. Minneapolis: University of Minnesota Press.

Qamar, Azher Hameed. 2022. "Social Value of the Child in the Global South: A Multifaceted Concept." *Journal of Early Childhood Research* 20 (4): 610–623.

Quinlan, E. 2008. "Conspicuous Invisibility: Shadowing as a Data Collection Strategy." *Qualitative Inquiry* 14 (8): 1480–1499.

Radhakrishnan, Vignesh, Sumant Sen, and Naresh Singaravelu. 2020. "Domestic Violence Complaints at a 10-Year High during COVID-19 Lockdown." *The Hindu*, June 22. https://www.thehindu.com/data/data-domestic-violence-complaints-at-a-10-year-high-during-covid-19-lockd own/article31885001.ece.

Raghuram, Parvati. 2016. "Locating Care Ethics beyond the Global North." *ACME: An International Journal for Critical Geographies* 15 (3): 511–533.

Rai, Shirin M. 2002. *Gender and the Political Economy of Development: From Nationalism to Globalisation*. Cambridge: Polity Press.

Rai, Shirin M. 2016. "Magic Numbers." Paper presented at Jawaharlal Nehru University, Centre for the Study of Law and Governance, January 21.

Rai, Shirin M. 2018. "The Good Life and the Bad: The Dialectics of Solidarity." *Social Politics: International Studies in Gender, State & Society* 25 (1, March): 1–19.

Rai, Shirin M. 2024. "Reflexive Solidarity." Paper presented at the International Studies Association Convention, San Francisco, April 3–6.

Rai, Shirin M., Benjamin D. Brown, and Kanchana N. Ruwanpura. 2019. "SDG 8: Decent Work and Economic Growth: A Gendered Analysis." *World Development* 113: 368–380.

Rai, Shirin M., Catherine Hoskyns, and Dania Thomas. 2010. "Depletion and Social Reproduction." Paper prepared for the Workshop on Depletion and Social Reproduction, Centre for the Study of Globalisation and Regionalisation, University of Warwick, April 21. https://warwick.ac.uk/fac/soc/pais/research/csgr/papers/workingpapers/2011/27411.pdf.

Rai, Shirin M., Catherine Hoskyns, and Dania Thomas. 2014. "Depletion: The Cost of Social Reproduction." *International Feminist Journal of Politics* 16 (1): 86–105. doi:10.1080/14616742.2013.789641.

Rai, Shirin M., and Jacqui True. 2020. "Feminist Everyday Observatory Tool." https://warwick.ac.uk/fac/soc/pais/research/wicid/cpml/feminist_everyday_observatory_toolkit_wicid.pdf.

Rai, Shirin M., Jacqui True, and Maria Tanyag. 2019. "From Depletion to Regeneration: Overcoming Structural and Physical Violence in Post-Conflict Economies." *Social Politics* 26 (4, Winter): 561–585. doi:10.1093/sp/jxz034

Ralph, Michael, and Maya Singhal. 2019. "Racial Capitalism." *Theory and Society* 48: 851–881. https://doi.org/10.1007/s11186-019-09367-z.

Rao, Smriti. 2021. "Beyond the Coronavirus: Understanding Crises of Social Reproduction." *Global Labour Journal* 12 (1): 39–53.

Rao, Smriti, Smita Ramnarain, Sirisha Naidu, Anupama Uppal, and Avanti Mukherjee. 2021. "Work and Social Reproduction in Rural India: Lessons from Time-Use Data." Working Paper Series No. 535. University of Massachusetts, Amherst. https://scholarworks.umass.edu/cgi/viewcontent.cgi?article=1250&context=peri_workingpapers.

Razavi, Shahra. 2007. "The Political and Social Economy of Care in a Development Context." United Nations Research Institute for Social Development, Gender and Development Programme, Paper No. 3. https://cdn.unrisd.org/assets/library/papers/pdf-files/razavi-paper.pdf, (Accessed February 29, 2024).

Reagon, Bernice Johnson. 2015. "Coalition Politics: Turning the Century." *Feministische Studien* 33 (1): 115–123. https://doi.org/10.1515/fs-2015-0115.

Redden, Stephanie M. 2018. "Feminist Engagements with 'Everyday Life.'" In *Handbook on the International Political Economy of Gender*, edited by Juanita Elias and Adrienne Roberts, 159–170. Cheltenham, UK: Edward Elgar.

Roberts Adrienne. 2015. "Gender, Financial Deepening and the Production of Embodied Finance: Towards a Critical Feminist Analysis." *Global Society* 29 (1): 107–127. doi:10.1080/13600826.2014.975189.

Roberts, Adrienne, and Ghazal Zulfiqar. 2019. "Social Reproduction, Finance and the Gendered Dimensions of Pawnbroking." *Capital & Class* 43 (4): 581–597. https://0-doi-org.pugwash.lib.warwick.ac.uk/10.1177/03098 16819880788.

Roberts, Jennifer, Robert Hodgson, and Paul Dolan. 2011. "'It's Driving Her Mad': Gender Differences in the Effects of Commuting on Psychological Health." *Journal of Health Economics* 30 (5): 1064–1076.

Robertson, Joshua. 2016. "Australian Mining Company Denies Role in Murder of South African Activist." *Guardian*, March 25. https://www.theguardian. com/environment/2016/mar/25/australian-mining-company-denies-role-in-of-south-african-activist.

Robinson, Cedric. 2023 [1983]. "Black Marxism." In *Social Theory Re-Wired: New Connections to Classical and Contemporary Perspective*, edited by Wesley Longhofer and Daniel Winchester. New York: Routledge.

Robison, O.M.E.F., G. Inglis, and J. Egan. 2020. "The Health, Well-being and Future Opportunities of Young Carers: A Population Approach." *Public Health* 185: 139–143. https://doi.org/10.1016/j.puhe.2020.05.002.

Robson, E., N. Ansell, U. S. Huber, W. T. S. Gould, and L. van Blerk. 2006. "Young Caregivers in the Context of the HIV/AIDS Pandemic in Sub-Saharan Africa." *Population, Place and Space* 12 (2): 93–111. https://doi.org/ 10.1002/psp.392.

Rose, Gillian. 2012. *Visual Methodologies: An Introduction to Researching with Visual Materials*. 3rd Edition. London: Sage.

Rose, Nikolas. 1991. "Governing by Numbers: Figuring Out Democracy." *Accounting, Organizations and Society* 16 (7): 673–692.

Rosen, Rachel, and Katherine Twamley. 2018 "Introduction: The Woman-Child Question: A Dialogue in the Borderlands." In *Feminism and the Politics of Childhood: Friends or Foes?*, edited by Rachel Rosen and Katherine Twamley, 1–20. London: UCL Press. http://www.jstor.com/stable/j,ctt21c4 t9k.6.

Royal Society for Public Health. 2016. "Commuter Health." https://www.rsph. org.uk/our-work/policy/wellbeing/commuter-health.html.

Rutledge, Christopher. 2020. "Mantashe Uses State of Disaster to Escape Accountability." *Daily Maverick*, March 30. https://www.dailymaverick. co.za/opinionista/2020-03-30-mantashe-uses-state-of-disaster-to-escape-accountability/.

Ruwanpura, Kanchana N. 2007. "Shifting Theories: Partial Perspectives on the Household." *Cambridge Journal of Economics* 31 (4, July): 525–538. https:// doi.org/10.1093/cje/bel032.

Ruwanpura, Kanchana. 2022. *Garments without Guilt*. Cambridge: Cambridge University Press.

Ruwanpura, Kanchana N., and Alex Hughes. 2016. "Empowered Spaces? Management Articulations of Gendered Spaces in Apparel Factories in

Karachi, Pakistan." *Gender, Place & Culture* 23 (9): 1270–1285. doi:10.1080/0966369X.2015.1136815

SABC News. 2018. "Xolobeni Activist Still Fears for Her Life." https://www.sabcnews.com/sabcnews/xolobeni-activist-still-fears-for-her-life/, (Accessed February 29, 2024).

Sacks, Karen Brodkin. 1989. "Toward a Unified Theory of Class, Race, and Gender." *American Ethnologist* 16 (3): 534–550. https://doi.org/10.1525/ae.1989.16.3.02a00080.

Safri, Maliha, and Julie Graham. 2010. "The Global Household: Toward a Feminist Postcapitalist International Political Economy." *Signs* 36 (1, Autumn): 99–125.

Said, Edward. 1978. *Orientalism*. New York: Pantheon.

Saito, Kohei. Marx in the Anthropocene: Towards the Idea of Degrowth Communism.

Samantroy, Ellina. 2022. "Women's Paid and Unpaid Work: Insights from the Time Use Survey and Methodological Issues." NLI Research Studies Series No. 154/2022. https://vvgnli.gov.in/sites/default/files/NLI%20Research%20Studies%20Series%20No.%20154-2022.pdf.

Sánchez de Madariaga, Inés, and Elena Zucchini. 2019. "Measuring Mobilities of Care: A Challenge for Transport Agendas." In *Integrating Gender into Transport Planning: From One to Many Tracks*, edited by Christina Lindkvist Scholten and Tanja Joelsson, 145–173. Cham: Palgrave Macmillan.

Sandow, Erika. 2014. "Til Work Do Us Part: The Social Fallacy of Long-Distance Commuting." *Urban Studies* 51 (3): 526–543.

Sandow, Erika, Olle Westerlund, and Urban Lindgren. 2014. "Is Your Commute Killing You? On the Mortality Risks of Long-Distance Commuting." *Environment and Planning A* 46 (6): 1496–1516.

Sangari, Kumkum, and Sudesh Vaid, eds. 1989. *Recasting Women: Essays in Colonial History*. Delhi: Kali for Women.

Sankey, D. 2014. "Towards Recognition of Subsistence Harms: Reassessing Approaches to Socioeconomic Forms of Violence in Transitional Justice." *International Journal of Transitional Justice* 8 (1): 121–140.

Sankey, D. 2015. "Gendered Experiences of Subsistence Harms: A Possible Contribution to Feminist Discourse on Gendered Harm?" *Social & Legal Studies* 24 (1): 25–45.

Sassen, Saskia. 2005. "The Global City: Introducing a Concept." *Brown Journal of World Affairs* 11 (2, Winter–Spring): 27–43.

Savage, Mike, and Roger Burrows. 2007. "The Coming Crisis of Empirical Sociology." *Sociology* 41 (5): 779–975. https://doi.org/10.1177/00380385070804.

Schelhase, Marc. 2021. "Bringing the Harm Home: The Quest for Home Ownership and the Amplification of Social Harm." *New Political Economy* 26 (3): 439–454. doi:10.1080/13563467.2020.1782363

Schmid, Caitlin B. 2022. "Neglecting Reproductive Labor: A Critical Review of Gender Equality Indices." *Social Politics: International Studies in Gender, State & Society* 29 (3, Fall): 907–931. https://doi.org/10.1093/sp/jxab009.

Schwanen, Tim. 2002. "Urban Form and Commuting Behaviour: A Cross-European Perspective." *Tijdschrift voor economische en sociale geografie* 93 (3): 336–343.

Schwanen, Tim, Martin Dijst, and Frans M. Dieleman. 2002. "A Microlevel Analysis of Residential Context and Travel Time." *Environment and Planning A* 34 (8): 1487–1507.

Schwendinger, Herman, and Julia Schwendinger. 1975. "Defenders of Order or Guardians of Human Rights?" In *Critical Criminology*, edited by Taylor, Walton and Young. London: Routledge and Kegan Paul.

Seabrooke, Leonard, and Eleni Tsingou. 2016. "Bodies of Knowledge in Reproduction: Epistemic Boundaries in the Political Economy of Fertility." *New Political Economy* 21 (1): 69–89. doi:10.1080/13563467.2015.1041482.

SEEA. 2012. "Environmental Activity Accounts." https://seea.un.org/content/environmental-activity-accounts.

Seguino, Stephanie. 2000. "Accounting for Asian Economic Growth: Adding Gender to the Equation." *Feminist Economics* 6 (3): 27–58.

Seguino, Stephanie. 2006. "Taking Gender Differences in Bargaining Power Seriously: Equity, Living Wages, and Labor Standards." In *Feminist Perspectives on Gender and the World*, edited by E. Kupier and D. Barker, 94–116. London: Routledge.

Sepulveda Carmona, Magdalena. 2013. "Report of the Special Rapporteur on Extreme Poverty and Human Rights. file:///C:/Users/sr86/Downloads/SSRN-id2437791.pdf.

Shah, Sonal, Kalpana Viswanath, Sonali Vyas, and Shreya Gadepalli. 2017. *Women and Transport in Indian Cities*. New Delhi: ITDP and Safetipin.

Sheller, Mimi. 2004. "Automotive Emotions: Feeling the Car." *Theory, Culture & Society* 21 (4–5): 221–242.

Sheller, Mimi. 2018. *Mobility Justice: The Politics of Movement in an Age of Extremes*. London: Verso Books,.

Shields, S. 2019. "The Paradoxes of Necessity: Fail Forwards Neoliberalism, Social Reproduction, Recombinant Populism and Poland's 500Plus Policy." *Capital & Class* 43 (4). https://doi.org/10.1177/0309816819880798.

Shilliam, Robbie. 2018. *Race and the Undeserving Poor: From Abolition to Brexit*. Newcastle upon Tyne: Agenda.

Siddiqui, Dina, and Hasan Ashraf. 2022. "Pandemics Politics: Class, Gender and Stigmatized Labor in Bangladesh's Garment Industry." *New Diversities* 24 (1): 47–65. https://newdiversities.mmg.mpg.de/wp-content/uploads/2022/10/2022_24-01_04_SiddiqiAshraf-1.pdf, (Accessed February 29, 2024).

Skovdal, M., Vincent Ogutu, Cellestine Aoro, and Catherine Campbell. 2009. "Young Carers as Social Actors: Coping Strategies of Children Caring for

Ailing or Ageing Guardians in Western Kenya." LSE Research Online. http://eprints.lse.ac.uk/25126/1/socialcarers_(LSERO).pdf.

Smith, Dorothy E. 1987. *The Everyday World as Problematic: A Feminist Sociology*. University of Toronto Press.

Smith, Julia. 2019. "Overcoming the 'Tyranny of the Urgent': Integrating Gender into Disease Outbreak Preparedness and Response." *Gender & Development* 27 (2): 355–369.

South Africa, Department of Statistics. 2021. "The National Household Travel Survey in South Africa (NHTS): South Africans Take 45 Million Trips, Mostly by Foot. https://www.statssa.gov.za/?p=14063.

South African History Online (SAHO). 2014. "Pondoland revolt–1950–1961." Updated 2019. https://www.sahistory.org.za/article/pondoland-revolt-1950-1961, (Accessed February 28, 2024).

Sparcpk. 2022. "Child Labour." https://www.sparcpk.org/SOPC%202021/CL.pdf, (Accessed February 29, 2024)

Squiers, Carol. 2006. *The Body at Risk*. London: International Centre of Photography. Berkeley: University of California Press.

Squire, Corrine, ed. 2020. *Stories Changing Lives: Narratives and Paths toward Social Change*. Oxford: Oxford University Press.

Srija, A., and S. S. Vijay. 2020. "Female Labour Force Participation in India: Insights through Time Use Survey." *Review of Market Integration* 12 (3): 159–199. https://doi.org/10.1177/09749292211031131.

Stack, Megan K. 2019. *Women's Work: A Personal Reckoning with Labour, Motherhood, and Privilege*. London: Scribe.

Stamatopoulos, Vivian. 2015. "One Million and Counting: The Hidden Army of Young Carers in Canada." *Journal of Youth Studies* 18 (6): 809–22. doi:10.1080/13676261.2014.992329.

Stamatopoulos, Vivian. 2018. "The Young Carer Penalty: Exploring the Costs of Caregiving among a Sample of Canadian Youth." *Child & Youth Services* 39 (2–3): 180–205. DOI: 10.1080/0145935X.2018.1491303.

Statista. 2024. "Distribution of Household Heads in India between 2019 and 2021, by Gender." https://www.statista.com/statistics/615599/household-by-gender-india/.

Stevano, Sara, Tobias Franz, Yannis Dafermos, and Elisa Van Waeyenberge. 2021. "COVID-19 and Crises of Capitalism: Intensifying Inequalities and Global Responses." *Canadian Journal of Development Studies/Revue canadienne d'études du développement* 42 (1–2): 1–17. DOI: 10.1080/02255189.2021.1892606.

Stevano, Sara, Suneetha Kadiyala, Deborah Johnston, Hazel Malapit, Elizabeth Hull, and Sofia Kalamatianou. 2019. "Time-Use Analytics: An Improved Way of Understanding Gendered Agriculture-Nutrition Pathways." *Feminist Economics* 25 (3): 1–22.

Stewart, Ann. 2023. "Gender and Aging: Caregiving and Receiving in African Legal Contexts." In *Handbook of Aging, Health and Public Policy*. Springer, Singapore. https://doi.org/10.1007/978-981-16-1914-4_90-1

Stocker, Stephanie, and Alexandre Hublet. 2022. "Sharma v Minister for the Environment: A Setback for Climate Change Claimants as Landmark Decision Is Overturned on Appeal." White & Case LLP. March 30. https://www.whitecase.com/insight-alert/sharma-v-minister-environment-setback-climate-change-claimants-landmark-decision, (Accessed February 28, 2024).

Sturgeon, Noel. 2009. *Environmentalism in Popular Culture: Gender, Race, Sexuality, and the Politics of the Natural.* Tucson: University of Arizona Press.

Svanberg, E., J. Stott, and A. Spector. 2010. "'Just Helping': Children Living with a Parent with Young Onset Dementia." *Aging & Mental Health* 14 (6): 740–751.

Swain, Dan. 2019. "Not Not but Not Yet: Present and Future in Prefigurative Politics." *Political Studies* 67 (1): 47–62. https://doi.org/10.1177/0032321717741233.

Tanyag Maria. 2018. "Depleting Fragile Bodies: The Political Economy of Sexual and Reproductive Health in Crisis Situations." *Review of International Studies* 44, part 4: 654–671.

Tapper, James. 2023. "'Never Again': Is Britain finally Ready to Return to the Office?" *Guardian*, August 12. https://www.theguardian.com/business/2023/aug/12/never-again-is-britain-finally-ready-to-return-to-the-office.

TGNP. 2009. *Who Cares for Us? Time Use Study of Unpaid Care Work in Tanzania.* Dar es Salaam: Tanzania Gender Networking Programme.

The Migration Observatory. 2018. "Migration Observatory Regional Profile: West Midlands." University of Oxford. https://migrationobservatory.ox.ac.uk/wp-content/uploads/2018/12/Migration-Observatory-Regional-Profile-West-Midlands.pdf, (Accessed February 27, 2024).

The Womin Collective. 2017. "Extractives vs Development Sovereignty: Building Living Consent Rights for African Women." *Gender & Development* 25 (3): 421–437. DOI: 10.1080/13552074.2017.1379782.

Tontoh, Elaine Agyemang. 2022. "The Triple Day Thesis: Theorising Motherhood as a Capability and a Capability Suppressor within Martha Nussbaum's Feminist Philosophical Capability Theory." *Journal of Human Development and Capabilities* 23 (4): 593–610. doi:10.1080/19452829.2021.201442

Topping, Alexandra, and Patrick Butler. 2023. "Hunt's Jobs Drive Will Push Mothers on Benefits to Work 30-Hour Week." *Guardian*, March 22. https://www.theguardian.com/society/2023/mar/22/jeremy-hunt-universal-credit-benefits-mothers-30-hour-weeks.

Törnberg, Anton. 2021. "Prefigurative Politics and Social Change: A Typology Drawing on Transition Studies." *Distinktion: Journal of Social Theory* 22 (1): 83–107. doi:10.1080/1600910X.2020.1856161.

Tricontinental. 2019. "The Fate of Xolobeni Would Be the Fate of Us All." Working Document no 2, Tricontinental. Institute for Social Research. https://thetricontinental.org/wp-content/uploads/2019/10/190928_Working-Document-2_EN_Web-1.pdf, (Accessed February 28, 2024).

Tronto, Joan. 2013. *Caring Democracy: Markets, Equality, and Justice.* New York: New York University Press.

True, Jacqui. 2012. *The Political Economy of Violence against Women.* Oxford University Press.

Truong, Thanh-Dam. 1996. "Gender, International Migration and Social Reproduction: Implications for Theory, Policy, Research and Networking." *Asian and Pacific Migration Journal* 5 (1): 27–52.

Tuck, Eve, and K. Wayne Yang. 2012. "Decolonization Is Not a Metaphor." *Tabula Rasa* 38: 61–111.

Twum-Danso Imoh, Afua, Lucia Rabello de Castro, and Orna Naftali. 2022. "Studies of Childhoods in the Global South: Towards an Epistemic Turn in Transnational Childhood Research?" *Third World Thematics: A TWQ Journal* 7 (1–3): 1–16.

UK Government. 2008. "Carers at the Heart of 21st-Century Families and Communities." https://assets.publishing.service.gov.uk/government/uplo ads/system/uploads/attachment_data/file/136492/carers_at_the_heart_ of_21_century_families.pdf.

UK Government. 2014. Children and Families Act 2014. http://www.legislat ion.gov.uk/ukpga/2014/6/section/96/enacted.

UK Government. 2021. "Adopted and Looked-After Children." https://www. ethnicity-facts-figures.service.gov.uk/health/social-care/adopted-and-loo ked-after-children/latest#main-facts-and-figures.

UK Government. n.d. "Carer's Allowance." https://www.gov.uk/carers-allowance.

UK National Audit Office. 2018. "Financial Sustainability of Local Authorities 2018." https://www.nao.org.uk/wp-content/uploads/2018/03/Financial-sustainabilty-of-local-authorites-2018.Pdf.

UK Office for National Statistics. 2014. "Commuting and Personal Well-being." https://webarchive.nationalarchives.gov.uk/ukgwa/20160105231823/ http://www.ons.gov.uk/ons/rel/wellbeing/measuring-national-well-being/ commuting-and-personal-well-being--2014/art-commuting-and-perso nal-well-being.html.

UK Office for National Statistics. 2016. "Women Shoulder the Responsibility of 'Unpaid Work.'" November 10. https://www.ons.gov.uk/employment andlabourmarket/peopleinwork/earningsandworkinghours/articles/ womenshouldertheresponsibilityofunpaidwork/2016-11-10.

UK Office for National Statistics. 2018. "Household Satellite Accounts 2015 and 2016." October 2. https://www.ons.gov.uk/releases/householdsatellite accounts2015and2016.

UN. 2015. "The Global Goals: Gender Equality." https://www.globalgoals.org/ goals/5-gender-equality/.

UN. 2017. "Household Size and Composition around the World 2017." house-hold_size_and_composition_around_the_world_2017_data_booklet.pdf.

UN. 2018. "UN Poverty Expert Says UK Policies Inflict Unnecessary Misery: UK Poverty Concerns." November 16. https://www.ohchr.org/en/press-releases/2018/11/un-poverty-expert-says-uk-policies-inflict-unnecessary-misery.

UN. 2020. "The Impact of COVID-19 on Women." https://www.unwomen.org/-/media/headquarters/attachments/sections/library/publications/2020/policy-brief-the-impact-of-covid-19-on-women-en.pdf?la=en&vs=1406.

UNICEF. 2016. "Collecting Water Is Often a Colossal Waste of Time for Women and Girls." https://www.unicef.org/press-releases/unicef-collecting-water-often-colossal-waste-time-women-and-girls.

UNICRC. 1989. The United Nations Convention on the Rights of the Child. https://www.unicef.org.uk/wp-content/uploads/2010/05/UNCRC_united_nations_convention_on_the_rights_of_the_child.pdf.

UNSNA. 1993. "System of National Accounts 1993." https://unstats.un.org/unsd/nationalaccount/sna1993.asp.

UNSNA. 2009. "System of National Accounts." https://unstats.un.org/unsd/nationalaccount/docs/sna2008.pdf.

UN System of Environmental Economic Accounting. 2012. "System of Environmental-Economic Accounting 2012: Central Framework." https://unstats.un.org/unsd/envaccounting/seearev/seea_cf_final_en.pdf.

UN System of Environmental Economic Accounting. n.d. "What Is the SEEA?" https://seea.un.org/#:~:text=The%20System%20of%20Environmental%2DEconomic,environmental%20assets%2C%20as%20they%20bring.

UN Women. 2020. "The Shadow Pandemic: Violence against Women during COVID-19." https://www.unwomen.org/en/news/stories/2020/5/press-release-the-shadow-pandemic-of-violence-against-women-during-covid-19.

UN Women. 2020. "World Survey on The Role of Women In Development | 2019 Why Addressing Women's Income and Time Poverty Matters For Sustainable Development. New York.

Varjonen, Johanna, Eeva Hamunen, and Katri Soinne. 2014. "Satellite Accounts on Household Production: Eurostat Methodology and Experiences to Apply It." Working Paper 1/2014, presented at the 32nd General Conference of The International Association for Research in Income and Wealth, Boston, USA, August 5–11, 2012. https://www.doria.fi/handle/10024/184229, (Accessed February 29, 2024).

Vizard, Polly, Polina Obolenskaya, and Tania Burchardt. 2019. "Child Poverty amongst Young Carers in the UK: Prevalence and Trends in the Wake of the Financial Crisis, Economic Downturn and Onset of Austerity." *Child Indicators Research* 12: 1831–1854.

Walker Gore, Clare. 2020. "'Unbroken Health and a Spirit Almost Criminally Elastic': Women's Work and Women's Bodies in the Autobiographies of Harriet Martineau and Margaret Oliphant." *Women's Writing* 27 (4): 473–483.

Warhurst, Amy, Sarah Bayless, and Emma Maynard. 2022. "Teachers' Perceptions of Supporting Young Carers in Schools: Identifying Support Needs and the Importance of Home–School Relationships." *Int J Environ Res Public Health* 19 (17): 10755. doi:10.3390/ijerph191710755.

Waring, M. 1988. *If Women Counted: A New Feminist Economics.* San Francisco: Harper & Row.

Waring, Marilyn, and Robert Carr. 2011. *Who Cares? The Economics of Dignity: A Case Study of HIV and AIDS Care-giving.* Commonwealth Secretariat.

Waring, M., and K. Sumeo. 2010. "Economic Crisis and Unpaid Care Work in the Pacific." Paper prepared for Conference on the Human Face of the Global Economic Crisis, UNDP, Port Vila, February 10–12.

Warren, Janet. 2007. "Young Carers: Conventional or Exaggerated Levels of Involvement in Domestic and Caring Tasks?" *Children & Society* 21 (2): 136–146.

Washinyira, Tariro. 2016. "Wild Coast Battle to Save Land from Mining." Ground Up. February 12. https://www.groundup.org.za/article/imbizo-xolobeni/.

WBG Commission on a Gender-Equal Economy. 2020. "Creating a Caring Economy: A Call to Action." https://wbg.org.uk/wp-content/uploads/2020/10/WBG-Report-v10.pdf.

Webb, C. J. R., and P. Bywaters. 2018. "Austerity, Rationing and Inequity: Trends in Children's and Young Peoples' Services Expenditure in England between 2010 and 2015." *Local Government Studies* 44 (1): 1–25.

Weeks, Kathi. 2011. *The Problem with Work: Feminism, Marxism, Antiwork Politics and Postwork Imaginaries.* Durham, NC: Duke University Press.

West, Robin L. 1987. "The Difference in Women's Hedonic Lives: A Phenomenological Critique of Feminist Legal Theory." *Wisconsin Women's Law Journal* 3: 81–146.

WHO. 2023. "Maternal Mortality." February 22. https://www.who.int/newsroom/fact-sheets/detail/maternal-mortality.

Wihstutz, Anne. 2011. "Working Vulnerability: Agency of Caring Children and Children's Rights." *Childhood* 18 (4): 447–459.

Winders, Jamie, and Barbara Ellen Smith. 2019. "Social Reproduction and Capitalist Production: A Genealogy of Dominant Imaginaries." *Progress in Human Geography* 43 (5): 871–889.

Wolf, Margery. 1985. *Revolution Postponed.* Stanford: Stanford University Press.

Wong, Sandy, Sara L. McLafferty, Arrianna M. Planey, and Valerie A. Preston. 2020. "Disability, Wages, and Commuting in New York." *Journal of Transport Geography* 87: 102818.

Woolf, Virginia. 2014 [1930]. "Street Haunting: A London Adventure." http://s.spachman.tripod.com/Woolf/streethaunting.htm.

World Bank. 2022. "Female Labor Force Participation." https://genderdata.worldbank.org/data-stories/flfp-data-story/.

Wright, A. J. 2018. "Technowelfare in Japan: Personal Care Robots and Temporalities of Care." Thesis, University of Hong Kong, Pokfulam. HKU Scholars Hub.

Yadav, Pooja. 2022. "Explained: Why Indian Women's Workforce Participation Is Still Considerably Low." *India Times*, July 17. https://www.indiatimes.com/explainers/news/why-indian-womens-workforce-participation-is-still-considerably-low-574847.html.

Yanomami, Adeina. In Richard Mosse, Broken Spectre, 30, September 2022–23 April 2023, 180 The Strand, London.

Yar, Majid. 2012. "Critical Criminology, Critical Theory and Social Harm," in *New Directions in Criminological Theory*, edited by S. Hall and S. Winlow. London: Routledge.

Yates, Luke. 2021. "Prefigurative Politics and Social Movement Strategy: The Roles of Prefiguration in the Reproduction, Mobilisation and Coordination of Movements." *Political Studies* 69 (4): 1033–1052.

Young, Iris Marion. 2013. *Responsibility for Justice*. Reprint edition. New York: Oxford University Press.

Yusoff, Kathryn. 2023. "Earth as a Medium of Struggle." In *Re/Sisters: A Lens on Gender and Ecology*, edited by Alona Pardo. London: Barbican Prestel.

Zalewski, Marysia, and Jane Parpart, eds. 2019. *The "Man" Question in International Relations*. London: Routledge.

Zbyszewska, Ania. 2018. "Regulating Work with People and 'Nature' in Mind: Feminist Reflections." *Comparative Labor Law and Policy Journal* 40 (1): 9–28.

Zelizer, Viviana A. 1989. "The Social Meaning of Money: 'Special Monies.'" *American Journal of Sociology* 95 (2): 342–377.

Zhu, X., Y. Liu, and X. Fang. 2022. "Revisiting the Sustainable Economic Welfare Growth in China: Provincial Assessment Based on the ISEW." Social Indicators Research 162: 279–306. https://doi.org/10.1007/s11205-021-02832-2.

Zuzanek, Jiri. 1998. "Time Use, Time Pressure, Personal Stress, Mental Health, and Life Satisfaction from a Life Cycle Perspective." *Journal of Occupational Science* 5 (1): 26–39.

Index